Endorsements for Organic M,

C000128082

"*Organic Marxism* is a fresh, energetic, anc
Clayton and Heinzekehr offer a combative stand against the geno-
cidal features of the modern project and develop a series of constructive resources drawing from the common historical lineage between
ecology and the critique of political economy. By combining process
philosophy with developments in China they find solutions beyond
traditional colonial dualisms (West vs. East) and make possible
otherwise unimaginable spaces for dialogue. This book is a must-
read for all interested in religion and globalization, process studies,
intercultural conversations, and critique of political ecology."

~Santiago Slabodsky
Assistant Professor of Ethics of Globalization
Claremont School of Theology
author, *Decolonial Judaism*

"What an unexpected, discomforting and important work! If Marxism
seemed to be abandoned in the West to a few academic leftists and nos-
talgic activists, the authors bring it roaring back into relevance. In the
face of an obscenely widened income gap and an insanely amplified climate threat, the critique of capitalism has never been so necessary. But
far from returning to a reductive mechanics of revolution, the authors
demonstrate how to graft socialism—never a static system—onto an
ecological model of dynamic interdependence. If their proposal has a
chance, it is through its mobilization of a potential China, where Marx
is a given and ecological civilization a stated ideal."

~ Catherine Keller
Drew University

"Globalization has linked China and the West as a community of
shared destiny. Dealing with ecological crisis has become the common
goal of constructive postmodernism, traditional Chinese culture, and
Marxism. *Organic Marxism* is a timely guide for responding to the
pressing issues facing us. In contrast to deconstructive Marxism,
Organic Marxism can help us not only to reinterpret traditional

Marxism, but also to reconstruct it. For all who wish to understand the future development of China and the world, this book provides profound insight."

~Qiang Naishe, Senior Editor of *Philosophical Trends,*
Chinese Academy of Social Sciences

"*Organic Marxism* will not only enrich the academic landscape in both China and the West. It will also play an important role in creating a new kind of civilization—an ecological civilization."

~Dr. Wang Zhihe, Executive Director,
Institute for the Postmodern Development of China

"In this highly original and provocative book, Clayton and Heinzekehr show how postmodern (organic) Marxism can be integrated with post-modern process philosophy and traditional Chinese thought into a worldview that provides the basis for a hopeful response to the coming climate chaos. The hope is not that our civilization can be spared; it is already too late for that. The hope is that the new worldview could lay the foundations for a new—an ecological—civilization."

~David Ray Griffin
author, *Whitehead's Radically Different Postmodern Philosophy*

"In *Organic Marxism* Philip Clayton and Justin Heinzekehr argue that Marxism constitutes a rich world of ideas and practices: a dialectic of social transformation embodying many vernaculars in many different countries. As such it remains the main hope of all those seeking to free the world from the destructiveness of capitalism, which now increasingly threatens planetary life itself. This is an unusual and provocative book. Don't miss it."

~John Bellamy Foster, editor, *Monthly Review;*
author, *Marx's Ecology*

"As a constructive alternative for a world hurtling full-speed towards planetary destruction, Clayton and Heinzekehr offer a compelling, context-specific, and highly readable vision. Weaving together Marxism, process philosophy, and Chinese thought, they highlight capitalism's fundamental relationship with environmental destruction as well as the inability of the "free market" to accurately value the planet and account for ecological risk. *Organic Marxism* should become a resource for all those who profess to love the world and those who dwell upon it as their neighbor."

~Timothy Murphy, Executive Director,
Progressive Christians Uniting

"A widespread reluctance to engage the full range of intellectual options has severely damaged the imagination not only in the United States but globally. For too long the orthodoxies of capitalism have successfully suppressed alternatives in all areas of life and thought, including religion. Clayton and Heinzekehr are part of a turning of the tide, as they provide the first sustained engagement of process and Marxian thought, set in conversation with key challenges and developments of our time. The resulting emphasis on organic perspectives, in contrast to abstractly imposed solutions, sets the stage for further engagements."

~Joerg Rieger, Wendland-Cook Professor of Constructive Theology
Perkins School of Theology, Southern Methodist University

"I've been looking for this book. Perhaps you have, too. We've been looking for a book that is clear in its examples, grounded in history, stretching in its ideas, amazing in its breadth, and hopeful in its projected possibilities. We've sought an alternative to capitalism that is flexible, good for people, good for communities, and good for the earth. We've wanted something that could make sense to people from many walks of life: academics, poets, farmers, and, yes, businesspeople. Who would have thought that this alternative could be called Organic Marxism? Who would have thought that it could provide hope for China and for other parts of the world, even North America? Don't let the word Marx scare you. You'll be on board early on and want, like me, to get going with the great work of helping build local communities that are creative, compassionate, participatory and diverse, with no one left behind. Philip Clayton and Justin Heinzekehr have given us a framework, a springboard, for doing our part in serving the common good."

~Jay McDaniel, Willis Professor, Hendrix College

Organic
Marxism

Organic Marxism

An alternative to capitalism
and ecological catastrophe

PHILIP CLAYTON
JUSTIN HEINZEKEHR

FOREWORD BY JOHN B. COBB, JR.

Toward Ecological Civilization Series

PROCESS CENTURY PRESS
CLAREMONT, CALIFORNIA 2014

ORGANIC MARXISM: An Alternative to Capitalism and Ecological Catastrophe

© 2014 Process Century Press

Process Century Press
An Imprint of the Center for Process Studies
A Program of Claremont School of Theology
1325 N. College Avenue
Claremont, CA 91711

ISBN 978-1-940447-02-5

Printed in the United States of America

Series Preface: Toward Ecological Civilization

We live in the ending of an age. But the ending of the modern period differs from the ending of previous periods, such as the classical or the medieval. The amazing achievements of modernity make it possible, even likely, that its end will also be the end of civilization, of many species, or even of the human species. At the same time, we are living in an age of new beginnings that give promise of an ecological civilization. Its emergence is marked by a growing sense of urgency and deepening awareness that the changes must go to the roots of what has led to the current threat of catastrophe.

In June 2015, the 10th Whitehead International Conference will be held in Claremont, CA. Called "Seizing an Alternative: Toward an Ecological Civilization," it claims an organic, relational, integrated, nondual, and processive conceptuality is needed, and that Alfred North Whitehead provides this in a remarkably comprehensive and rigorous way. We propose that he can be "the philosopher of ecological civilization." With the help of those who have come to an ecological vision in other ways, the conference will explore this Whiteheadian alternative, showing how it is sufficiently advanced to provide the shared vision so urgently needed.

The judgment underlying this effort is that contemporary research and scholarship is still enthralled by the 17th-century view of nature articulated by Descartes and reinforced by Kant. Without freeing our minds of this objectifying and reductive understanding of the world, we are not likely to direct our actions wisely in response to the crisis to which this tradition has led us. Given the ambitious goal of replacing now dominant patterns of thought with one that would redirect us toward ecological civilization, clearly more is needed than a single conference. Fortunately, a larger platform is developing that includes the conference and looks beyond it. It is named Pando Populus in honor of the world's largest and oldest organism, an aspen grove.

In preparation for the conference, and in support of the larger initiative of Pando Populus, we are publishing this series, appropriately named "Toward Ecological Civilization."

John B. Cobb, Jr.

Contents

Foreword

JOHN B. COBB, JR.

This is an astonishing book. Many of its positive ideas are found elsewhere, but here they are brought together as a new form of "Marxism." One would have thought that in the United States that would be the wrong way to attract interest and support. But as one reads, the reason becomes clear. What is needed now is different from any past form of society. But it is not a revision of the now dominant ideology, capitalism. That provides the wrong starting point. The critique of capitalism in these pages is not simply of some ways in which it operates but of its most fundamental nature and goals. It cannot be salvaged by reforms. In this critique the authors build on the thought of Marx.

The errors of Marxism, deriving more or less from Marx himself, have been serious. They are clearly stated. Marxism in its Leninist and Stalinist forms did not work and will not work. This fact is in no way obscured. But the basic assumptions and purposes of Marx are not invalidated. To achieve a healthy and sustainable society today is to realize the goals of Marx. That is why the book is calling for a new form of Marxism.

Today more and more people recognize that global capitalism is destroying itself and in the process rendering the planet uninhabitable. It is time to turn away from efforts to modify it and, instead, to look for a new starting point. Perhaps we can sufficiently overcome the prejudices into which we have been socialized to recognize that Marx offers us this new starting point.

Far more than American and British scholars, European intellectuals have attempted to update and make positive use of Marx. On the European continent there exists a rich literature proposing new forms of Marxism that are (the authors claim) free from the errors that have led to the demise of politically important Marxist parties. Too often, however, those who have written thoughtfully treat Marxism as a stimulus for criticism but not as a real option. A few American Marxists have shown that an ecological Marxism can find grounding in Marx, and this is surely important. But this book goes much further. One can wish that it would become the basis of a vigorous discussion of this basic alternative to capitalism.

Both capitalist and Marxist thinkers present themselves as scientific. However, the science on which they model themselves is "modern" science. Actually science has moved on. Its findings have broken out of the modern boundaries and call for radical rethinking of the nature of the world. Organism is replacing mechanism in contemporary models. Marxism needs to base itself on contemporary postmodern science rather than on an outdated modern one. Hence the call for "organic Marxism." The clear implication of the book is that this is a move that Marxism can make, whereas capitalism is inherently stuck with outdated models.

The book will have a much easier time gaining a hearing in China than in the United States. China is not now trying to implement any past form of Marxism. It knows the problems from painful experience. But it has not given up on Marxism itself. Some of the directions of development of Marxism for which this book calls are already being considered in somewhat scattered ways. To have a coherent statement of a form that Marxism could take in China may well be appreciated as a direct contribution to the present discussion among leading politicians and intellectuals there. Adopting this term with the understanding offered here could have historic importance in China, and what happens in China is of historic importance for the world.

Although the authors list specific policies and practices that would implement organic Marxism, they do not endorse a single set of policies for all cultures and governments. This limitation is the consistent consequence of their understanding. Organic Marxism calls for an economy that grows organically out of the existing cultural and economic situation. With regard to China in particular, the authors do not claim to have the detailed knowledge needed to press specific policies. Chinese, and specifically Chinese in various parts of that vast land, are much more likely to be qualified. Only the knowledge of specific situations can suffice to identify promising next steps. Organic Marxism does not seek to impose solutions on any country from outside. It seeks to empower those best able to make decisions to do so. But suggestions can be made by outsiders to stimulate the thought of those who are locally involved. This book offers many such suggestions.

I would myself draw from organic Marxism a more impassioned critique of much that has been done in China in the last decade or two. Organic Marxism is serious about the critique of capitalism, whereas China has opened the door quite wide to that capitalism. This has enabled its economy to grow at an amazing speed, but it has also created false expectations over which it now has little control. It has listened to capitalist experts from the United States, and it has failed to bring a Marxist critique to bear on the capitalist assumptions of their advice. It has copied the American "value free" research universities, thereby preparing capitalist leaders for China's future. I believe China still has the opportunity to check this rush into the arms of global capitalism, but it will not be easy. This book could be an important ally in that resistance.

I hope that the depiction in these pages of a new form of Marxism that grows authentically out of China's own traditions will help it to change course. May it do so soon! The chances of a serious move toward socialism in the countries of Europe and North America are far more slim. One can nevertheless hope that this book, together with the growing awareness of what capitalism is doing to the 99 percent and to the world's ecosystems, will have some effect even here in slowing the headlong rush toward global destruction.

Preface

"Why Marx?" many Americans ask us.

This is not a question that my Chinese friends ask. They understand that Marxism is written into the Chinese Constitution. The governing philosophy of China in the years to come may look quite different from the socialist philosophy that Karl Marx formulated almost two hundred years ago. It will still be called Marxism.

Things look different to most Americans. They often respond, "But the West tried Marxism, at various times in various forms, and it failed. Why do you still think it's a viable option?" It's a good question. Although Americans know that the Communism of Russia and China is derived from Karl Marx, very few have ever read Marx seriously. They believe that socialism and Communism are identical, and for decades they have heard that both are bad. Basically, Americans been told that these words mean that the state owns everything and that there is no private property, free market, or human rights. The attempts to implement either socialism or Communism, most Americans believe, have shown that the theories are false.

We believe these judgments are mistaken, and in the following pages we offer an alternative.

We wish to lay our seven central claims on the table right at the outset: It is urgent that people around the planet recognize the situation that the human race now faces and that we take steps to implement the solutions. Capitalism as a social and economic system has created massive injustices and has devastated the global environment. As we will show, there are real alternatives to capitalism. Far preferable to it, we will argue, is a hybrid system that limits market forces within the context of socialist communities structured for the common good. It is inevitable that global climate change will produce social and economic collapse on many parts of our planet. Out of the dust of that collapse, a new ecological civilization can arise. It's far better for humans and for the planet, however, that we act now, rather than waiting for the full force of the calamity to strike.

In the process of naming the problems and moving toward solutions, a form of open Marxism that we call *Organic Marxism* can and must play a crucial role. Here are three reasons why:

(1) The core ideas of Marx's work remain compelling. Probably no thinker in the modern period wrote more insightfully on what it would mean to construct society and economics for the common good—and on the ways that power and wealth create government for the Few, not the Many.

Of course, working 150 years ago, Marx made some assumptions that we now know are false. Some of his solutions were composed for the industrial age, not for the post-industrial information and technological age in which we now live. It's not difficult, however, to reformulate Marx's work without these assumptions.

The reform program that results, we hope to show, is pretty compelling. If you want to understand the dynamics of multinational corporations today, or the way that the wealthy exercise power over entire societies and the global economy, or how rapidly growing class differences make the upper class increasingly inaccessible to the rest of us, then Marx remains a prescient guide. Part of the American dream, for example, is to deny that there are class lines drawn through the middle of American society. Each year, however, the widening gap between the 1 percent and the 99 percent turns that persistent American dream into more of a myth. Particularly instructive in this regard is the famous boast by Warren Buffett (quoted by the Marxist theorist Joerg Rieger) that "there is such a thing as class warfare and that his class is winning it."[1]

(2) What one learns growing up in America is a caricature of socialism. One is taught that socialism means a police state, Stalin and his death camps, the crumbling factories in East Germany in the 1980s—and, again, the denial of all private property, human rights, and the free market. But none of these allegations is true of contemporary (postmodern) socialist theory. Many readers who are attracted to the idea of a relational worldview for the common good have probably never realized that socialism is the social-political philosophy most closely aligned with their own ideals for human society.

(3) The world faces a series of crises that capitalism, by itself, will never be able to solve. Consider just two. The first is the excesses of capitalism itself. Corporate selfishness and greed, the ability of the rich to buy votes and hence mold the policies within democracies, the growing inequities between the rich and poor, the increasing vulnerability of the middle class—these are the realities of our global situation today. Twenty years ago they were scarcely named within mainline North American society. (They *were* being named in Europe, South America, and Asia.) Today, however, they are widely recognized realities.

The second crisis is even more urgent. A nearly universal scientific consensus has emerged that human development is causing a global disruption of our planet's climate system. Among the effects already manifesting are more violent storms, flooding, droughts, rising temperatures, and a rising sea level. With each passing decade, the effects will become more devastating.

The problem is not that experts disagree about the future, nor that people don't care. The problem is that the way the global system is currently set up—allowing individuals to amass whatever wealth they can and to spend it as they wish—makes it impossible for the human species as a whole to take the actions that we need to take. *For the first time, capitalism has faced a crisis that it is fundamentally incapable of solving.*

Since the time of the failed "Glorious Revolution of 1848," some socialists (though never the majority) have been guilty of an idealism verging on utopianism. There is however nothing idealistic about the pages that follow. Thanks to the comforts of growing economies and new technologies, the reach of capitalist assumptions has continued to grow over the last 50 years. Were circumstances to remain as rosy as they have been for citizens of Europe, North America, and a few of the developing countries, the global economic system would not change.

But circumstances *are* changing. Climate disruption has arrived. Scientists tell us it's just the beginning. We should expect to see catastrophic storm damage, flooded coastal cities, loss of fresh water for billions of people, mass animal extinctions, and increasing starvation due to crop failures. This is not science fiction or religious apocalypse; it's what is in store for the residents of our planet in the coming few decades.

If the collapse of civilizations in the past is any guide, we can be fairly sure that three things will happen. Rich people and nations will use their wealth to (try to) buy the resources they want, their technology to (try to) get the water and food that they need, and their power to fight off poor people and nations who want what they have. People without food, water, or government support will take up whatever weapons they have and begin moving toward the nations that have the food and water that they need. Governments, in battle against their hostile neighbors and an increasingly hostile planetary system, will reduce civic freedoms and increase their control, doing whatever they deem necessary to protect their interests and their citizens.

If this is the future that lies ahead of us—and the scientific models seem to agree that it is—then there are, we fear, only two options. We can do nothing until the full crisis is upon us, at which point those in power will use their power as they see fit. By and large, the rich with power will survive and the poor without power will die. Or we can act before the situation becomes desperate. In either case, humanity will be forced to limit the excessive consumption of the rich, whether through taxes, rations, or confiscations. It is just a question of when.

We offer this manifesto of society built for the common good, then, as the better of two options. This is what it will look like if humanity acts in its own long-term interest, and in time. When change is inevitable and the other options are worse, the most rational course of action is to do the right thing, even when it's hard.

In short, we put this book in your hands as a wager. We wager that, while we still have time, humans will do what is in the best interests of the species as a whole, which means: what is in the interest of sustaining life on this planet. We wager that ours is not a suicidal species, an irrational species, or a fundamentally selfish species. Admittedly, no small amount of evidence supports betting on the other side. But maybe, just maybe, these pages will play some role, however small, in increasing the odds that our species will choose life over death, sustainability over extinction.

* * *

We have written this book not just for scholars but primarily for policymakers, government leaders, and lay people. We acknowledge many authors in the notes to whom we are deeply indebted; without their great work this book would be impossible. But we have fought the temptation to give long expositions of their positions in the text. Nor do we take pains to point out every disagreement we have with authors whom we quote and have learned from. Without any theory, enduring reform is not possible. But too much academic talk can also block action.

A note to readers: This book observes the Chinese naming convention of surname, first name, except in those instances where a Chinese author has been published by a Western press and is identified by Western standards. This occurs mostly in the bibliographic references in the notes.

We gratefully acknowledge the people without whom this book could not have been written:

- Karl Marx and Alfred North Whitehead, the two main theoretical sources of the argument.

- John B. Cobb, Jr., David Ray Griffin, and Jay McDaniel, who have helped to synthesize process thought and constructive postmodernism into an intellectual and practical program. In particular, we have been deeply influenced by their commitment to support ecological and sustainable development in China. John Cobb has written that "China is the place most likely to achieve ecological civilization."[2] We share his conviction that, in the entire world, China today is the most fertile soil for the growth of process and constructive postmodern thought.

- Wang Zhihe and Fan Meijun, directors of the Institute for the Postmodern Development of China <www.post-modernchina.org/>. With their work on constructive postmodernism in China and on the Chinese "Second Enlightenment," they have been pioneers in supporting discussion of these themes in the People's Republic of China.

- John Bellamy Foster and Joerg Rieger, Western Marxists whose work has taught and inspired us. Prof. Rieger's critique of an earlier version of this book added immensely to the quality of the final product.

- Elizabeth McDuffie, who assisted us with checking and assembling the text.

- Our editor, Jeanyne Slettom, for her constant encouragement and her professional supervision of the publishing process.

Philip Clayton
Justin Heinzekehr
Claremont, California
July 4, 2014

NOTES

1. Joerg Rieger, ed., *Religion, Theology, and Class: Fresh Engagements after Long Silence* (New York: Palgrave Macmillan, 2013), 4.

2. Liu Junxian, "China is the Place Most Likely to Achieve Ecological Civilization—An Interview with Constructive Postmodern Thinker John Cobb," *Journal of China Executive Leadership Academy Pudong* 3 (2010): 5-10, quoted in Wang Zhihe, "Constructive Postmodernism, Chinese Marxism, and Ecological Civilization," paper presented at the 9th International Whitehead Conference in Krakow, Poland, September 2013.

Part One

Why Marxism?

Chapter One

INTRODUCING ORGANIC MARXISM

Many people in developed nations believe—we think wrongly—that they have nothing to learn from Karl Marx. Their governments and their media have told them that it's impossible to implement socialist principles in political and economic systems. The collapse of East Germany and the USSR, the decreased role of Communist parties in the European nations, the difficulties faced by socialist governments and parties in Latin America and elsewhere—these are the developments that critics point to in arguing that Marxism has failed as a socio-economic system. Even in the People's Republic of China, where Marxism is enshrined in the national constitution, one hears skepticism about the continuing relevance of Marxist analyses.

In practice, most of global economics now functions according to the principles of the so-called free market economy—with disastrous consequences for the planet and much of its population. The domination of capitalist principles has been so thorough that Francis Fukuyama proclaimed "the end of history" in 1992, arguing that humanity has finally attained its highest and ultimate form of government, Western-style capital-based democracy.[1] Many commentators, especially in the United States, appealed to Fukuyama (inaccurately, as it turned out) to support their belief that free market principles had won a final and decisive victory over every other form of economic system.

The advocates of Fukuyama's thesis in the early 1990s would have been surprised to hear that, just two decades later, the public outcry against unrestrained capitalism, and against the government policies that support it, has grown in volume and influence. Of all the factors causing this change, none has served to highlight the limits of the capitalist system more than the global environmental crisis.

Global capitalism has created the greatest ecological and humanitarian catastrophe in the history of human civilization. The unrestrained pursuit of wealth on the part of those with economic power has left approximately half the world's population—over three billion people—living on less than $2.50 a day.[2] At least eighty percent of humanity lives on less than $10 a day.[3] Whereas forty years ago the gap between the richest twenty percent and the poorest twenty percent on the planet stood at 50 to 1, today the disparity in wealth has risen to 80 to 1. The evidence is overwhelming that the wealthiest nations have designed the world economic system to bring maximum gains to themselves. Under the present system, it is virtually impossible for the poor nations to catch up. Multinational corporations are able to utilize tax loopholes, cheap raw materials, inexpensive labor, "free trade" agreements, and lax enforcement of existing treaties in order to continually produce the highest possible profits for their shareholders. Unfortunately, the United States is a leader in allowing unequal conditions at home and in supporting unequal conditions abroad.

As if the human consequences of capitalism were not enough, the planet itself now moans under the unbearable burden of these practices. No pillaging army in its drive for conquest has had as devastating an effect upon global ecosystems as international corporations have in their drive for profit. Wealthy individuals and companies continue to use their positions of dominance to rack up short-term gains at the long-term expense of the planet.

Now that the Intergovernmental Panel on Climate Change (IPCC) has brought the conclusions of climate science to public attention, no one can claim *not* to know the consequences for the planet, and for human civilization, if we continue to produce carbon emissions at present levels. Yet, unfortunately, our present capital-based economic system requires continually expanding markets. The science is clear: "growth economics" has run up against the absolute limits to its growth—planetary limits. It has been approximately three million years since the earth experienced atmospheric carbon levels of the present magnitude (over 400 parts per million). These "greenhouse gases" have turned our planet into a hothouse—or better put, a pressure cooker.

Because of these global developments, support has been growing for a radical shift of the political and economic models that we use to structure human civilization. Central to such a paradigm shift are the society-based economic principles derived from Marx and the history of Marxism. The time is ideal for a return to the enduring insights of Marxist analyses for a very simple reason: unrestrained capitalism is now threatening civilization as we know it. Diminishing resources, global climate disruption, weakening economies in both the developed and developing nations—these are present-day realities. As humanity draws nearer and nearer to the edge of the cliff, massive social unrest and political disruptions will push human societies ever more quickly over the edge.

The severity of our planetary situation is a present and urgent reason for forward-looking thinkers to seek solutions beyond the status quo. *Nothing less than a shift in the global economic paradigm* will allow human nations, cultures, and civilizations to survive in anything like the forms in which we have known them heretofore. If you see that your car is heading off the road and toward a brick wall, you do not keep your foot on the accelerator. The vehicle of the capitalist growth economy has left the old, safe road and will soon hit its wall. The consequences forecast by scientists are almost incomprehensible: melting ice caps, rising sea levels, lack of food and drinking water for hundreds of millions of people, mass starvation, and the extinction of thirty to forty percent of the planet's species. If this situation is not sufficient reason for nations to begin instituting new socioeconomic practices, it is hard to say what *would be* a sufficient reason.

MARXIST SOCIOECONOMIC POLICIES AFTER "INDUSTRIAL MARXISM"

At the same time that unrestrained capitalism threatens to destroy the planet, its major alternative, Marxism, has come under increasing criticism. Many theorists in the West seek to give the impression that it has been largely discredited. In light of this situation, it is not sufficient merely to point out the false promises of capitalism. One must also engage in a careful process of sorting through the legacy of Karl Marx's work in order to establish what a viable Marxism will mean in the twenty-first century. The program of Organic Marxism calls for a number of important revisions and updates of classical Marxist thought and practice:

(1) *Marxism is not a universal predictive science.* The dream of social determinism was one of the many myths of European modernism that must now be left behind. We may not be able to list the objective factors that will predict a global revolution of the proletariat and the advent of a purely utopian socialist society. It follows that no national economy can be managed and controlled by central planning alone. Human ideals and philosophies, and even human religions, play crucial roles in motivating personal and social behaviors across cultures and nations. Marxists today do not dismiss ideas as a mere "superstructure," and we do not believe that the forces of production are the only real causal factors in history.

(2) *Marxists do not need to insist only on state ownership, state-run businesses, and the abolition of all market forces.* Most actual socioeconomic systems are "mixed" or "hybrid" systems and are in this sense "impure." The push by wealthy individuals and businesses to increase their profits must be constrained and restrained by social policies and institutions at the government level; hence central planning and government restraints must play some role. But twenty-first-century Marxists also make room for a limited role for market

forces at the local, national, and international levels. Governments that strive for just social and economic conditions for all their citizens do not have to eliminate competition and private ownership.

Marx wrote in the context of early industrialization in the West. The solutions he proposed addressed exploitation of workers in the industries of his day—the kind of exploitation that continues today, for example in the garment industry in developing nations such as Bangladesh. Other parts of the global economy are post-industrial. Marxist analyses still reveal truths about these economic systems (such as global financial markets and the service sector), even though the solutions may not be identical to those that Marx proposed.

(3) *Marxism was never meant to be a purely theoretical dispute among university professors.* The European debate over Marxist theory, long dominated by modernist assumptions, has in recent decades splintered into literally dozens of competing schools. Scholars engaged in increasingly abstract debates concerning the minutiae of their various competing theories, often with little obvious relevance to the realities of governing cities and countries. Theories divided into sub-theories and schools into sub-schools until in the end (some critics say) each scholar has become the chief advocate of a school consisting of himself or herself alone. When major Marxist figures and movements did arise—the Frankfurt School, Althusser, Habermas—whose insights began to influence public policy, their followers inevitably began to quarrel amongst themselves, decreasing the practical influence of their teachers. Too few Marxist authors have submitted their theories to rigorous testing in the fires of *realpolitik*, and those who have tried to do so in recent years—in Europe, Asia, and Latin America—have tended to work within the assumptions of the present-day global economic system. Only a radical blending of theory and practice in the study and implementation of Marxism will correct the imbalances of the past.

(4) *Critics are wrong in their claim that Marxism has become a meaningless label for whatever random practices a socially-oriented*

government chooses to impose. A "Marxism without real content" will not help human civilization through the crisis that it now faces. Not only will its capitalist opponents quickly realize that it is empty of content; the intellectuals, the students, the businessmen, and eventually even the bureaucrats of a nation will recognize it as well. It is all too easy to recognize when Marx's terms are used in a rote fashion and do not actually provide a substantive guiding framework for government policies and initiatives. When one fails to draw clear lines that lead from theory and practice, others begin to wonder whether the language is being used only to maintain the status quo. By contrast, updated Marxist analyses of the dynamics of wealth and power can help leaders to modify unjust systems and to implement wise policies.

One can welcome positive features in the traditions stemming from Marx's work, while still insisting that many of the classic forms of Marxism need updating, including German, Soviet, and early Chinese theories and practices. From this it by no means follows that Marxism as such has been superseded or that its core principles no longer have any significant meaning. As the coming chapters will show, the central Marxist insights remain as vital as ever—in fact, given the global situation today, perhaps more so.

(5) *A vibrant, living Marxism cannot be "one size fits all."* According to modernist European assumptions, only a universal theory—a theory that is applicable everywhere and at all times—can be a true theory. As constructive postmodernism has shown, however, theories grow in, through, and out of their particular contexts, just as a plant grows in a particular soil and ecosystem. [4] The only useful Marxism for our time will be a *postmodern* Marxism, which means that it will exist only as adapted to a particular time and place: this nation, this culture, this language and history, these particular needs of these particular people. In these pages we defend a *culturally embedded Marxism*: a set of core commitments that take different forms as they are applied in different political and economic contexts.

8

ORGANIC MARXISM AND "ECOLOGICAL CIVILIZATION"

> [People] make their own history, but they do not make it
> just as they please; they do not make it under circumstances
> chosen by themselves, but under circumstances directly
> encountered, given and transmitted from the past. The tradi-
> tion of all the dead generations weighs like a nightmare on
> the brain of the living.[5]

In the second decade of the twenty-first century, we find ourselves in a new world, facing challenges that humanity has never
faced before. Many around us ignore the writing on the wall, others
turn inward to their own private pleasures and gains, and the most
dangerous spend their careers promising that the problems are not
really there because science and technology will make them magically
disappear. Avoiding planetary disaster will take men and women of
courage who think change, advocate for change, and work sacrificially
to bring about change.

The leaders of the new ecological civilization will need conceptual resources adequate to this daunting task. For their overarching
framework, they require a social, economic, and political philosophy
that places *the common good*—of humanity, and of the planet—above
all else.

Given this goal, it becomes a top priority to diagnose and deconstruct those assumptions of European modernism that history has
shown to be inadequate. Unfortunately, Marx uncritically accepted
many of these assumptions. If his work is to speak to the needs of
our postmodern world, it will need a bold reformulation that draws
on newly available conceptual resources. Fortunately, the natural alliance between Marxism and environmental philosophy has long been
recognized. Already in the 1960s Ernst Bloch was linking Marxism
to the ecological movement, using the expression, "transcending
without transcendence."[6]

CONTEMPORARY CHINESE MARXISM

This book has been written with particular attention to the situation in China today. We made this decision not only because of the sheer size of China's population and its political, economic, and technological power; not only because China is the largest nation in the world to be defined by its constitution as a Marxist state; and not only because the environmental decisions made by the people and the leaders of China will reverberate across the entire planet. It's also because the contemporary Chinese situation raises particularly complex questions about the future of Marxism and capitalism. The somewhat different questions facing Marxists in Russia and Latin America are not less important, but they will not be our primary focus here.

That said, we should add an important caveat: the authors are scholars, not politicians; and we are "China watchers," not Chinese nationals with special expertise in China's internal affairs. One cannot insist that political theory in a postmodern world is radically contextual while at the same time making pronouncements from the outside on how China should be run. We limit ourselves to the somewhat more general task of reconstructing Marxist thought in this emerging postmodern context, recognizing that internal issues and day-by-day management decisions are the domain of Chinese leaders.

What makes China particularly important for Organic Marxism is that two things are happening simultaneously. One encounters deep reflection about what the next phase will be in the "Sinoization of Marxism," and one also sees a turn to the concept of ecological civilization. As scholars and environmentalists, we believe that the combination of Marxism and ecological thinking represents the most hopeful orientation for political theory and human policymaking. In that sense, this book is no abstract exercise. Since the 17th Congress of the Communist Party of China, the idea of creating an "ecological civilization" has been an official part of the Party's platform and plans. As one reads in Hu Jintao's report, the goal is to form "an energy and resource efficient, environment friendly structure of industries, pattern of growth, and mode of consumption."[7] With the rapidly growing ecological crisis in China, the urgency of establishing an ecological civilization is becoming a top priority from government leaders to the common people.

The idea of "ecological civilization" reflects an important change in the model of economic development in China. As Dr. Wang Zhihe writes, "Rather than emphasizing economic construction as the core of development, as it did in the past, the Party authorities have come to realize that sustainable development must be based on an understanding of an intertwined relationship between humanity and nature."[8] During the 18th Congress (November 2012), President Hu Jintao made "ecological civilization" a central theme in his report. At this Congress the Party wrote the task of building an ecological civilization into the Chinese constitution. As President Hu insisted, "We must give high priority to making an ecological civilization, work hard to build a beautiful country, and achieve lasting and sustainable development of the Chinese nation."[9]

President Hu's 2012 report integrated these priorities into the plans for China's development over the coming years. Emphasizing the importance of preserving farmland for farmers, he held up the goals of green fields, clean water and blue sky. Xi Jinping, the new leader of China, has voiced the same priorities. Building an ecological civilization, he has said, is a cause "benefiting both contemporaries and future generations."[10]

It is the thesis of this book that the goal of building an ecological civilization is not foreign to China's Marxist tradition; it is part of a natural evolution of Marxist thought, both in China and around the world. We thus echo the assessment of Dr. Wang Zhihe:

> These comments can help us understand why Constructive Postmodernism has been so well received in China. ... Constructive Postmodernism has deep convergences with

Chinese Marxism, such as putting emphasis on process, taking an organic stance, having a strong consciousness of social responsibility, caring for the poor, defending justice, and pursuing the common good. I argue that it is these deep convergences that make some open Chinese Marxists enthusiastic about Constructive Postmodernism.[11]

No one inside or outside China is under any illusions about how difficult it will be to build an ecological civilization, especially when nations and multinational corporations are resistant to changes in the present system. Still, the evidence suggests that the statements by China's leaders reflect substantial commitments. Western leaders, NGOs, and businesspeople will take them even more seriously as they come to understand the growing together of Marxism and an ecological worldview—hence our focus on Organic Marxism.

CONCLUSION: NEW RESOURCES

The good news is that new conceptual resources are now available for constructing a significantly revised form of Marxism. In these pages we will explore the developments in the sciences and in the philosophy of science that support this emerging postmodern, organic paradigm. Among them, ecosystem studies and ecological philosophies play a particularly important role. We have also drawn from cultural studies, which traces the different ways that cultural beliefs, norms, and practices are embedded and embodied in different societies. Too often Marxism has been taught and implemented as if it were "one size fits all." Without sensitivity to cultural dynamics and divergences, neither this nor any other political philosophy can be successfully applied.

The final resource that appears in these pages is process philosophy. To our knowledge, this is the first book on Marxism written from a process perspective. Some Chinese Marxists are already interpreting process philosophy as a new school within contemporary Western Marxism. As process philosophy begins to play a larger and larger role in China, it is important to think carefully about the ways that it leads to a deeper understanding of Marxist principles. For example, it is highly significant that process thinking appears in many places in traditional Chinese philosophy, in Confucian and Daoist thinkers, and even in the most ancient text in the Chinese philosophical tradition, the *I Jing*.

In the end, the work of all political and economic theories will be judged by the fruits of their application. No one denies that radical changes are necessary; indeed, it's increasingly clear that they must come quickly. Even non-Marxists know the most famous sentence Karl Marx ever wrote: "The philosophers have only interpreted the world, in various ways: the point, however, is to change it."[12] We dedicate this book to all those men and women around the world, young and old, who are dedicated to building a sustainable ecological civilization in our time.

NOTES

1. Francis Fukuyama, *The End of History and the Last Man* (New York: Free Press, 2006).

2. <http://www.globalissues.org/article/26/poverty-facts-and-stats#src1>.

3. Shaohua Chen and Martin Ravallion, "The developing world is poorer than we thought, but no less successful in the fight against poverty," World Bank, August 2008, <http://www.globalissues.org/article/26/poverty-facts-and-stats#src1>.

4. David Ray Griffin, ed., *The Reenchantment of Science: Postmodern Proposals* (Albany, NY: State University of New York Press, 1988); David Ray Griffin and Richard Falk, eds., *Postmodern Politics for a Planet in Crisis: Policy, Process, and Presidential Vision* (Albany, NY: State University of New York Press, 1993); Griffin, *Whitehead's Radically Different Postmodern Philosophy: An Argument for its Contemporary*

Relevance (Albany, NY: State University of New York Press, 2007); Philip Clayton, *Science and Ecological Civilization: A Constructive Postmodern Approach,* forthcoming in Chinese translation (Beijing, 2014).

5. Mark Cowling and James Martin, eds., *Marx's Eighteenth Brumaire: (Post)modern Interpretations* (London: Pluto Press, 2002), 19.

6. See Ernst Bloch, *Atheismus im Christentum: zur Religion des Exodus und des Reichs* (Frankfurt am Main: Suhrkamp, 1968).

7. Hu Jintao's Report at 17th Party Congress, <http://www.china.com. cn/17da/2007-10/24/content_9119449_4.htm>.

8. "International Whitehead Conference Discusses Ecological Civilization in China," *Global Times,* September 13, 2013, <http://www. globaltimes.cn/DesktopModules/DnnForge%20-%20NewsArticles/ Print.aspx?tabid=99&tabmoduleid=94&articleId=811013&moduleId =405&PortalID=0>.

9. <http://v.china.com.cn/18da/2012-11/11/content_27074139.htm>.

10. Xi Jinping, "Further Deepen the Construction of Ecological Civilization" <http://www.forestry.gov.cn/portal/main/s/195/con-tent-531588.html>.

11. Wang Zhihe, "Constructive Postmodernism, Chinese Marxism, and Ecological Civilization," paper presented at the 9th International Whitehead Conference in Krakow, Poland, September 2013.

12. Karl Marx"Theses on Feuerbach" (first published in 1843), in Marx, *The German Ideology* (Albany, NY: Prometheus Books, 1998). Marx's "Theses on Feuerbach" are also available online, <http://www.marxists. org/archive/marx/works/1845/theses/>.

Chapter 2

WHY NOT CAPITALISM?
HISTORICAL ORIGINS

In the following chapters we describe and advocate for Organic Marxism as a framework for social, political, and economic decision-making. Developments in the natural and social sciences, in ecology, and in cultural studies make this position a serious contender in the current debate. This postmodern version of Marxism deserves serious attention not only because of its strengths, however, but also because of the weaknesses of the alternatives. In particular, it should be assessed in light of the palpable shortcomings of its capitalist competitor, which are becoming more and more visible to observers around the world.

One cannot undertake this comparison without acknowledging how deeply capitalist assumptions have formed the backdrop for most thinking about economics and politics since the dawn of the modern age. Unless one pauses to carefully evaluate these background assumptions, it is impossible to seriously study and evaluate the alternatives.

The criticism that is most often raised against any alternative to capitalism is that it is idealistic and utopian. The last decades have provided numerous examples of the collapse of socialist experiments. Usually, as nations fall under the increasing dominance of unrestrained capitalist practices, little attention is paid to the drawbacks of canceling policies that were in place for the common good. As wealthier individuals focus on their access to higher profits and greater diversity of buying choices, they usually pay little attention to what is being lost as the capitalist kingdom grows.

Perhaps a short anecdote will help. One of this book's authors was studying in Germany in the period leading up to the fall of the Berlin wall. Because of the abuses and mismanagement of the East German government, the German Democratic Republic (DDR), little attention was paid to the dashed hopes of this socialist experiment on German soil. On the morning following the collapse of the Berlin wall, German newspaper reporters interviewed the East Germans who began pouring into West Berlin through the new openings in the wall. They asked, "What is it like for you to come to the West for the first time? What does it mean to you?" One expected to hear emotional comments about the importance of freedom, self-government, and the need for a more open socialist democracy. Instead, the answers were uniformly about access to products. "I need spark plugs for my moped" and "I want to buy bananas for my family" were the first answers in the article; and most of the comments that followed were similar. Only one woman said, "I just want to wander under the Linden trees on the Kurfürstendamm," the famous broad avenue in West Berlin.

How did the assumptions of capitalist political and economic systems become "just obvious"? Why do so many falsely assume that "there *is* no alternative"? Only when we have sketched the birth and history of this worldview can we begin to understand its contemporary manifestations, and only then can we accurately assess whether there are more positive alternatives.

DEFINING CAPITALISM

American authors like to define capitalism as the rejection of state ownership. Thus the Merriam Webster dictionary suggests as its primary definition that capitalism is "a way of organizing an economy so that the things that are used to make and transport products (such as land, oil, factories, ships, etc.) are owned by individual people and companies rather than by the government."

But rejection of state ownership is actually a subsidiary feature. At its most basic level, *capitalism means an economic system in which the most central value and goal is the creation and increase in wealth.* In such systems, wealth is measured not primarily in terms of the labor that is required to produce goods, or the use-value that these goods have for real people. Instead, it's measured in terms of an independent economic reality: the exchange value of these goods on the open market. Capital is the fluid currency by means of which goods are bought and sold, and in terms of which they are valued. The exchange of currency therefore becomes the dominant reality; other aspects of economics—the banking system, exchange, economic institutions, work, and even social institutions—are assessed by the amount of capital that the market will pay for them.

Put differently, capitalism is a way of valuing items and services that abstracts from the labor that produces them and from the real-world uses to which they are put—the rice that is eaten, the clothes that are worn, the house that a family lives in. Instead, the amount of money that investors will pay for an item is allowed to determine its value. As the scope of capitalism grows, this criterion informs value judgments for ever larger spheres of daily life. More and more of the lived experience of human social systems, and of the people who participate in them, comes to be evaluated based upon the market's decision concerning values.

Perhaps an anecdote will help to make this point. Some years ago we were guests at the house of a wealthy gentleman in Connecticut. We had heard that he used his house to display and sell art and furniture, but we were completely unprepared for what we found when we arrived. Not only every painting on the walls, but every piece of furniture in his own home had a number on it. Guests were given a price list and asked to consider making purchases during their visit. No attention was paid to the value of friendships, discussions, or the experience of sharing food together at the table. The "free market" had come to dominate this gentleman's home, so that everything in his "private sphere" was now valued according to the price that the visitors would pay for it. (We did not ask whether his wife and children were also for sale.)

Many people—especially those who possess the most wealth— believe that the best means for structuring human society is to build it upon market-based means for assigning value. One can only evaluate this suggestion, however, by contrasting it with the alternative. What is lost when market mechanisms supersede the more ancient ways of determining the value of products: the labor that was required to produce them, and the uses that they are put to by ordinary humans (food, clothing, shelter)? What happens when we turn things that are valuable in and of themselves—family, community, ecosystems, even the planet itself—into commodities to be bought and traded, so that market value replaces inherent value? One will understand the present world situation only when one has come to recognize what has been lost as the "global market" has come to dominate human societies and the planet.

To understand the implications of the shift to a capitalist worldview, some historical analysis is necessary.

THE IDEAL OF THE STATE: A BRIEF HISTORY

To some readers it might appear obvious that an economic and political system based on the principle of selfishness—acquisition for oneself and one's family, apart from the question of what is best for the community as a whole—would be an inferior system. After all, we already know that human beings tend to be selfish. We tend to see the world through only one pair of eyes, our own; we naturally think of our own desires before we think of the desires of others; and our own pain quickly blinds us to the concerns of others around us. If this is the kind of animal that we are, why would we want a political system that encourages us to be even more selfish than we already are?

Indeed, given the evidence of the selfishness of human beings—their tendency to use their power to benefit themselves, or their friends and family, over the needs of others—wouldn't we desire exactly the opposite from our political system? Ideally, one would think, the function of the state should be to help make us *better* than we are. Governments, it would seem, should pass policies that help educate and cultivate their citizens. By word and example, they should encourage us to greater deeds than we would otherwise have achieved. Likewise, governments should take steps to restrain those citizens whose selfishness has made them rich and powerful at the expense of other citizens. One thinks, for example, of the hedge fund traders and managers on Wall Street whose greed caused a global economic crisis in 2008.

Much higher ideals for government were formulated early in the history of most of the world's great civilizations. Consider the example of China. It was believed that the Emperor ruled the dynasty not for his own gain but for the good of all citizens. (Even though many rulers clearly failed to achieve this goal, the standard was clear.) Confucius's description of the noble person was really a description of the virtues expected of every good government official in his work. When one is strong, it is to make the whole community strong; where there is knowledge, it is knowledge for all; and where there are values and cultivation, the goal is to foster harmony across the society. The Emperor is nothing without the state, and the state finds its greatest happiness and fulfillment in the Emperor. Or so, at any rate, it was said.

From the beginning of Western civilization, the ancient philosophers also held that the state and its rulers exist for the good of the entire society. In Athens in the sixth century BCE, the ruler Solon recognized that laws must take into account both economic and moral values in order for the society to remain healthy. As a result, Solon encouraged citizens to expand foreign trade and to make sure their children found productive work; he also forgave the debts of the poorest people in Athens in an attempt to create a more equal society. One poem attributed to Solon says:

Some wicked men are rich, some good are poor,
We will not change our virtue for their store:
Virtue's a thing that none can take away;
But money changes owners all the day.[1]

In the *Republic*, Plato offered detailed analogies to show that the health of individuals and families is dependent on a healthy state. "Also ... the State, if once started well, moves with accumulating force like a wheel. For good nurture and education implant good constitutions, and these good constitutions, taking root in a good education, improve more and more."[2] The *Republic* provides detailed instructions for the training of future leaders, so that they will offer wise direction to the state as a whole. Plato carefully lays out the standards, the training, and the educational requirements that future rulers need if they are to become wise and benevolent. His ideal is the "philosopher-king," a moral and well-educated person who can help to establish and retain the perfect balance between the working class, military, and administrators of the society.

Aristotle's *Politics* are if anything even more clear. Those who lead the state must have the highest virtue, *aristos*, or excellence. When a nation based on excellence (an aristocracy, i.e. rule by the excellent) loses this virtue and leaders begin to rule by power alone, the state devolves into oligarchy and eventually into totalitarian rule. Aristotle warned stringently about this danger and sought to ward it off with political theory, historical analysis, a theory of constitutions, and wise educational advice. Unfortunately, stable aristocracies devoted to the good of the people have been the exception rather than the rule over the course of human history.

In the medieval period in the West, a ruler was expected to be a representative of God. Because the central attributes of God were said to be love and justice, the excellent ruler was the one who exemplified both these qualities. In the medieval Islamic tradition, this requirement was generalized into a Muslim theory of human nature (theological anthropology): humans are created by God to be his "vice-regents"—creatures who reign on earth on God's behalf, wisely leading each other and all living things. According to the Christian theologians of the medieval period, the purpose of the state was to function as a microcosm of God's kingdom, manifesting the order that is reflected in the nature of God and in the creation itself. These ideals dominated political theory during the approximately 1,000 years of the Middle Ages in the West.

As we will see in a moment, the "libertarian" tradition in modernist Europe and North America eventually broke from this tradition. But even the modern liberals and libertarians retained reference to these higher values, at least at the beginning. Consider the Declaration of Independence, which the settlers in the British colonies in North America composed in order to justify their fight for freedom from the British monarch, George III:

> We hold these truths to be self-evident, that all men are created equal, that they are endowed by their Creator with certain unalienable Rights, that among these are Life, Liberty and the pursuit of Happiness. That to secure these rights, Governments are instituted among Men, deriving their just powers from the consent of the governed, That whenever any Form of Government becomes destructive of these ends, it is the Right of the People to alter or to abolish it, and to institute new Government, laying its foundation on such principles and organizing its powers in such form, as to them shall seem most likely to effect their Safety and Happiness.

When Thomas Jefferson penned these words, and when the founding fathers of the United States of America adopted them as their motto, they grounded the authority of the state in its ability to preserve and promote "life, liberty, and the pursuit of happiness" on behalf of all its citizens.

In short: since the dawn of civilization, virtually every great civilization in both East and West has affirmed that rulers lead on behalf of the good of the people. The core values of each civilization have been articulated by its leaders, as well as by the philosophers, religious leaders, artists, poets, and great writers of that society. The idea of a value-free state—one that encourages the citizens to pursue their own gain outside any broader system of values—would have been completely foreign to the ways that these civilizations defined themselves. The American president John F. Kennedy gave a concise expression to this standard: "Ask not what your country can do for you. Ask what you can do for your country."

THE BIRTH OF CAPITALISM

We began with this short section on the history of political philosophy in order to point out the anomaly of capitalism as a political theory. The justification of the state offered by the modern capitalist philosophers stands in marked contrast to the ideals that underlay the great civilizations in both East and West. How did this revolutionary change come about?

To understand what happened, we need to return to the words that Thomas Jefferson used in the Declaration of Independence in 1776. All humans, he said, are "endowed by their Creator with certain unalienable Rights," most especially "Life, Liberty and the pursuit of Happiness." Jefferson drew this list of core human rights from the influential *Two Treatises of Government*, published anonymously by the British political theorist John Locke in 1689. But Jefferson made an important change to Locke's wording: he substituted the word "happiness" for the word "property." In the *Second Treatise*, Locke had actually said that the purpose of the state is to protect the "life, liberty, and *property*" of the male property-holders, who (according to his proposal) were the only persons who should be allowed to vote.[3] In the influential work of John Locke, the protection of wealth—in this case, property—served as the major justification of the state.

Why this sudden change? Undoubtedly the imperial expansion of the European nations had something to do with it. Thanks to their massive military and naval power, they had begun taking raw materials (and, when they could, slaves) from Africa, Asia, and the Americas, which brought a rapid increase in wealth to Britain's upper classes. With the new influx of capital, someone needed to justify why laws should favor the exploitation of foreign resources and their flow across national borders.

The early capitalists had inherited a rather negative view of human nature. One cause was the stress on sin in the Catholic and Protestant churches: "All men have sinned and fallen short of the kingdom of God," writes Paul in the Christian New Testament (Romans 3:23), and "the wages of sin is death" (Rom. 6:23). Others argue that the many wars and plagues that had dominated Europe, such as the Thirty Years War (1618-48), had darkened the European view of human nature. After all, it's estimated that a *quarter* of the population of northern Europe had died as a result of the wars and plagues.

For whatever reason, the view of human nature held by the philosopher Thomas Hobbes, published in his famous book *Leviathan* in 1649, came to dominate the political thinking of his age. The natural state of man, he argued, is "the war of all against all." What we have to expect, he continued, is that life will be "nasty, brutish, and short." As a result, it is in our interest to support a ruler, no matter how harsh he is, who is able to amass enough power to prevent civil war and anarchy among the population. Virtually the only value that citizens should impose on the leader of the state is that he be powerful enough to win victory over his opponents.

John Locke, whose *Two Treatises* are arguably the founding document for capitalist political theory, was deeply influenced by Hobbes. Indeed, he generalized Hobbes' "state of war" into what he called the "state of nature" for human beings. Locke's definition is clear: "Men living according to reason, without a common superior on earth to judge between them, is properly the state of nature." This is the situation that we find ourselves in before we agree to form a political state. According to Locke, it is "want of a common judge, with authority," that "puts all persons in a state of nature."[4] Locke shared with Hobbes the assumption that, left in the state of nature, humans will fall into warfare with each other and no one will be safe.

For Locke, the existence of the state was justified by a sort of social contract. The ruler wants power over the society, and the citizens want protection from the state of nature, which is the worst possible state for humans to live in. So the citizens transfer some of their natural powers—their powers over their own bodies, and their powers of production—to the ruler, in return for his protection. The government keeps up its end of the bargain only as long as it offers these protections: protecting the citizens from physical harm ("life"), protecting them from being imprisoned by or coming under the control of other citizens ("liberty"), and protecting their possessions from theft or damage ("property"). Locke bases all other, "higher" functions of the government upon this one foundation.

Through the influence of Hobbes and Locke, *government in the capitalist tradition was initially defined in primarily negative terms*. Its task is to protect citizens from each other and from the "state of nature" into which they would otherwise fall. When citizens are protected in this way, they are free to pursue their goals of acquiring more property. It follows that, with the exception of its role as protector, the less that government does, the better.

In this sense capitalism is closely aligned with the work of the Italian political theorist Niccolò Machiavelli (1469-1527). In Machiavelli's famous book, *The Prince*, he exhorts the ruler (the Prince) to take whatever steps are necessary to stay in power. His view of human nature is similar to Hobbes' "war of all against all":

> And here comes the question whether it is better to be loved rather than feared, or feared rather than loved ... [I]f we must choose between them, it is far safer to be feared than loved. For of men it may generally be affirmed, that they are thankless, fickle, falsely studious to avoid danger, greedy of gain, devoted to you while you are able to confer benefits upon them ... but in the hour of need they turn against you.[5]

Like Hobbes, Machiavelli argues that the main task of the ruler is to amass as much power as possible, so that he will be the undisputed authority in all things: "Therefore if a Prince succeeds in establishing and maintaining his authority, the means will always be judged honourable and be approved by everyone. For the vulgar are always taken by appearances and by results, and the world is made up of the vulgar."[6] By no means does the leader rule for the common good; he rules for himself. His only obligation to the people is to prevent them from being destroyed by their enemies or destroying each other. If the ruler carries out these negative functions, by whatever means, he will stay in power: "He who becomes a Prince through the favour of the people should always keep on good terms with them; which it is easy for him to do, since all they ask is not to be oppressed."[7]

It is interesting to compare this truncated view of the government's role with the values that the European Enlightenment philosophers embraced a short time later. The leaders of the Enlightenment have sometimes been criticized for focusing exclusively on rationality and science, at the expense of values and literature, but that judgment only tells part of the story. Enlightenment authors also argued that the state has the responsibility to recognize and develop the *humanum*—the essence of what it is to be human. Human communities need not merely physical protection but also the sorts of cultural, artistic, and educational institutions that support the formation of cultivated persons. So even within the Western liberal tradition, it was not obvious that a negative definition of the role of government had to dominate political philosophy.

A few examples will suffice. In France, Jean-Jacques Rousseau defended a version of the social contract that diverged significantly from his British predecessors. Whereas Hobbes and Locke argued that humans exist naturally in a state of violence and misery, Rousseau believed that it is *civilization* which actually corrupts humans from their original harmony. He held that, when humans in the "state of nature" agree to form a state, they relinquish their private desires in order to pursue the general good of the community. For Rousseau, the power of the state stems from the general will (*volonté générale*) of the entire population. Citizens retain their general will; it should not be transferred away from them onto an all-powerful ruler (such as Hobbes' Leviathan). Because Rousseau believed that the people themselves always continue to play a role in constituting the power of the state, he insists that education and the cultivation of virtue are important parts of governance. It is the role of the legislator, he writes, to inspire the people to support those laws that will transform them and future generations into better citizens:

> By themselves, the people always desire what is good, but do not always discern it. The general will (*volonté générale*) is always right, but the judgment which guides it is not always enlightened. The general will must be made to see objects as they are, sometimes as they ought to appear; it must be shown the good path that it is seeking, and guarded from the seduction of private interests; it must be made to observe closely times and places, and to balance the attraction of immediate and palpable advantages against the danger of remote and concealed evils. ... All alike have need of guides.[8]

The German philosophers called this training of the general will *Bildung*, which means forming and molding persons as a whole, developing their minds and their character. Thus the German philosopher Georg W.F. Hegel began his great work, *The Phenomenology of Mind* (*Die Phänomenologie des Geistes*) with a discussion of cultivation:

> Culture or development of mind (*Bildung*), regarded from the side of the individual, consists in his acquiring what lies at his hand ready for him, in making its inorganic nature organic to himself, and taking possession of it for himself. Looked at, however, from the side of universal mind qua general spiritual substance, culture means nothing else than that this substance gives itself its own self-consciousness, brings about its own inherent process and its own reflection into self.[9]

26

For the French and German Enlightenment thinkers, then, the state exists for more than the protection of property; culture matters also. Civic-mindedness and a focus on the common good require the careful formation of citizens. For the Enlightenment philosophers it was clear that the government and its institutions have some responsibility to contribute constructively to the flourishing of society and culture.

THE "INVISIBLE HAND" OF CAPITALISM

Of course, the philosophers of capitalism gradually learned not to present their political philosophy in solely negative terms. The most important of these reformulations came in Adam Smith's famous book, *The Wealth of Nations*. Coincidentally, *The Wealth of Nations* was published in 1776, the same year as Thomas Jefferson wrote the Declaration of Independence, which justified the revolutionary war against England that led to the formation of the United States of America. Capitalism, it appears, has been built into the very DNA of the United States more than any other nation in the history of this planet.

Adam Smith builds his case for capitalism by analyzing the division of labor. According to Smith, the members of any social group will naturally begin to differentiate themselves into different employments. Workers, he claims, become more efficient when they perform fewer tasks. As a result, productivity rises, and the society is able to generate more wealth. In his analysis, the more "advanced" societies are those that have divided their labor more distinctly.[10]

This division of labor in turn gives rise to the need for some means of exchange, so that workers can trade their surplus products for those produced by other workers. Capital (currency) is therefore invented as a convenient means of exchange.[11] Adam Smith claims that the price of any given product arises as a function of the amount of work it takes to produce it. From that initial point, the price will rise when there is a scarcity of the product, and it will fall when an over-abundance of the product is available.[12]

It is a fundamental assumption for Adam Smith that every individual will seek to maximize his or her own profit. Based on this premise, he views it as a basic law of economics that workers will continue to produce their product as long as its price compensates for the work of producing it. When the price of a product falls, fewer people will have incentive to produce that product. At that point, he claims, the market will naturally balance itself out. Over the long run, prices will tend to stabilize at the precise level where the workers are compensated for their work and receive a reasonable profit for it. In other words, the market will show a wisdom greater than any human person or policy could ever establish.

Adam Smith's economic philosophy produced a doctrine known as *laissez-faire* capitalism, from the French phrase for "to let it be" or "to allow to do." This economic philosophy instructs the government not to interfere or intervene in the markets in any way. Ironically, this doctrine came to be known as the "free market" doctrine, confusing the "freedom" of human rights and basic human liberties with the "freedom" of the wealthy to accumulate as much wealth as they can.

Note that, according to Smith, this natural balance will establish itself at the international level as well as at the local level. Put in more contemporary terms, this amounts to the claim that microeconomics and macroeconomics work in the same way. By establishing a system of free trade, Smith argues, nations will maximize their own profits, and hence the good of their citizens. The international market will evidence the same stability that Smith believes is the natural byproduct of any local system, such as when farmers grow rice on their farm and bring it to the local market to sell to villagers.[13]

Adam Smith acknowledged that there is something surprising, even miraculous, about this outcome. Each of us can act purely in our own self-interest; and yet the outcome, when we come together in markets, will be the best possible result for our village, our country, and for all humans on the planet. Smith viewed this outcome as a deterministic law, analogous to the physical laws of Newton, which had made an incredible impact on the European mind in the early eighteenth century. Yet he did not use the terms of physics. Instead, he presented his idea as if there were a God who magically transforms our selfishness into the best possible outcome for the whole. Smith called this transformation "the invisible hand":

> [The rich] consume little more than the poor, and in spite of their natural selfishness and rapacity . . . they divide with the poor the produce of all their improvements. *They are led by an invisible hand* to make nearly the same distribution of the necessaries of life, which would have been made, had the earth been divided into equal portions among all its inhabitants; and thus without intending it, without knowing it, advance the interest of the society, and afford means to the multiplication of the species.[14]

Or, even more clearly:

> Every individual . . . neither intends to promote the public interest, nor knows how much he is promoting it . . . [H]e intends only his own security; and by directing that industry in such a manner as its produce may be of the greatest value, he intends only his own gain, and *he is in this, as in many other cases, led by an invisible hand* to promote an end which was no part of his intention.[15]

What is remarkable in this foundational text for capitalism is that it not only allows each citizen to be selfish; *it exhorts them to be so.* Smith wants us to believe that no one needs to act consciously in the public interest and that policies aimed for the common good are doomed to fail. Nevertheless, miraculously, those who promote their own private interests, those who seek to become as wealthy as possible, end up producing the highest possible level of common good:

> It is not from the benevolence of the butcher, the brewer, or the baker, that we expect our dinner, but from their regard to their own interest. We address ourselves, not to their humanity

but to their self-love, and never talk to them of our necessities but of their advantages.[16]

What should worry one the most about this political philosophy is not just the negativity that permeates it. It is also the truncated view of the human person that it presupposes and fosters. The famous libertarian philosopher of the nineteenth century, John Stuart Mill, offers a similar set of priorities:

> [Political economy] does not treat the whole of man's nature as modified by the social state, nor of the whole conduct of man in society. *It is concerned with him solely as a being who desires to possess wealth*, and who is capable of judging the comparative efficacy of means for obtaining that end.[17]

Of all the complex desires that constitute our being as humans, it is only our "desire to possess wealth" that comes into focus here. According to Mill, only one kind of reasoning is necessary for this activity: means-ends reasoning, or what Max Weber would later call instrumental reasoning (*Zweckrationalität*), the rationality of picking the best means to achieve a desired goal. *Wertrationalität*, or the ability to reason about which goals are really of the greatest value, here falls out of the picture. Mill admits that he is putting forward "an arbitrary definition of man, as a being who invariably does that by which he may obtain the greatest amount of necessaries, conveniences, and luxuries, with the smallest quantity of labour and physical self-denial with which they can be obtained."[18]

CONCLUSION

In sum, Adam Smith introduced the idea of production for profit, measured not primarily in terms of the inherent values of the work and what is produced, but rather in terms of an independent economic reality known as currency or capital. According to this economic philosophy, the creation and exchange of currency becomes the primary goal, and all the other "goods" that human work can produce are consequences of the quest to acquire capital.

It is important to remember that Adam Smith was writing in the eighteenth century, almost 250 years ago. Social and economic change occurred much more slowly at that time, and most citizens believed that kings and queens ruled over the people by "divine right," by the will of God.

These facts help to explain Smith's naïve view that there is a natural stability and morality to the free market, but they do not justify it. Even at that time, the capitalist ideology was used to defend the injustices of the European nations, who were colonizing most of the world and profiting from their colonial rule. For instance, the early capitalists argued that it was actually in Africa's best interest that the slave traders should purchase men, women, and children and ship them to the New World. Did not the slave trade bring large amounts of capital to the tribal rulers and kings in the African nations? Was not this currency crucial for them to move away from their savage lifestyles, so that they could convert to Christianity and begin to become players in an emerging global market? Were not "costs" such as slavery and colonization well worth paying, given the many benefits that would come from being a part of the Europe-based capitalist system? Clearly the early capitalists believed that their system would be better for all nations, not only for the colonizing nations. Of course, one may wonder to what extent Britain, France, Spain, and Holland were blinded by the immense financial profits that they were reaping from colonizing Africa, South America, and much of Asia.

Today, more than two hundred years later, the injustice and abuse that the European empires forced upon the colonized peoples have become much clearer. Also, the inaccuracies of the founding story of capitalism are now obvious to all. State-sponsored terrorism, whether supported by fascist Spain and Germany or (in more hidden ways) by North American operatives in South America in the 1950s, has produced atrocities equal to or worse than what humans supposedly did to each other in the "state of nature." Moreover, the rapidity of change in today's world has falsified Adam Smith's belief in the natural harmony and stability of markets both at the local and at the international level. Most importantly, the immense population growth of the nineteenth and twentieth centuries has demonstrated that limited natural resources, which seemed inexhaustible in the eighteenth century, in fact set a planet-wide constraint on growth.

These and other factors, which we will explore in greater detail in the following chapters, run counter to Adam Smith's assertion that he had uncovered the unchanging natural laws of value and exchange. Above all, the "invisible hand" of the free market, like the hand of God, turned out not to bring the sort of justice for all persons that Smith claimed it would bring. Unrestrained capitalism has brought at least as much damage to people and to the planet as has unrestrained colonialism, and indeed for many of the same reasons. The magic that Adam Smith believed in—that if all are economically selfish, all will win—turned out to be, quite simply, false. In the next chapter, we examine the consequences of capitalist systems and the effects that they have wrought on human beings, nations, and the way we live with each other.

NOTES

1. Plutarch, *Lives*, ed. Arthur Hugh Clough, trans. John Dryden, vol. 1 (Boston: Little Brown and Co., 1906), 170.

2. Plato, *The Republic*, trans. Benjamin Jowett (Hoboken, NJ: Capstone, 2012), 133.

3. The American states also restricted voting rights to male property owners until these restrictions began to be lifted in the early 1800s.

4. John Locke, *Two Treatises on Government and A Letter Concerning Toleration*, ed. Ian Shapiro (New Haven: Yale University Press, 2003), 108.

5. Niccolo Machiavelli, *The Prince*, trans. Ninian Hill Thompson (Hoboken, NJ: Capstone, 2010), 125.

6. Ibid., 133.

7. Ibid., 74.

8. Jean-Jacques Rousseau, *The Social Contract; And, The First and Second Discourses*, ed. Susan Dunn (New Haven: Yale University Press, 2002), 180.

9. Georg Wilhelm Friedrich Hegel, *The Phenomenology of Mind*, trans. J.B. Baillie, 2nd ed. (New York: Macmillan, 1949), Preface.

10. Adam Smith, *An Inquiry into the Nature and Causes of the Wealth of Nations* (New York: The Modern Library, 1937), 5.

11. Ibid., 22.

12. Ibid., 30.

13. Ibid., 419.

14. Adam Smith, *The Theory of Moral Sentiments* (New York: Penguin Books, 2009), 184-85, italics added.

15. Smith, *The Wealth of Nations*, 456, italics added.

16. Ibid., 26-27.

17. John Stuart Mill, "On the Definition of Political Economy, and on the Method of Investigation Proper to It," first published in the *London and Westminster Review* (October 1836); republished in Mill, *Essays on Some Unsettled Questions of Political Economy*, 3rd ed. (London: Longmans, Green, Reader & Dyer, 1877), 137, italics added.

18. Ibid., 144.

Chapter 3

WHY NOT CAPITALISM? CONTEMPORARY PRACTICES AND THEIR CONSEQUENCES

Pure and Impure Forms of Capitalism

In the previous chapter we saw that capitalism is a type of economic and social system in which the most central driver is the accumulation of capital—the creation and increase in wealth. In a "pure" capitalist system, the only public institutions that would exist (apart from the military and a minimal government) would be the ones that property holders pay for. We also saw that, ideally, the capitalist state would not place any limits on the markets, since market forces by themselves are supposed to be the best way to establish what services should exist and how much they should cost.

In today's world capitalism rarely exists in this pure form. Governments and international organizations now play a wide variety of important roles: they provide some services on behalf of their citizens; they partially control currency values and interest rates; they limit businesses and investors from abusive behavior; they own buildings and parks; and they administer programs, such as the military and educational systems, that are viewed as essential to the good of the nation. Government ownership can be a means for achieving these goals, but it need not be seen as an end in itself.

(For this reason it is misleading to *define* socialism as the advocacy of government ownership. Such definitions are used by opponents in order to create the impression that socialists are out to take things away from people. We would prefer to define as *socialist* those social, economic, and political systems that seek to provide social services to citizens for the common good. We return to this question below.)

Most governments in the world today mix socialist and capitalist elements in the ways they structure and run their economies. As a result, capitalism is present today only in "impure" forms, constrained by socially motivated policies. This fact makes it more difficult to evaluate where market forces are helpful and where they are damaging. For example, when medications are available to citizens of a country, should we give credit to capitalist principles? Is it the quest for profit on the part of the various drug companies that has made it possible for sick people to get the medicine they need? Or do governmental guidelines, drug standards and testing (mandated in the U.S. by the Food and Drug Administration), national education policies, or government-sponsored insurance policies (such as Medicare and Social Security) play a more important role in meeting the health needs of the citizens? In a "mixed" system, neither capitalists nor socialists alone can claim the credit, since the medical system as a whole functions as a blend of the two systems. When defenders of capitalism point to positive consequences of the free market, they invariably ignore the role of governments in regulating market competition and preventing abuses.

EXAMPLES OF PURE CAPITALISM

For this reason, one has to step back a century or two in order to find examples of "pure" capitalism. Although the beginning of manufacturing can be traced back to the late eighteenth century, it was only with the rapid expansion of factories in the Second Industrial Revolution, roughly 150 years ago, that the full effects of unrestrained capitalism began to be felt. By this time the industrialists were able to amass large amounts of capital, to transform the lives of a significant number of citizens, and to begin to change the face of society. Because the revolutionary changes were unexpected, there was little government control at this time. For these reasons, this era offers good examples of the effects of market forces—the profit motive in its purest form—without governmental interventions to restrain and adapt market forces for the common good.

The period of the construction of the first trans-Continental railway across America provides a good first case study. No laws regulated this industry, the quality of the construction, or the treatment or salary of the laborers. Several different companies participated. Among them, the Central Pacific Railroad faced a shortage of workers in the Western United States. Recruiters traveled to China and brought over men to do the most brutal and dangerous construction. Working under inhumane conditions, the Chinese laborers built the first railroad line over the high Sierra Nevada mountains and across Nevada in order to meet up with the tracks that had already been laid in northern Utah. The Chinese immigrants were paid pennies a day. During the "blasting"— the placing of dynamite and the huge explosions that leveled obstacles along the way—little care was paid to their safety, and many were killed and maimed. By contrast, the existence of railroad connections brought great profits to the owners of the railroads and the businesses that depended on them.

As industrialization expanded in the United States, similarly inhumane working conditions arose in most of the industries and factories. Twelve-hour work days were not unusual, and the factory owners relied increasingly on children and poor women. Workers were paid at levels comparable to Bangladeshi garment workers today, and they worked in similarly dangerous conditions. Poor families would live in tenements built and owned by the factories where they worked. Subjected to high prices for housing and food, these families would sometimes find themselves owing more to the capitalist owners than they were paid for their work. As a popular folk song from this period describes it, one had to "Work all day for the pennies in your tea, Down behind the railway, And drill ye Tarriers drill, And blast, And fire."

As a result of these abuses, local, state, and federal governments began to pass some laws protecting workers, blending capitalist and socialist principles. For the first time, the governments of European and American nations began to develop a "mixed" model of capitalism. Of course, individuals and companies still owned the factories, and the workers did not share in ownership or enjoy any percentage of the profits. But the newspapers began to publish stories about the abuses, which increased public outcry against the brutal working conditions. Public protest led to new laws, which placed some constraints on what the factory owners could do to their workers. A religiously inspired protest movement began, which came to be known as the Social Gospel movement. Led by Walter Rauschenbusch, the Social Gospel movement increased public protest against the abuses, further encouraging new legislation and limiting what the owners could do to decrease costs and increase profits.

Financial legislation brought the first limitations on the power of companies. The Sherman Antitrust Act, passed by Congress in 1890, limited the power of a single corporation to create a monopoly. But currency speculation still remained largely uncontrolled. The 1920s (the "Roaring '20s") brought such rapid growth of the stock markets that average Americans began pouring their excess capital into speculative stocks. Banks would guarantee the investment, sometimes committing to pay two or even three times the value of the customer's investment if the market should fall. The promise of quick profits led to a frenzy of buying; in a single year, for example, the value of steel stocks doubled.

The great collapse of the European and American stock markets in October 1929 was in large part the result of the "pure" capitalism of the 1920s. In America, the Dow Jones Industrial Average lost 89 percent of its value over a three-year period, and it would take until late 1954 for the market to regain the value it had lost. I can well remember the stories my father's father told about the stock market crash, and in particular about October 29, 1929, the day they called "Black Tuesday." A bank owner and stock broker, he had invested large amounts of his and his clients' funds in the market. For him, as for the vast numbers of Americans who had staked their hopes in the unlimited growth of their capital through the markets, it was as if the world were ending. My grandfather described stockbrokers, including some of his friends, committing suicide by jumping out of the windows of their office buildings. All the capital they had amassed was wiped out. Having lost their house and most of their possessions, he and his wife moved into a small apartment. I remember his describing how they put bricks into their suitcases, so that the porters wouldn't know that their suitcases were mostly empty.

The greatest move toward a "mixed" capitalist/socialist economy in the United States occurred during the Great Depression, after the crash of the markets and the bankruptcy of many financial institutions. The massive unemployment and poverty of the Great Depression would last for almost 10 years. In response to the excesses of capitalist speculation, President Franklin D. Roosevelt began a series of social reforms known collectively as the "New Deal." His Social Security program, for example, represented the first government-sponsored insurance programs for elderly, unemployed, and sick Americans. The Fair Labor Standards Act of 1938 set maximum hours and minimum wages for most categories of workers.

These and other measures protecting workers and the public came to be known as the social "safety net." In this analogy, the participants in the capitalist system are like acrobats swinging on a trapeze far above the floor of the circus tent. When they lose hold of the trapeze, as is bound to happen from time to time, the safety net catches them before they hit the ground, so that they do not fall to their death. Similarly, the social policies that are established and funded by the government protect workers when the market lets them drop, so that they are not left destitute.

Of the many implications of the "safety net" metaphor, we note just two. First, by this time references to Adam Smith's "invisible hand" have disappeared. The bitter experience of industrialization and the growing control of the capitalists in the nineteenth and twentieth centuries was ample evidence that the free market does in fact destroy lives and create abuses. A society can either look the other way as individuals and families are crushed by wealthy corporations and individuals, or it can offer workers some protections from the brutal consequences of business competition. The social services provided by the safety net keep people and families alive when market forces would otherwise destroy them.

The second implication of the metaphor is less encouraging, however. Why would governments do nothing more than to construct a safety net? Why would they allow the markets themselves to remain unregulated enough that they can create abuses of this sort? Failing to address the *causes* of the class system that capitalism creates, governments have often sought only to mitigate a few of the *effects* of the unrestrained market system on the least fortunate of its workers.

One should find it puzzling that governments, which exist for the good of their citizens, would limit their interventions only to the effects and not to the causes of harm. Imagine that an extremely dangerous section of highway causes multiple accidents, leaving many drivers and passengers dead or wounded. We cannot imagine that leaders would simply keep ambulances waiting at the side of the road to transport the wounded off to hospitals after each accident. We expect them to modify the highway so that it will cause less damage to drivers. Why, in the case of capitalist speculation, would governments choose to help mitigate the negative consequences only after the fact?

CAPITALISM, SOCIAL DARWINISM, AND RELIGION

We suggest that many have been blinded by an ideology that the defenders of unrestrained markets have created in order to keep governments on the sidelines. Ever since it turned out that (*contra* Adam Smith) there is no "invisible hand" to protect workers from the byproducts of competition, defenders of "free" markets have used science on the one hand, and religion on the other, to make their case. Let's consider each of these two strategies in turn.

In 1859, in the midst of the Industrial Revolution, Charles Darwin published his famous *On the Origin of Species.* Viewed as science, Darwin's groundbreaking work did much to launch the biological sciences as we know them today. Taken as ideology, however, it did massive damage. Darwin's scientific insights were simple but brilliant. He postulated that there must be some mechanism of "random variation" in organisms. (Biologists later discovered the structure of DNA and the details of genetic mutations to explain this phenomenon.) The environment then brings about a "selective retention" of some of these genotypes. The organisms with the greatest "reproductive fitness" multiply, playing a larger and larger role in their ecosystem, while other species become extinct over time.

Darwin's second book, *The Descent of Man* (1871), included a major role for cooperative behaviors. It shows that Darwinian biology is far from a philosophy of individualism. Instead, Darwin had a deep understanding of the crucial role that groups, social behaviors, and cooperation play in the evolution of life.[1]

But Darwin's contemporaries chose to overlook the social and cooperative features of his scientific breakthroughs. Already in the early reception of Darwin's work, Victorian writers focused on the idea of "the survival of the fittest." The early popularizer of evolutionary theory, Alfred Lord Tennyson, wrote a poem that captured the public imagination of that time:

> Are God and Nature then at strife
> That Nature lends such evil dreams?
> So careful of the type she seems
> So careless of the single life ...

> "So careful of the type?" but no.
> From scarped cliff and quarried stone
> She cries a thousand types are gone;

I care for nothing, all shall go. [...]

                       shall he,
Man, her last work, who seem'd so fair
Such splendid purpose in his eyes,
Who roll'd the psalm to wintry skies,
Who built him fanes of fruitless prayer,

Who trusted God was love indeed
And love Creation's final law—
Tho' Nature, red in tooth and claw
With ravine, shrieked against his creed...[2]

On this view, which became the dominant interpretation of Darwinism, evolution was about the harsh battle of all against all—very much like the "nasty, brutish, and short" view of nature that Thomas Hobbes had championed in 1649. Nature is "red in tooth and claw," the Victorians believed, because it is about the stronger animals killing the weaker animals.

A major school in social and economic theory known as "Social Darwinism" was born out of this misrepresentation of Darwin. If the "the survival of the fittest" is natural law, the capitalists argued, then the same rule should also guide the way we build and structure human society. Those who have wealth must be rich because they are more "fit" for survival, and those who lack wealth must be poor because they are "unfit." In the most vicious forms of Social Darwinism, theorists argued that those in power ought to let the poor simply die, preferably before they have the chance to reproduce. After all, they are the weak links in the evolutionary chain; the species as a whole will be stronger if the rich are allowed to have many children and the poor have none. Incidentally, similar arguments have been used to defend nationalism: the country that conquers other countries must be more fit and therefore deserves to rule over the others as an imperial power. During the colonial period, British, French, and German theorists each used this language in defending their empires.

One of Darwin's cousins, Francis Galton, turned this attitude into a specific program soon after Darwin's death, which he named "eugenics." The eugenics movement (from the Greek for "well born") advocated social and government programs to improve the quality of the human gene pool. Specifically, Galton sought to introduce programs to increase the number of children for people with desirable characteristics and to prevent reproduction for people with undesirable characteristics. His American follower William Goodell, for example, argued that mentally ill men should be castrated and the ovaries should be removed from mentally ill women. If women with undesirable traits became pregnant, they should undergo forced abortions, and women with desirable traits should be forcibly impregnated by men whose traits are considered to be advantageous.

Racism played a major role in the eugenics movement. Because the British Victorians considered white people to be more highly evolved than dark-skinned people, they argued that light-skinned people should be given reproductive advantages. The more extreme advocates of eugenics programs sought to decrease or even exterminate undesirable ethnic groups (genocide) on the grounds that they were more primitive than the more advanced, light-skinned ethnic groups. Adolph Hitler and the Nazis later adopted this same ideology of social eugenics for what they claimed to be scientific reasons. Famously, they used pseudo-Darwinian language to justify their efforts to exterminate all members of the Jewish religion, which they (falsely) treated as a race.[3]

In Chapter 9 we will explore the developments in recent biology that have undercut the Social Darwinist interpretation of evolution. Social Darwinism is, unfortunately, a prime example of science being used as ideology in order to defend the status quo of those in power. Although the scientific justification for this application has long since been undercut, it continues to surface in libertarian defenses of market forces, however harsh the consequences are for the poor.

It is perhaps not surprising that Darwinism was and is still used to provide the scientific justification for capitalism. But it is a bit more surprising, or at least disappointing, that Christian theologians have also given their own religious backing to the capitalists. In offering their support, the theologians often appeal back to the sixteenth-century Reformation theologian John Calvin. Calvin believed that God predestined some to eternal salvation and others to eternal damnation. But how does one know whether he is among the saved or the damned? Well, the theologians argued, surely God will shower blessings on those whom he has chosen for eternal life in heaven, while withholding blessings from those who are destined to go to hell. The Calvinists knew that they could not change the outcome of God's decision. But if they worked hard, they could become rich; and riches would be a sign that they were probably among the "elect" of God. The great German sociologist Max Weber named this phenomenon "the Protestant work ethic" and demonstrated the immense influence that it had on the development of capitalism in modern Europe.[4]

In fact, Christianity and capitalism have often worked as close allies. This marriage is difficult to understand, since Jesus, the founder of Christianity, gave many warnings to the rich and proclaimed that the Kingdom of God is for the poor (Luke 6:20). Perhaps the reason is that Christianity has also emphasized personal choice and individual responsibility. The religion asks each person to choose between heaven and hell, teaching that one's decision will have inescapable consequences. Sometimes the New Testament even uses analogies with money to explain the outcome of one's choice: if you invest your resources well, you will be rewarded, but if you invest badly, you will be punished (Matthew 25:14-30). This sort of logic leads people to think that economic success or failure must be a consequence of personal decisions.

THE CONSEQUENCES OF CAPITALISM

In short, the standard capitalist argument is that all the good developments in the modern period—science, technology, increased comfort, increased standard of living, and increased lifespan—are the result of free market capitalism. This argument has a corollary: those who work hard will succeed, and those who have not succeeded have not worked hard.

We believe both claims are false. Let's begin with the second. One of the most foundational myths of capitalism is that wealth is earned through hard work and natural abilities. Those who have talent and apply it towards the pursuit of wealth will rise above the economic class into which they were born. Thomas Piketty's recent book, *Capital in the Twenty-First Century*, shows that even in the current era, inheritance is a stronger predictor of wealth than earnings. In other words, capital continues to be controlled by family dynasties much more than by those with natural talent. Piketty's research shows that economic inequality will continue to grow unless we make changes to our economic structure, perhaps through a progressive tax system.[5] In short, the actual data undercut the capitalist myth that outcomes in the competition for wealth are determined primarily by your virtue, character, intelligence and skill, and by how hard you work.

It turns out that other factors determine wealth, generally trumping individual factors of the sort just mentioned. Consider these four examples.

(1) Your access to capital. Obviously, those who have no money cannot make money on investments, whereas people who are rich can use their money to make more money. In an age of technology, and in a global economic system that increasingly favors large businesses, significant capitalization is increasingly the indispensable condition for success in business. Globally, people from the upper classes have far greater access to wealth, while people from lower classes don't have it and have a far harder time borrowing it. In many Western countries it is more difficult for people of color to procure major loans, and in most countries women have a more difficult time with financing than men. Access to capital is also significantly easier in the global North than in the South.

(2) *Your education and training.* In general, salary rises as one's educational level rises.[6] Graduates from the MBA program at Harvard University in 2013 began work with an average starting salary of $120,000. MBA graduates from the University of Madras, one of India's strong programs, begin work at $85,000.[7] People trained in high tech professions and in business have the highest earning power. Teachers earn less, and their ability to earn decreases still further when they teach younger children. Farm workers and non-skilled workers earn the least. Many living in rural settings, especially in developing nations, have little to no access to educational opportunities. But income correlates with education worldwide.

(3) *The region of the world you come from.* Your region does not determine whether or not you can be a successful capitalist, but it does have some effects. If you are born in a developed nation, you probably have greater access to lucrative markets and better odds of financial success. According to data from the Organization for Economic Co-operation and Development (OECD), Estonia ranks lowest among the OECD member countries (mostly developed nations), with an average annual wage of $17,323.[8] Worldwide, however, the median *household* income is only about $10,000, according to Gallup.[9] And the World Bank estimates that in 2010 about 21 percent of people in the developing world, 1.22 billion people, lived at or below $1.25 a day.[10]

Another comparative measure used to compute purchasing power parity (PPP) is the gross domestic product divided by a country's population, which yields per capita GDP. According to the International Monetary Fund, when one uses this measure Qatar ranks the highest in the world at $100,889, and the Democratic Republic of Congo ranks the lowest in the world at $365.[11] Put differently, the PPP is *276 times higher* in Qatar than it is in the Republic of Congo.

(4) *Your race.* Around the world, race and ethnicity influence one's income. According to the U.S. Census Bureau, "While White Americans made up roughly 75.1% of all persons in 2000, 87.93% of all households in the top 5% were headed by a person who identified

as being White alone. Only 4.75% of all households in the top 5% were headed by someone who identified him or herself as being Hispanic or Latino of any race, versus 12.5% of persons identifying themselves as Hispanic or Latino in the general population."[12]

One could easily extend this list; the data are readily available. But the message is hard to deny: *numerous factors that are outside the individual's own control determine his or her fate in the "free" market.* Generally speaking, men have advantages over women, white people over darker-skinned people, the already wealthy over the poor, developed nations over developing nations, and urban dwellers over farmers. If your country has a stable currency, a low crime rate, a strong educational system, and a well-developed infrastructure, then you are likely to outperform those who lack these advantages—even if you both bring the same skills and effort to your business ventures.

CONCLUSION

Americans like to use the traditional expression, "May the best man win!" But in the sometimes brutal world of global markets, it is frequently *not* the best man who wins. Indeed, multiple examples suggest that it is often the *less* virtuous people who win the battle to become rich.

These facts also undermine the claim that we should give credit to capitalism for the achievements of the modern period. It is not unguided and unrestrained human competition that has provided the social goods which add the most quality of life for the greatest number of people. Instead, the greatest gains come when people organize themselves into *societies that serve the common good in both word and deed*—that is, in their core beliefs as well as in their actual practice. As we will see in the next chapter, successful socialist systems can retain an appropriate place for entrepreneurial activities. *Contra* traditional Marxism, hybrid systems work; suitably constrained market forces can benefit the public good.

Most people find it counterintuitive that a system motivated exclusively by greed and cutthroat competition would bring the greatest benefits to the greatest number of people. We now see that there is a good reason people find this claim counterintuitive: it is false. Abuses are only overcome when governments, multinational agencies, labor groups, consumer advocates, and a well-organized system of checks and balances all serve as watchdogs over market competition. As we will see in the next chapter, the best solution is neither *laissez-faire* capitalism nor state ownership of all major industries. As the climate crisis deepens, new kinds of solutions will have to be found that focus on the common good, blending the needs of society, humanity as a whole, and the planet on which we depend.

NOTES

1. More recent work has brought further evidence of the role of cooperative behaviors and of "group selection" in evolution. See Elliott Sober and David Sloan Wilson, *Unto Others: The Evolution and Psychology of Unselfish Behavior* (Cambridge, MA: Harvard University Press, 1998).

2. Alfred Lord Tennyson, "In Memoriam A.H.H." The famous phrase, "Nature, red in tooth and claw," occurs in Canto 56.

3. Robert Jay Lifton, *The Nazi Doctors: Medical Killing and the Psychology of Genocide* (New York: Basic Books, 1986); see especially the introduction.

4. Max Weber, *The Protestant Ethic and the Spirit of Capitalism: The Talcott Parsons Translation Interpretations,* ed. Richard Swedberg (New York: W.W. Norton & Co., 2009).

5. Thomas Piketty, *Capital in the Twenty-First Century,* trans. Arthur Goldhammer (Boston: Harvard University Press, 2014).

6. For data from the U.S., see: <http://en.wikipedia.org/wiki/Household_income_in_the_United_States.>

7. <http://www.payscale.com/research/US/School=University_of_Madras/Salary>.

8. <http://en.wikipedia.org/wiki/List_of_countries_by_average wage>.

9. <http://www.gallup.com/poll/166211/worldwide-median-household-income-000.aspx>.

10. <http://www.worldbank.org/en/topic/poverty/overview>.

11. <http://en.wikipedia.org/wiki/List_of_countries_by_GDP_(PPP)_per_capita>.

12. <http://en.wikipedia.org/wiki/Household_income_in_the_United_States>.

Part Two

*From Modern to
Postmodern Marxism*

Chapter 4

MARXISM IN THE INDUSTRIAL AGE
AND ORGANIC MARXISM

"Power Corrupts ..."

In the preceding two chapters, we have taken a close look at the flaws in capitalism, both in theory and in practice. As a theory of human nature, it endorses the view that humans are fundamentally combative, much more prone to competition than to cooperation. Hence it assumes that the mechanism of market competition, rather than incentives for shared cooperative action, will bring the best result. As a social and political theory, capitalism presupposes a minimalist view of the state, whose primary purpose is negative: to fight off attacks from without and corruption from within. The government's primary responsibility is to allow the markets to function independently, with little to no government protections or guidance in the public interest.

As we saw in Chapter 2, this is the economic philosophy known as *laissez-faire* capitalism. Historically, *laissez-faire* policies have been combined with government investment in military buildup and the manufacture of arms—as one would expect from a protection-based theory. Philosophically, the two policies go together: the government's role is to protect the nation from any hostile attacks, so that its capitalists can amass more wealth, since in theory their wealth is good for the nation and all of its citizens. Also, winning wars tends to be good for a nation's economy, as is evidenced by economic statistics for the United States between 1917 and 1945. *Laissez-faire* governments tend to place less emphasis on education, support of the arts, socialized medicine, or the other means by which governments normally work for the common good and add to the quality of life of their citizens. Instead, such governments have traditionally invested primarily in their military forces and in infrastructures that contribute to the financial success of their major businesses.

Similar to the theories of capitalism, the practices of capitalist systems since Adam Smith have been what one would expect from a philosophy of this sort. Over and over again, when humans are given unlimited power, they use it to enrich themselves, their friends, and their families, no matter what the effects on others around them. The ancient Romans, whose system of emperors (Caesars) has much to teach us about the exercise of absolute power, used to say, "Power corrupts, and absolute power corrupts absolutely." From the dawn of the Industrial Revolution through the practices of banks and multinational corporations today, persons and businesses that amass large amounts of wealth and power have very often used them for their own gain—at great cost to other people, other nations, and the environment.

As we know from organized sports, when human competition is carefully regulated according to clear rules, when it is assigned a specific playing field, and when everyone on the field has equal access to the ball, great performances can result. By contrast, sporting events without a referee often spiral out of control, especially if the stakes are high, and people are likely to get hurt. Why would we expect it to be different when "free" markets are left to function without constraints, unguided by restraints and broader social goods? One does not have to look very deeply into the history of industrialization in the West or into the behavior of multinational corporations today to recognize that unconstrained market forces are a recipe for disaster.

Since these principles seem so obvious, one has to ask why they have been ignored. Two reasons come to mind. First, powerful people and corporations don't want to be restrained in the practices they can employ and the money they can earn. They exercise their influence in multiple ways to keep governments and intergovernmental organizations from limiting their activities.

The other reason is that many people do not believe that there is any alternative. This response is strange, since socialists through the ages have proposed ways to limit the super-rich for the sake of society as a whole. It's not surprising that capitalists have sought to disparage Marx and his followers; the last thing they want is for people to get the idea that societies might be run in ways that favor the 99 percent. But it is surprising that they have been successful, up until now, in much of Europe and North America. More and more people have become "capitalist by default"; they know the system favors the richest citizens, but they see no alternative.

This is a tragic situation. An increasing percentage of the world's population now recognizes that unrestrained capitalism is impoverishing nations, supporting vast injustices, and leading the planet toward environmental destruction. Marxist analyses of the power of the wealthy and the flow of capital, such as the recent book on *Capital in the Twenty-First Century* by Thomas Piketty,[1] reveal that the "free" market is not what it claims to be. Socialist alternatives lie ready at hand. Why are they not seen as live options?

MARX'S MODERNIST ASSUMPTIONS

It is not surprising that economic proposals developed over 150 years ago would need to be updated; what's surprising is that so many of them still turn out to be accurate in the twenty-first century. Marx wrote early in the Industrial Age, when its abuses were just becoming visible. Economies had not yet diversified, the service sector was small, and globalization was in its infancy. Private banks, though powerful, exercised a small fraction of the control that they currently exert over global money supply. Each of these more recent developments suggests updates to the "Industrial Marxism" that Marx bequeathed to his followers. In particular, four updates from Marx's modern, industrial context to the "postmodern" context of our day deserve our attention.

(1) *In the mid-nineteenth century, many people believed that the principles of history are deterministic; they can be grasped and codified in a single, all-comprehensive system.* Karl Marx wrote in the context of the great systematic philosophies of Germany and their assumptions about knowledge. On the one hand, these assumptions helped him to conceive an alternative to the capitalist philosophy of Adam Smith. On the other, they also made it more difficult for him to see the specificity of his own context and historical age.

The towering influence on the early Marx was Georg W.F. Hegel (1770-1831), the greatest of the German Idealist thinkers. Inspired by the deterministic laws of Newton's physics, Hegel interpreted the flow of history as an inevitable process. His *Phenomenology of Spirit* and *Encyclopedia* describe each of the steps by which one stage of history gives rise to the next. For Hegel, the outcomes of history are predictable not because they are determined (*bestimmt*) by the necessities of natural science; instead, history and society manifest *their own* determinism, their own invariant stages of development.

At the same time, Hegel was a rationalist. As he wrote, "the real is the rational and the rational is the real."[2] Because the progression of human history is at the same time the progression of rationality or "the concept" (*der Begriff*), Hegel claimed that the various stages in the historical process can be known in advance by philosophers, once they develop a universal philosophical science. Or at least, he thought, *he* could know them.

Marx famously "turned Hegel on his head." Instead of the progression of "Absolute Spirit" unfolding itself in history, he interpreted socio-economic conditions as being the driving force of history. For this reason, *Das Kapital* offers a study of the unfolding of the logic of capital, as manifested in the progressive stages of socio-economic development and, in particular, stages in the means of production. Nonetheless, it was still Hegel who provided the framework for his thinking. As a result, Marx accepted Hegel's deterministic picture of history without revision.

We have since learned that the deterministic view of human history is inaccurate. Physicists have shown that determinism does not even hold for fundamental physics; many phenomena of the quantum world are indeterministic. Scientists now study "chaotic systems," in which the conditions at a given moment can never be established with enough precision to predict the future states of the system.[3] The conclusions of the chaos theorists became famous through the so-called "butterfly effect," in which a single flap of a butterfly's wings in China could have large and unpredictable downstream consequences, such as affecting the weather over Los Angeles. Biological systems are built upon the same principles of chaos theory, while also adding new layers of complexity that further undercut predictability.[4]

Social systems multiply the unpredictability exponentially. Not only do they further build upon the complexity principles of the biological world; they also add the even greater complexity of symbolic structures and ideas. No laws can predict the great works of fiction or the idiosyncracies of the powerful leaders who have changed the course of history. Because so many random factors contribute to emerging economic and social developments, it's misleading to speak of necessary stages of social development. Postmodern Marxists still study the power relations of class, wealth, and capital, as well as the ways that workers and their work are devalued and "commodified," that is, treated like products that can be bought and sold. But these empirical studies do not need to presuppose a deterministic picture of history.

Today, human societies and practices are evolving into a postmodern age. Capitalists have been quick to drop (or at least to disguise) the modernist assumptions of Adam Smith and his predecessors Thomas Hobbes and John Locke, who created the myth of the capitalist subject, "the isolated individual who produces and consumes."[5] For example, leading capitalist theorists of the twentieth century, such as Friedrich Hayek and John Maynard Keynes, were careful to avoid Adam Smith's claims about deterministic systems.[6] By contrast, spokespersons for the large socialist economies have not so carefully distanced themselves from Marx's deterministic language. Because these particular modernist assumptions are now widely viewed as inaccurate, misleading, and undesirable, it's important to develop a postmodern (post-industrial, post-deterministic, culturally embedded) Marxism for the socio-economic realities of the twenty-first century.

(2) *Marx and his early followers believed that workers, once they are sufficiently informed, will act in their own best interest and rise up against the injustices of their employers and the capitalist system.* They were optimistic that a more equitable socialist society could then be built.

These claims of traditional Marxism reflect in part the determinist view of history that we have been discussing. But they also reveal several other assumptions of European modernism. The first is a linear view of time and history. Time, the modernists held, is like an arrow; it moves in a straight line from an origin to a final outcome. By contrast, traditional views of time in Chinese and Indian civilization tend to be cyclical; history is built out of a series of cycles.[7] The Europeans then added the belief, known as *meliorism,* that things are getting better and better over time. In addition, they were deeply influenced by the Jewish and Christian assumption that there would be a final point in history when God would send a Messiah or Savior, who would intervene and bring about "heaven on earth." According to secularized Messianism, social conditions will get better over time, until eventually a utopia, an ideal society, will arise.

Partly because of his Jewish background, Marx was influenced by these assumptions. Of course, as an atheist he created a secular version of this history: socio-economic forces, not God, will lead to higher and better stages. Moreover, the final stage will not be heaven but a *secular* utopia: the "withering away" of the state and the formation of something like the ideal society. In this society, he wrote, one can hunt in the morning, fish in the afternoon, and talk philosophy at night.[8] Marx looked forward to a future when workers will no longer be alienated from the products of their labor. The value of products will be tied to the real labor that it took to produce them and to the uses for which they were designed (food, clothing, shelter), instead of being set by the profit-making activities of massive corporations as they move products and currency around the global markets.

Marxists today are far less likely to use utopian language. We have seen how powerfully the wealthy fight against reforms of the current system, and how subtly employers and the market can hypnotize workers to believe that, if they just work hard enough, they will someday share in the luxury. The evidence is now clear that global capitalism creates and relies on a permanent underclass, living at or below the poverty line. Yet those with even moderate wealth seem willing to accept the injustices of the system, as long as they have enough comforts and access to the latest technologies. The billions of people who lack wealth, comfort, and safety are not so happy about living in destitute conditions; but they lack the education and the power to bring about change.

In short, the experience of the last 150 years should make us far less sanguine about the prospects for change. It hasn't helped that some socialist governments have adopted the language of the perfect society and made unreasonable promises to their citizens based on it. At the same time, workers have seen that their governments are not perfect; many of the old difficulties continue to arise even in Marxist states. In many cases workers lost faith in the promises that their governments made, and scholars became disillusioned even more quickly. Defenders of capitalism have been more than happy to point out the failures of Marx's predictions. Instead of separating out the enduring truths of Marxist analyses from the contingent features of Marx's early industrial context, many people have been ready "to throw out the baby with the bathwater."

In light of this history, postmodern Marxists have learned to temper our claims. The utopianism and secular Messianism of the nineteenth century lie in the distant past. We are under no illusions about the growing power and influence of the one percent, the world's most wealthy. It's true that the global climate crisis is producing a growing outrage about the wasteful lifestyles of the wealthy classes around the planet. Still, although this outrage increases the chances for reforms, it does not guarantee them. There is little that is utopian about our current situation.

(3) *Marx's work as a social theorist, a historian of economics, and a student of the class struggle remains relevant. These insights can be separated from Marx's role as a modernist philosopher. His efforts (especially in his earlier writings) to prove the doctrine of dialectical materialism using the categories of Hegel's philosophy are less enduring. At worst, they produce a "vulgar Marxism" that clashes with the scientific spirit of his work and with core assumptions of an ecological civilization.*

Karl Marx engaged in a rigorous study of economic systems across history and of the effects of capital on working conditions. His interests were not abstract, however; he intended his results to bring about revolutionary changes for the working class. It is thus unfortunate that Western philosophers have focused on his early philosophical writings as the essence of his work.

When one ignores Marx's commitment to careful empirical study and presents his thought as a philosophical system, it sounds arbitrary and dogmatic. On this view, all human history is the consequence of socio-economic structures. Where Hegel had been a strict idealist, this Marx becomes a strict materialist. In order to avoid Hegel's claim that Absolute Spirit is the real causal force in history, one denies that ideas have *any* direct causal effects. Instead, ideas and ideologies are merely a "superstructure" that has no real influence on history; the dialectical history of production and capital alone determines the flow of human affairs. Ideas are merely "epiphenomenal," that is, they are mere appearances, results of the real causes, which are social and economic. Religion and philosophy in particular are entirely illusory.

Although we recognize that such sentences exist in Marx's early writings, they should not be taken as expressions of his mature view; nor do they represent his enduring legacy. After all, it would be self-contradictory to write a Marxist philosophy if you believed that ideas have no effects and all philosophies are pointless! Marx knew that careful analysis can reveal the (often hidden) power of wealthy people and their money, and he sought to undercut capitalist structures through his publications. Hence he clearly did not believe that human thought is completely impotent.

Not every theory in science or philosophy serves an ideology. But Marx's work is a good reminder that *some do.* The wealthy classes create justifications to make others think that it's fair and just that they own the vast majority of assets and that we work for them. As Marx wrote in *The German Ideology*:

> The ideas of the ruling class are in every epoch the ruling ideas, i.e. the class which is the ruling material force of society, is at the same time its ruling intellectual force. The class which has the means of material production at its disposal, has control at the same time over the means of mental production, so that thereby, generally speaking, the ideas of those who lack the means of mental production are subject to it. The ruling ideas are nothing more than the ideal expression of the dominant material relationships, the dominant material relationships grasped as ideas.[9]

Some things have changed since Marx penned these words. For example, teachers are much more likely to belong to the 99 percent, earning less than carpenters and plumbers. The "intellectual class," which since the 1960s has largely turned against the upper class, has been largely disenfranchised and dismantled. (In the United States today, 76 percent of the college and graduate school courses are taught by teachers who are hired for one course or semester at a time, like day-laborers.[10]) Wealthy businessmen (and the economists who serve their interests) now write their own justifications of the system that makes them rich.

(4) According to classical Marxism, *the natural world forms a backdrop to the class struggle, but only as the "stuff" of materialism, the contributor of raw materials, and the occasion for work. It may be the stage on which the human struggle is played out, but in the classical presentations it is not in itself sufficiently incorporated into the analysis.*

In Chapter 11 we will examine John Bellamy Foster's case that Marx himself pushed beyond these limits. But few of Marx's modernist followers recognized the ecological features of his thought. According to traditional presentations, Marx focused primarily on human social conditions. They argue that, although Marx presented humanity as an integral part of the natural world, he did not extend his concerns about unjust conditions, or his ideas about how to fix them, to nonhuman animals.

The exclusive focus on the human is symptomatic of European thought in the modern period. The "father of modern philosophy," René Descartes, asserted that animals are mere machines. This philosophy of human exceptionalism, which holds that humanity must be analyzed according to separate principles than other living things, dominated European philosophy for several centuries afterwards.

Postmodern Marxists reject this stance. On our view, it's not consistent for a materialist to categorize humans as unique based on soul, spirit, or any other mental qualities, since empirical studies reveal numerous parallels between humans and other animals. Indeed, animals clearly suffer as severely from capitalist excesses as do humans, if not more so. Also, resources such as land, water, and air do play a central role in defining the nature of and need for work. Humans *and* nonhumans can remain organically connected to the cycle of work and the products that it produces, or both can be relegated to mere means for others to accumulate wealth. Capitalist systems alienate people from their own work *and* from their home in the natural world.

Authors are fond of citing Marx's 11th Thesis on Feuerbach: "Philosophers have hitherto only interpreted the world in various ways; the point is to change it."[11] The call to change applies not merely to the social world, however, but to the natural world as well. One can well understand how the ruling assumptions of Marx's age tended to focus his attention on human systems. But this one-sided emphasis makes it all the more urgent that we bring out and formulate the ecological dimensions that are implicit in Marx's analysis (see Chapter 11 below). Not only is it inconsistent to stop with human systems; it's also clear that the needs of the natural world today cry out for a more robust response than political theorists have made in the past. Humans are not the only victims of capitalist excesses.

POSTMODERN ORGANIC MARXISM

Given the vast changes over the last 150 years, it is not surprising that many of the modernist assumptions from Marx's day are no longer credible today. What *is* surprising is that, despite the changes, so many of Marx's insights have stood the test of time.

Most people today do not believe that history is a linear progression. Things are not simply getting better and better (meliorism), as the modernists claimed they would. Workers know that most will never own the beautiful houses and luxury cars that appear on their TV screens and on billboard advertisements, yet they have not (yet) pushed back against their oppressors in the ways we once expected. Indeed, many of the poorest people in the world are the greatest advocates of capitalism. To a great extent, the "toys of technology" and the pleasures of even small ownership have hypnotized the middle class, even as they lose more than they win. Technology has also produced a rise in the standard of living for the working class, creating the illusion that they will someday be wealthy and powerful like the upper classes. Humans often do not act for their own long-term good, much less for the common good of the planet and of society as a whole.

What we have learned is that government "for the common good" requires balancing market forces and social principles, the needs of humans and the needs of the environment. We have learned that the dialectics of *culture* are as important as the theory of dialectical materialism, for history also manifests a dialectical relationship between culture and economic conditions. Culture—which includes not only physical structures but also a vast range of ideas, values, practices, mores, and religious beliefs—deeply molds every aspect of the class struggle. As we will see in the next chapter, the radical transformations of Marxism in Russia and China had everything to do with deep and longstanding features of Russian and Chinese culture, features unique to the history of a particular people.

To reject modernism is to inaugurate a distinctively postmodern form of Marxist analysis that seeks to learn from the dynamics of culture in order to bring about societal reforms. Here Marxist principles and cultural studies become allies. Cultural studies reveal how greatly policy decisions are influenced by cultural differences, even within different regions of the same country. It takes immense cultural sensitivity to apply socio-economic insights to different cultural "ecosystems." Marxist theory faces vastly different cultural worlds as it is applied in Western Europe, Latin America, Russia, China, and elsewhere.

Organic Marxism grows out of these more recent insights. We retain the core principles of Marx's social and economic analyses, but we break with the modernist assumptions that dominated European thought in the nineteenth century. The question is not whether Marx has been "verified" or "falsified" by subsequent history. After all, we note that the bestselling nonfiction book in the United States as we revise this chapter is a book on Marxist economics, Thomas Piketty's *Capital in the Twenty-First Century*.[12] Instead, the question is what one can learn from the last 150 years. By combining the best of Marx's insights with the evolving postmodern worldview, we obtain the basic platform of Organic Marxism:

(1) *History is not deterministic but open-ended. No single, all-comprehensive system can ever capture the complexities of civilizational change.* Change occurs as part of organic processes, in human social systems as much as it does in the biosphere. The metaphors for unpredictable processes are drawn from networks, webs, and ecosystems, not from the deterministic and closed systems of Newtonian physics. Because all of these are open-ended processes, postmodern Marxism is best understood as a form of process philosophy.

Interestingly, this is an insight that one finds also in the work of Engels. In his "Socialism: Utopian and Scientific," he wrote, "The great merit of Hegel's philosophy was that for the first time the whole world, natural, historical, intellectual, is represented as a process."[13] This insight that process permeates all reality also lies at the heart of traditional Chinese thought (see Chapter 10 below). In a genuinely Chinese reformulation of European Marxism, one expects to find that open-ended processes are given an increasingly prominent role.

(2) *There are no promises that human history will simply get better and better over time. Neither changes in class structure, nor improvements in technology, nor more selfless human beings are likely to produce a utopia on this planet.* Organic Marxism emphasizes growth and the striving for a healthy, blossoming society. But one can conceive societal improvement without needing to imagine some ideal, utopian state in the future. In the postmodern context, processes of improvement replace progress toward perfection.

Managing a society is not like assembling a puzzle out of perfectly designed pieces. It is more similar to *bricolage*, "construction ... achieved by using whatever comes to hand" (from the French *bricoler*, to putter about).[14] The French philosopher Jacques Derrida famously utilized this notion to explain his deconstructive postmodern position:

The bricoleur, says Levi-Strauss, is someone who uses "the means at hand," that is, the instruments he finds at his disposition around him, those which are already there, which had not been especially conceived with an eye to the operation for which they are to be used and to which one tries by trial and error to adapt them, not hesitating to change them whenever it appears necessary, or to try several of them at once, even if their form and their origin are heterogenous.[15]

This is a very different model of social management than either the *laissez-faire* approach of the early capitalists or the "social engineering" approach of social philosophers in the tradition of Max Weber. The model is closer to the gardener or farmer who labors in his fields, surrounded by a profusion of growth. One has to work *with* the plants and the soil and the weather. The farmer has clear goals in mind: healthy plants and a good harvest. But he is not an engineer, building and assembling everything he touches; he works organically, cooperatively, and symbiotically with the growing things around him.

This model also draws on more cautious predictions about the working class. The more impoverished classes, like all other groups of humans, will often act contrary to their own best interests. Nevertheless, real reforms are possible at every level. Societies can be structured for the common good, or they can continue to be organized to produce wealth for small numbers of citizens. Governments can serve the 1 percent, or they can serve the 99 percent of the population. The art of management, both in the private sphere and in the public sphere, is to deal skillfully with the reality that people often make badly informed decisions and focus too much on short-term gains. The goal of reforms is to create conditions so that people know their options and the long-term consequences of their decisions.

(3) *Marxist social and economic analyses include, but also extend far beyond, matters of production and capital. Human beings are thinking, symbolizing creatures, and what we think has huge effects on how*

we structure our societies. Ideas, beliefs, art and literature, philosophy and even religion—all of these can play major roles in addressing the inequities of wealth and poverty and the injustices between the classes.

Part of the excitement of the organic, process approach to Marxism is that it includes all dimensions of reality within its framework. Contemporary Marxists are able to adapt the traditional language to semi-capitalist systems, to the social democracies of Northern Europe, to the volatile societies of Latin America and Africa, and to increasingly technologized populations with a comfortable and satisfied middle class (to name just a few examples). In each case one is able to trace the roles played by class, capital, and power. The vocabulary changes, but the core dynamics are the same.

As Marx saw, humans are social animals, embedded in and influenced by history, culture, social class and rank, economic conditions, and type of work. Culture includes far more than the material conditions of our existence. Organic analyses of interconnections do not treat any one dimension as foundational; they lay out the entire range of what Marx (following Feuerbach) called our "species being" (*Gattungswesen*) in its connection with other agents in our biological and social ecosystems. Only from this synoptic perspective can one guide and manage human development for the common good.

(4) *Any viable Marxism for the twenty-first century will consider humans in the* entire *context of their existence on earth. All living things, all natural resources—in short, the entire planet—is relevant to the class struggle.* Capitalist structures and practices have raped and pillaged the entire planet, not just human beings. Marxism therefore is and must be, at its core, an ecological and environmental philosophy.

For example, the Marxian concept of "alienation" offers a framework for thinking about the human relationship to nature, not just the relationship of some humans to other humans (see Chapter 11). In the postmodern context we are learning to recognize the applicability of Marx's alienation theory far beyond the contexts of work, production, and capital. The widespread sense of dissatisfaction on the part of the middle classes in multiple cultures begs for Marxist analysis: "Look, I have achieved all of this; what now? Having all this, why do I still feel empty? Why do I sense that there must be something else, something higher, to live for?"

The planetary ecological crisis, climate disruption, the rapid loss of biodiversity, the dangerous pollution of the earth's air and soil— these are issues that call for urgent responses from governments and the global community. Already nations are being forced to manage the secondary social and economic consequences of these primary challenges. It is increasingly likely that the disruptions that lie ahead will lead to revolutionary changes in the roles and responsibilities of governments and the global community. *The coming crisis is an unprecedented opportunity for rethinking what it means to structure societies for the common good.* Only a Marxism built on organic principles will be able to respond productively to these demands for new political theories and new roles for governments in an era of environmental catastrophe. Over the coming decades, as governments are managing the fallout from ecological mismanagement, we predict that the principles of Organic Marxism will play an increasingly important role.

NOTES

1. Thomas Piketty, *Capital in the Twenty-First Century* (Cambridge, MA: Belknap Press of Harvard University Press, 2014).

2. Hegel, *Lectures on the Philosophy of Right,* Introduction.

3. See James Glieck, *Chaos: Making a New Science* (New York: Penguin Books, 1987).

4. Stuart Kauffman and Philip Clayton, "On Emergence, Agency, and Organization," *Philosophy and Biology* 21 (2006): 501-21. See also Charles Lineweaver, Paul C.W. Davies, and Michael Ruse, eds.,

Complexity and the Arrow of Time (New York: Cambridge University Press, 2013), including the concluding chapter by Clayton, "On the Plurality of Complexity-Producing Mechanisms," 332-51.

5. Halden Doerge, "Modernism and Postmodernism or Early and Late Capitalism?" <http://www.inhabitatiodei.com/2008/02/25/modernism-and-postmodernism-or-early-and-late-capitalism/>.

6. See for example, Friedrich Hayek, "The Use of Knowledge in Society," *American Economic Review* 35 (1945): 519-30; John Maynard Keynes, *The General Theory of Employment, Interest and Money* (London: Macmillan, 1936).

7. Stephen Jay Gould, *Time's Arrow, Time's Cycle: Myth and Metaphor in the Discovery of Geological Time* (Cambridge, MA: Harvard University Press, 1987).

8. Karl Marx, *The German Ideology*, 78.

9. Ibid., 92.

10. As reported on the national United States website <www.Inside HigherEd.com> in April 2014.

11. Marx's "Theses on Feuerbach" are available online at <http://www.marxists.org/archive/marx/works/1845/theses/>.

12. Thomas Piketty's *Capital in the Twenty-First Century* tops the New York Time's Bestseller list in the nonfiction category for the week of May 19, 2014.

13. Friedrich Engels, *Socialism: Utopian and Scientific*, trans. Edward Aveling (New York: International Publishers, 1975); Karl Marx and Friedrich Engels, *Selected Works* (Moscow: Progress Publishers, 1970), 413; Marx and Engels is now online at <https://www.marxists.org/archive/marx/works/1875/gotha/ch01.htm>.

14. <http://www.merriam-webster.com/dictionary/bricolage>.

15. Jacques Derrida, *Writing and Difference*, trans. Alan Bass (Chicago: University of Chicago Press, 1978), 285.

Chapter 5

FROM GERMAN MARXISM TO CULTURALLY EMBEDDED MARXISM

THE MANY MARXISMS

One of the central claims of the "organic" framework we are considering is that struggle for an equitable and sustainable society is always embedded and embodied within a particular cultural context. Societies do not develop according to universal laws, and not every society progresses through the same stages in the same order. Technological advances on the one hand, and environmental catastrophes on the other, may alter the dynamics of the class struggle.

Based on the evidence available to them, Marx and Engels expected that Communist reforms would come most quickly in industrialized societies, since they represent later stages in the evolution of capitalism. In order for the proletariat to develop its class consciousness, society must develop to the point where the capitalist owners severely exploit the workers, taking away the value of their labor as profits:

> [N]ot only has the bourgeoisie forged the weapons that bring death to itself; it has also called into existence the men who are to wield those weapons—the modern working class—the proletarians. In proportion as the bourgeoisie, i.e., capital, is developed, in the same proportion is the proletariat, the modern working class, developed—a class of labourers, who

live only so long as they find work, and who find work only so long as their labour increases capital.[1]

As it happened, however, Communism found its most famous applications in nations that had not yet developed into full-fledged industrial societies—nations that Marx and Engels would have defined as "feudal." Marxism moved eastward, first to Russia and later to China, despite these countries' lack of a large industrialized working class. Communism was attractive in these contexts not because these societies were "ready" for this transition (by Marx's criteria), but because they contained a large set of people who were frustrated with the blatant injustices in their societies. "It [turned] out that poverty and oppression constituted the best soil for Marxism to grow in."[2]

Each time Marxist principles have become embodied in a new cultural context, they have been modified to suit the economic, social, and cultural characteristics of that place and time. The implementation of Communism has differed very significantly in the Russian and Chinese contexts. Although later versions of Communism do not exactly match Marx's original vision, they have all drawn on the ideal of a more just and equitable society. Marx's principles ask leaders to institute reforms for the sake of those who are the most disadvantaged. They call for constructive alternatives to capitalist exploitation of workers and of nature. The basic social and economic ideals do not change, even though the means for implementing them, and the specific solutions that are implemented, vary greatly from country to country.

In order to underscore the crucial role of these cultural differences, in this brief chapter we sketch the evolution of Russian and Chinese Marxism. Even for experts, it's helpful to pause and consider the implications of these narratives of historical and cultural adaptation, *for they take us to the heart of the new postmodern Marxism.* In each case, Marx's thought was applied in new ways, consistent with cultural and religious patterns that predated the arrival of Marxist ideas. Even when Marxist leaders themselves believed that they were making a complete break with their nation's past, key elements of that past continued to appear in their efforts to build a communist state.

In China in particular, this adaptation to a unique cultural context is giving rise to a distinctively postmodern Marxism, which sometimes contrasts sharply with the cultural context of Marx's own nineteenth-century German context. One of the surprising phenomena, in both Russia and China, was that some leaders did not acknowledge the debt that Marxism in their country owed to the great traditions of their own past and to the unique cultures of their people. Essentially, they treated Marxism as a modern paradigm even while their efforts were transforming it into a postmodern one. Chinese leaders are now correcting for this modernist prejudice. We believe they are paving the way for a new understanding of Marxism in China that takes into account its constructive postmodern potential.

MARXISM IN RUSSIA

In the nineteenth century, Russia was experiencing rapid social change. It lagged behind Western Europe in science and industry, and its agricultural system still relied on a rural peasant class that constituted over ninety percent of the population.[3] The Tsar ruled the country with absolute authority and there was little opportunity for others to influence public policy. Between the peasants and the tsar stood rigidly defined social classes, including the nobles who owned the land, clergy, state officials, merchants and urban workers. In short, the form of Russian society was, as Marx would say, feudal—it was made up of many distinct, fixed classes and was mostly rural.[4] After Russia's defeat in the Crimean War (1856), Alexander II began to make sweeping reforms in Russian society, abolishing serfdom, allowing greater freedom to courts and local government, expanding industry, and encouraging capitalist investment.

> The expansion of industrial capitalism brought Russia into closer contact with Europe, exposing her still further to

73

Western ideas ... [H]er leaders were driven by a desire to catch up with Europe—to compress within a few decades the scientific and technological progress that had taken other nations centuries to achieve. Drawing upon European experience, Russia was able to leap quickly from an economy still medieval in many respects to one employing the most advanced methods of production.[5]

But this rapid development had many negative consequences. With the shift of power from rural to urban areas, many of the former peasants found themselves worse off than before. Those who moved into the cities were exploited even more heavily in industrial work than they had been in agriculture. The tsarist government was also unprepared for the movement of society towards liberalism and attempted to continue governing in an autocratic style.[6] The combination of these factors made Russian society very unstable by the end of the nineteenth century.

In this environment, Marxism seemed attractive to many as a way to improve the lives of the majority of Russians, since it criticized the social disruption and suffering that capitalism was creating, while also promising modernization and social equality. The problem was that traditional Marxism required a strong capitalist society to lay the groundwork for the emergence of communism from the proletariat. "Autocracy, Marxists would agree, was a feudal rather than a bourgeois institution. Russian capitalism was still weak. Marxism thus might seem to require that its followers first strive for a capitalist Russia—a preposterous suggestion."[7] One of the ways of overcoming this problem was to suggest that class consciousness should be brought to the workers by the intelligentsia. This was the proposal of Lenin and the Bolsheviks. Since Russia did not have a developed proletarian class, the party would be "the vanguard of the proletariat," providing the necessary leadership and ideology to transform Russia into a communist nation.

Lenin's contributions to Marxism were actually quite significant because, over time, they created a separation between the Communist Party, which promoted state ideology and ran a strongly centralized government, and the working class, which was supposed to follow the direction of the Party. In this way, Lenin (and Stalin after him) actually ended up emulating many features of the tsarist model, setting up an autocratic party in place of the tsar. This was not as great a shift as one might have expected. For example, even under Alexander's reforms, the state was already the primary investor in and funder of industrial projects, so a state-owned economy was not completely foreign to the Russian people:

> [The government] was the largest single employer, directing a huge bureaucracy and commanding the involuntary services of many of its subjects, including state serfs. Even those areas of the economy left to private operation were expected to gear their activities to the state's military and economic needs. Thus, under tsarism the state grew at the expense of its citizens, establishing a pattern of absolutism upon which the Communists were later to build.[8]

Russian Marxism also retained some key characteristics of Orthodox Christianity, even though the official ideology of the party suggested a complete break with Russia's religious history. For one, Orthodox Christianity was a much more communal religion than its Western counterpart; the religious person was thought of first as a member of the congregation, and individual religious experience was deemphasized. Orthodoxy also tended to support the absolute authority of the national ruler (unlike Roman Catholicism, which looked to the pope as the religious leader of society).[9] "Despite its Marxist roots, the Communist society erected by the Bolsheviks must be understood as deriving in part from a Russian tradition that was fundamentally at variance with Western values and habits. ... Soviet society parallels so many of the traditional Russian modes that the influence of the latter appears to be significant."[10]

The introduction of Marxism into Russia resulted in a transformed Marxism. To be sure, the impulse for Russian Marxism was still the liberation of workers from exploitation, but the method of implementation was deeply Russian. Unfortunately, because Lenin and other leaders assumed that they were bringing a predetermined, universal Marxism to the people, it was not possible for them to see that many of the cultural resources they needed were already present within Russian society. Had they thought of Marxism in a postmodern way, perhaps they could have seen that the rural peasants had much to offer the movement. Of course, not everything about Russian culture would have been desirable as the nation moved forward (such as the tendency to absolutism), but it would have made a great difference if Marxist leaders would have used their energies to connect Marxism with those cultural values that did support a society geared toward the common good (including the Russian emphasis on communalism over individualism). Had communist leaders recognized the way that Russian Marxism was building upon existing cultural and religious patterns, they might have been able to avoid the separation between party and proletariat that led to many abuses of the poor and to dissatisfaction on the part of many citizens.

MARXISM IN CHINA—MAO ZEDONG THOUGHT

The Chinese context produced an even more complicated revision of Marx's view of history. In the first place, Marx himself defined Asiatic societies differently at different points in his work.[11] In the *Grundrisse*, Marx argued that Asiatic societies were characterized by villages where land was owned communally, with the state exercising purely formal ownership. He believed that these communities were not necessarily organized in a feudal system.[12] But in *Das Kapital*, Marx returned to the more common European view of his time, in which the Asiatic mode of production was said to depend on imperial ownership of land. Here, Marx assumed that Chinese society required a despotic government in order to construct and maintain the extensive hydraulic works for agriculture. He believed that this fact necessarily prevented any private ownership of land in China, placing the country again in the category of a feudal society.[13] Since the *Grundrisse* remained unpublished for many years after Marx's death, it was Marx's views in *Das Kapital* that were available to early Chinese Marxists.

Many Chinese scholars believe that Marx's idea of Chinese history, especially in *Das Kapital*, was Eurocentric and overly simplistic. In reality, China has always had a dynamic history, which has included vast changes in its economy and social structures over time. For much of its history, Chinese agriculture was actually characterized by a mixture of private and state ownership, even in those empires that undertook large public works. For example, irrigation was often made possible by investments from large landowners rather than the state itself.[14] Certainly China could not be called "feudal" in the same sense as Western Europe in the Middle Ages. "Not since the Tang and Northern Wei dynasties had Chinese society consisted of patrimonial fiefdoms in which serfs were tied to the land, obtaining protection in exchange for service on the lord's estate. Even then, the bulk of the economy was outside the estate system."[15] Likewise, over the centuries China's economy had developed in ways that did not fit the European model of history that Marx knew from his own context, although it did include a significant inequality between the rural peasants and the mostly urban gentry and landlords.

As in Russia, Marxism was attractive to many Chinese people in the early twentieth century because it promised an alternative to the inequality of capitalist systems as well as a constructive route towards the future. China had suffered for many years under the exploitation of English and Japanese imperialism and needed to find a way to strengthen the nation. At the same time, the inequalities of the past social order were unacceptable to the majority of the people, who were rural farmers. As Mao Zedong wrote, "The ruthless economic exploitation and political oppression of the peasants by the landlord class forced them into numerous uprisings against its rule ... It was the class struggles of the peasants, the peasant uprisings and peasant wars that constituted the real motive force of historical development in Chinese feudal society."[16] Mao and others adapted Marxism to their particular context by making rural areas the center of the Marxist movement in China, instead of relying on an urban proletariat:

> The serious problem is the education of the peasantry. The peasant economy is scattered, and the socialization of agriculture, judging by the Soviet Union's experience, will require a long time and painstaking work. Without socialization of agriculture, there can be no complete, consolidated socialism.[17]

As in Russia, the Chinese cultural context affected the way that Marxism was applied. In particular, Confucian morality had a great effect on Mao's thought, even as he rejected its role in maintaining the oppressive social structures of the past. Confucianism has always emphasized the need for leaders of the country to be virtuous, censuring those who do not measure up to its standard. Each individual must conform to a demanding code of conduct in order to be able to act according to the Confucian ideal.[18] Although Mao was critical of many elements of Confucianism, he maintained these forms of thought in his adaptation of Marxism. "[L]ike Confucianism before it, Maoism teaches a commitment to transforming the world by applying the lessons of a utopian ideology to the actions and institutions of everyday life. This is not to claim that Mao was a 'closet Confucian,' but to emphasize that the Confucian way was virtually synonymous with the Chinese way. Both Confucianism and Maoism are uniquely Chinese."[19] Confucian patterns of thought have remained very important to Chinese society, even during times when leaders have sought to cut all ties with previous cultural values.

CHINESE MARXISM TODAY

China today is facing new challenges that require new adaptations of Marxism. The context is very different from Germany in the 1840s, when Marx began fighting back against the controlling capitalist powers. China's economy has become far more complex than it was in the past, especially in light of the "One Country, Two Systems" policy of Deng Xiaoping. At the same time, Chinese leaders are seeking to find a pragmatic balance between the core principles of both Marxism and Confucianism, which call for a virtuous state and a virtuous people. Leaders are seeking to find creative extensions of core Marxist principles in order to provide guidance through these new economic and social realities.

One of the new crises that postmodern Chinese Marxism is now confronting is the injustice that humans have wrought on the environment. Just as traditional Marxism sides with the workers in the face of exploitation by the capitalists, so the new Marxism must act to prevent the exploitation of nature on the part of those who seek to maximize short-term profits and GDP. (This raises questions about the value and agency of nature, to which we return in Chapter 11.)

Today the global context is characterized by ever greater inequities between rich and poor, limits on economic growth imposed by the depletion of resources, and a disruption of the planet's climate patterns that is now affecting ecosystems and their inhabitants (both human and nonhuman) around the world. As grave as it is, this crisis also provides humans with a new opportunity: to implement Marxist principles "for the common good," utilizing positive resources from the past while firmly renouncing those aspects of each culture that have created oppressive relationships between persons and nations.

In the past, Marxism has shown itself capable of adapting to the cultural forms of each new situation and context. Although the first process of cultural adaptation began as soon as Marxism began travelling eastward from Germany into Russia, today's global context calls for even more complex and radical adaptations. In particular, the relationship between Marxist thought and cultural values needs to be conceived in a genuinely dialectical fashion. Under the influence of Hegel, Marx conceived dialectic as a "synthesis" of thesis and antithesis, in which differences are "transcended yet preserved" (*aufgehoben*). Traditional Chinese thought, influenced by Daoist thought, describes the process as (re)establishing the harmony between complementary principles. When Western and Eastern notions of dialectics can be harmonized, a stronger political philosophy results.

What has *not* worked is the construction of a Marxism free of all cultural influences. Claims to have invented a purely universal political philosophy usually hide the influences of the author's particular time and place. However much one denies them, history and culture persist in often unconscious ways.[20] Attempts to eliminate the past, as in Lenin's creation of a Party-centered Communism or the excesses of Mao's Cultural Revolution, often cause it to manifest in particularly destructive ways. By contrast, Marx's original vision—to create a more just and equitable society—actually requires cultural resources and a constructive retrieval of the past.

NOTES

1. Karl Marx and Friedrich Engels, *The Communist Manifesto*, trans. Samuel Moore (London: Pluto Press, 2008), 43.

2. Robert Service, *Comrades!: A History of World Communism* (Cambridge, MA: Harvard University Press, 2007), 46.

3. Herbert McClosky and John E. Turner, "The Russian Legacy," in *Comparative Communism: The Soviet, Chinese, and Yugoslav Models*, ed. Gary K. Bertsch and Thomas W. Ganschow (San Francisco: W.H. Freeman, 1976), 41.

4. See Marx and Engel's discussion of the transition from feudalism to capitalism. Marx and Engels, *The Communist Manifesto*, 35-40.

5. McClosky and Turner, "The Russian Legacy," 48-49.

6. Ibid., 49.

7. Theodore H. Von Laue, "Leninism," in *Comparative Communism: The Soviet, Chinese, and Yugoslav Models*, 21.

8. McClosky and Turner, "The Russian Legacy," 40-41.

9. Ibid., "The Russian Legacy," 43-44.

10. Ibid., "The Russian Legacy," 46.

11. Bill Brugger and David Kelly, *Chinese Marxism in the Post-Mao Era* (Stanford, CA: Stanford University Press, 1990), 22-23.

12. "Amidst oriental despotism and the propertylessness which seems legally to exist there, this clan or communal property exists in fact as the foundation, created mostly by a combination of manufactures and agriculture within the small commune, which thus becomes altogether self-sustaining, and contains all the conditions of reproduction and surplus production within itself. A part of their surplus labour belongs to the higher community, which exists ultimately as a *person*, and this surplus labour takes the form of tribute etc., as well as of common labour for the exaltation of the unity, partly of the real despot, partly of the imagined clan-being, the god. Now, in so far as it actually realizes itself in labour, this kind of communal property can appear either in the form where the little communes vegetate independently alongside one another, and where, inside them, the individual with his family work independently on the lot assigned to them . . . or the unity may extend to the communality of labour itself." Karl Marx, *The Grundrisse* (New York: Vintage, 1973), 473.

13. "In Asia . . . the fact that state taxes are chiefly composed of rents payable in kind depends on conditions of production that are reproduced with the regularity of natural phenomena. And this mode of payment tends in its turn to maintain the ancient mode of production." Karl Marx, *Capital: A Critique of Political Economy*, trans. Samuel Moore and Edward Aveling (Moscow: Progress Publishers, 1995), 88, <http://www.marxists.org/archive/marx/works/download/pdf/

Capital-Volume-I.pdf>. Also see Brugger and Kelly, *Chinese Marxism in the Post-Mao Era*, 22-23.

14. Ibid., 23.

15 Ibid.

16. Mao Zedong, *Quotations from Chairman Mao Tsetung* (San Francisco: China Books, 1972), 9.

17. Ibid., 29.

18. John K. Fairbank, "The Chinese Pattern," in *Comparative Communism: The Soviet, Chinese, and Yugoslav Models*, ed. Gary K. Bertsch and Thomas W. Ganschow, 58.

19. Judith A. Berling, "Confucianism," *Focus on Asian Studies* 2, no. 1 (1982): 5-7.

20. "To some extent the nature of every revolution is determined by the society that gives rise to it ... Ancient cultures are not easily extinguished, and no society, however revolutionary, can escape from carrying forward some of the traditions, habits, and patterns of organization of the previous social order. Once transplanted in the new society, the customs of the past tend to persist and to reinforce themselves." McClosky and Turner, "The Russian Legacy," 38.

Chapter 6

DECONSTRUCTIVE POSTMODERNISM
AND CRITICAL MARXISM

How do contemporary Western interpretations of Marxism address the realities of the history we have just considered? In this chapter we look at two well-known Western movements that have written positively about the legacy of Karl Marx: deconstructive postmodernism and Critical Marxism. We focus in on three of the most influential representatives of these movements: Jacques Derrida, Slavoj Žižek, and David Harvey. These authors provide creative, even startling interpretations of Marx and Marxism. What remains less clear, however, is to what extent they offer practical guidance in addressing urgent global issues. Can policymakers find constructive guidance here as they seek to adapt Marx to the very different demands of the twenty-first century?

Jacques Derrida

In the West, postmodernity is often linked to the work of one philosopher: Jacques Derrida (1930–2004). His method of deconstruction has become one of the best known alternatives to modern thought. Deconstruction is a way of challenging the hierarchies of concepts that have characterized Western thought since Plato, but have been more pronounced since the advent of modernity. Deconstruction includes both a reversal of this hierarchy of concepts and a recognition that competing concepts somehow include each other.

Therefore we must proceed using a double gesture, according to a unity that is both systematic and in and of itself divided, a double writing, that is, a writing that is in and of itself multiple … On the one hand, we must traverse a phase of *overturning*. To do justice to this necessity is to recognize that in a classical philosophical opposition we are not dealing with the peaceful coexistence of a *vis-à-vis*, but rather with a violent hierarchy. One of the two terms governs the other (axiologically, logically, etc.), or has the upper hand. To deconstruct the opposition, first of all, is to overturn the hierarchy at a given moment. To overlook this phase of overturning is to forget the conflictual and subordinating structure of opposition. Therefore one might proceed too quickly to a *neutralization* that *in practice* would leave the previous field untouched, leaving one no hold on the previous opposition, thereby preventing any means of *intervening* in the field effectively.[1]

The classic example that Derrida uses is the binary opposition between speech and writing in Western philosophy. Many philosophers have assumed that speech and writing constitute different forms of language, and that speech is the more authentic form. But Derrida points out that there are no characteristics of speech that cannot also be attributed to writing; in particular, both speech and writing can be said to be derivative of other sign systems. This means that neither speech nor writing can be called the "natural" way of expressing oneself. In fact, Derrida argues that writing could be said to be the basis for speech instead of the other way around:

Now from the moment that one considers the totality of determined signs, spoken, and a fortiori written, as unmotivated institutions, one must exclude any relationship of natural subordination, any natural hierarchy among signifiers or orders of signifiers. If "writing" signifies inscription and especially the durable institution of a sign (and that is the only irreducible kernel of the concept of writing), writing in general covers the entire field of linguistic signs. In that field a certain sort of instituted signifiers may then appear, "graphic" in the narrow and derivative sense of the word, ordered by a certain relationship with other instituted—hence "written," even if they are "phonic"—signifiers. The very idea of institution—hence of the arbitrariness of the sign—is unthinkable before the possibility of writing and outside of its horizon.[2]

In Derrida's sustained reflection on Marxism at a conference in 1991 (now published as *Specters of Marx*), he links his own project of deconstruction with certain tendencies in Marx and Engel's original vision of communism. This famous conference took place only a few years after the fall of the Berlin Wall (1989), when many Western scholars were ready to declare the end of Marxism and the triumph of capitalism. According to Derrida, Marxism is relevant now more than ever because the disintegration of the concrete structures of communism allow for Marx's original criticisms of capitalism to "haunt" us. He says, "When the dogma machine and the 'Marxist' ideological apparatuses (States, parties, cells, unions, and other places of doctrinal production) are in the process of disappearing, we no longer have any excuse, only alibis, for turning away from this responsibility."[3] Derrida believes that the "triumph" of capitalism in the West has only served to highlight its own failures, as human suffering continues and environmental catastrophe appears inevitable. Western economic systems have only exacerbated the plagues of underemployment, foreign debt, arms trade, and inter-ethnic violence.[4]

For Derrida, Marxism is still relevant not because it represents a possible political program that could be implemented. Instead, it provides us with a set of important ideals that are clearly far from being realized—and indeed are *impossible* to realize—under the system of global capitalism.[5] It acts as a "specter" that continues to make us dissatisfied with the shortcomings of our current reality. Marxism becomes a deconstructive principle: it never "arrives" in order to be put into practice, but remains relevant only in the sense that it prompts us to ask critical questions about systems and practices that are now in place. "It can never be always present," Derrida writes, "it can be, only, if there is any, it can be only possible, it must even remain a can-be or maybe in order to remain a demand."[6] Marxism is able to serve as a critique of the current world order precisely because it is now no longer a real option for providing such order itself as a positive, constructive philosophy.

Derrida's analysis creates a deconstructive space for political theory, and for Marxist theory in particular. This space is characterized by the assumption that Marxism (or any other particular school of thought) is best used as critical theory rather than as a set of practical policies. Partly because of the past abuses of communist leaders like Stalin and the imperialism of the West, Derrida and other Western deconstructive philosophers seem to have lost faith in the possibility that a philosophy could actually help to implement a sustainable, harmonious society.[7]

SLAVOJ ŽIŽEK

Slavoj Žižek, although he is critical of Derrida's version of deconstruction,[8] lives in this space that deconstruction has created in the West. Žižek is a senior researcher and cultural critic at the University of Ljubljana, Slovenia. His influences include Jacques Lacan and psychoanalysis, Marxism, Hegel and German idealism, and the Frankfurt School of philosophy. He studied at Ljubljana and at the University of Paris, returning to Ljubljana in 1971 as a researcher. For a time he was an active member of the communist party of Slovenia, and then was involved with the Committee for the Defense of Human Rights. Žižek's controversial theories and confrontational style have made him one of the most visible Western philosophers of our time.

In his book *In Defense of Lost Causes*, Žižek outlines his suggestions for a new version of Marxism that could help us respond to the looming environmental crisis. He agrees that traditional Marxism has identified the main problems with global capitalism that are leading us toward this crisis: every citizen is pressured to consume as much as possible; no one feels personally responsible for the consequences of the circulation of capital or the depletion of natural resources; and, because the market is the product of a huge number of interactions between individuals, each individual feels as though he or she is powerless to change the system.[9] But Žižek does not believe that traditional Marxism is an adequate philosophy either. Instead, he claims that traditional Marxism does not go far enough to deconstruct the way that we think about humanity, history, and ecology. Unfortunately, the proposal that Žižek puts forward in its place is, like Derrida's, more deconstructive than practical.[10]

In his adaptation of traditional Marxism to the current social and political situation, Žižek deconstructs the concepts of humanity, history, and nature. First, he identifies a new possible global "proletariat" made up of people excluded from state economies and administrations. Given the current state of affairs, Žižek believes that the biggest factor that determines the quality of a person's life is not the difference between owner and laborer, but between those who are formally included in the economy and those who are excluded or informally connected. The "excluded" are found primarily in the urban slums that exist worldwide outside most big cities. Here they receive no benefits from the state; there is no law or infrastructure, no insurance, etc. They may be integrated into the economy informally (as day laborers or self-employed entrepreneurs), but they are not recognized as workers by the state. According to Žižek:

> if the principal task of the emancipatory politics of the nineteenth century was to break the monopoly of the bourgeois liberals by politicizing the working class, ... the principal task of the twenty-first century is to politicize—organize and discipline—the "destructured masses" of slum-dwellers.[11]

This means, however, that in Žižek's proposal the state is always going to be part of the problem, not the main agent of transformation.[12]

Next, Žižek deconstructs the concept of history. Traditional Marxism expects the working class to perform a political act that will bring about a more just economic order. Žižek says this foundational aspect of Marxism depends on a linear, "historical" view of time, in which "at each moment of time, there are multiple possibilities waiting to be realized; once one of them actualizes itself, others are canceled."[13] In this view of history, the goal is to look at the various possibilities that may occur in the future and choose the one that appears to lead toward the best outcome. The problem, Žižek claims, is that the rise of global capitalism appears to be inevitable, leaving individuals and nations with no choice but to adapt or to be left behind.

This hopelessness can lead people to believe that there is nothing that they can do to prevent the environmental crisis that comes along with capitalism. In response, Žižek suggests that we view history as *circular*. It is possible, he suggests, that our actions retroactively change past possibilities, that they introduce something radically new into history, that they break free of the set of possible actions that we are led to believe in from past experiences. In this case,

> we should first perceive [environmental catastrophe] as our fate, as unavoidable, and then, projecting ourself onto it, adopting its standpoint, we should retroactively insert into its past (the past of the future) counterfactual possibilities ("If we had done this and that, the catastrophe we are in now would not have occurred!") upon which we then act today.[14]

Extending this idea even further, Žižek also suggests that we deconstruct our ideas of ecology or nature. On his view, one of the greatest obstacles to significant political change is the environmental movement itself. One of the myths of environmentalism, he claims, is that of a natural world that exists in a harmonious balance until humans arrive and destroy this balance. Žižek believes that what we call "nature" is actually nothing more than a series of "catastrophes," arbitrary changes of direction that include great loss of life. Human behavior is simply an extension of this natural imbalance—though admittedly one that threatens to be more destructive than any past event in the earth's history.[15]

Žižek suggests, therefore, that we come to terms with two facts: first, that there is no such thing as "nature" independent of human influence; and second, that our actions can permanently disturb the ordinary state of our world. As a result, we should try to influence our environment in such a way that we avoid catastrophe—not by returning to an original state of balance, but by making collective, radical political choices to change our patterns of consumption.

Žižek's method allows him to make some brilliant observations about the assumptions that underlie both capitalism and traditional Marxism. It allows him to gesture towards a possibility of political change, which includes more specific recommendations than would be possible with Derridean deconstruction. Žižek suggests that radical political change should occur through a mobilization of those excluded from the apparatus of the state; it should institute severe, but egalitarian, measures that limit consumption and pollution; and it may use violence, even terror, to accomplish these things.[16]

At the same time, the radical nature of Žižek's proposal means that it functions more as a theoretical critique of existing systems than as a real possibility for action. The ideal political response for Žižek would be one that breaks completely from the usual idea of what is possible or even desirable. But because nearly all political action contains elements of the past and builds on common social wisdom, he ends up dismissing any actual political program in favor of an abstract, idealized radical program.[17] Žižek's political "action" is therefore always deferred action, not action that can be put into practice in our existing context.[18]

DAVID HARVEY

Another current interpretation of Marxism claiming to offer an alternative to global capitalism is that of David Harvey. Harvey, who teaches at the Graduate Center at City University of New York, has been extremely influential in his own field of human geography, as well as in the humanities more generally. His book *Social Justice and the City* (1973) was one of the first to suggest that the field of geography should not remain objective in the face of economic inequality. With books such as *Limits to Capital* (1982) and *The New Imperialism* (2003), Harvey has become an outspoken critic of unregulated capitalism. Harvey was listed in 2007 as one of the top 20 most cited authors in the humanities and social sciences.[19]

In some ways Harvey's use of Marx is diametrically opposed to that of Žižek; he pursues a systematic, scientific critique of capitalism,[20] as opposed to the anti-systematic Žižek. As much as Harvey criticizes the postmodern lack of metanarrative and its deconstructive tendencies, however, his own proposal also fails to provide a real alternative vision, especially for non-Western contexts. Harvey's work offers excellent explanations of the way that capitalism functions, but it remains too general to be able to make concrete suggestions about how to utilize the cultural differences that inevitably play a role in political systems.

Harvey's project is nicely summarized in his famous text:

> There are laws of process at work under capitalism capable of generating a seemingly infinite range of outcomes out of the slightest variation in initial conditions or of human activity and imagination. In the same way that the laws of fluid dynamics are invariant in every river in the world, so the laws of capital circulation are consistent from one supermarket to another, from one commodity production system to another.[21]

Harvey attempts to uncover these laws and expose the violence that allows capitalism to continue. According to his influential critique, the major problem of capitalism is that wealth tends to be accumulated faster than it can put to use. This over-accumulation manifests itself both as unused capital and unused labor, underemployment or unemployment.[22] In the resulting scenario, excess capital and excess labor exist side by side with no way of being brought back together.[23] In order to restore a stable rate of profit, some capital must be eliminated. These crises can be solved in various ways: by creating fictitious capital or credit,[24] by exporting capital to other locations, or by expanding the circulation of products and capital to new markets.[25]

The effect of the latter two alternatives is to push the devaluation of capital or labor onto different geographical locations (generally, developing nations) rather than to suffer the effects of devaluation in the original location (generally, the developed nations). When the potential devaluation is severe enough, conflicts arise as to who is going to bear the burden of this devaluation: "Trade wars, dumping, interest rate wars, restrictions on capital flow and foreign exchange, immigration policies, colonial conquest, the subjugation and domination of tributary economies, the forced reorganization of the division of labour within economic empires, and, finally, the physical destruction and forced devaluation of a rival's capital through war are some of the methods at hand."[26] Harvey believes that these violent actions are an inevitable part of capitalism. In the end, he argues, capitalism can only be sustained by expanding violent conflict, which will eventually involve the entire world in immense destruction.

David Harvey's work focuses on a close analysis of Marx's original writings, especially *Das Kapital*, and therefore tends to neglect the important variants among Marx-inspired systems of government around the world, each one responding in unique ways to the historical, social, and cultural situation that they face. If anything, Harvey goes to the opposite extreme. At times, he dismisses specific Marxist movements as being "militantly particular." He writes negatively about the sociocultural location of particular political movements, which keeps them from achieving "sufficient critical distance and detachment to formulate global ambitions."[27] As Alex Callinicos writes in his important critique of Harvey's work:

Harvey…is an intellectual based in the academy, participating in and reflecting on social movements that develop outside it and that usually lack, as the phrase "militant particularism" implies, the comprehensive programme possession of which is surely one defining characteristic of a party.[28]

Writing at a fairly abstract level allows Harvey to take a wide view of the problems of capitalism and to make general criticisms that apply to global economic systems. At the same time, this approach leaves Harvey less flexible in addressing the specific contexts in which economic policies are always instantiated. This means that his work is mainly useful as a critical commentary on global capitalism. As effective as it is for this purpose, it lacks a specific platform that could be used to construct new paths beyond the capitalist system. Worse, in a sort of antithesis to *Realpolitik*, Harvey explicitly criticizes attempts to achieve an organic integration of Marxist principles with the ethos of specific civilizations and histories, such as the Chinese people. In contrast to this view, we argue that each national history, each specific context of a developing nation, is like the particular soil within a particular ecosystem. The wise farmer, knowing his soil, will select the appropriate seeds, plant them in the appropriate density, and cultivate them for maximal growth and sustainability.

Derek Gregory asks, "If the world doesn't come as clean as you can think it, as A.N. Whitehead almost said (and Harvey holds his work in high regard too), and if in consequence we need to recognize and respect the diversity and variability of life on earth, what worlds are lost in Harvey's explorations?"[29] If one takes Harvey as his sole guide, one would certainly lose the "world" of cultural particularity, the resources that make each nation and people different from one another. In a certain sense, Harvey's theory works in the same way that imperialist capitalism does: it maintains its own value by expanding its reach to cover more and more of the globe. Most importantly, since this theory does not take account of the differing cultural features within different contexts, it will be more difficult to implement his suggestions; as we saw in Chapter 3, theories must always be adaptable to new contexts in order to be practicable.

CONCLUSION

Derrida, Žižek, and Harvey represent three of the most well-known Western interpreters of Marxism of the last few decades. The first two embed Marxism in the context of European postmodernism in order to encourage radical political imagination, whereas Harvey uses it scientifically to uncover the underlying structure of capitalism.

We have found reason to worry that these approaches do not produce a constructive version of Marxism that is able both build upon the past *and* to create new ways forward into the future. The work of Derrida and Žižek focuses on the idealized possibility of radical change in ways that obscure the potential of existing political structures and social wisdom. Harvey's analysis remains at a generalized or global level, which keeps him from constructing concrete, practical programs for improving particular socioeconomic systems.

We have purposefully combined these sharply contrasting thinkers into a single chapter. Each one has been highly influential in the Western discussion, and each one has generated much attention and commentary. The first two represent the movements of deconstruction and post-structuralist thought—two movements that tend to be anti-scientific, or at least openly suspicious of scientific claims to knowledge. Harvey, by contrast, claims to utilize a scientific approach and to draw deeply from the resources of social scientific study.

As later chapters will show, much of the Western discussion has been imprisoned within one or the other of these two approaches. The scientific approaches limit themselves to stringent empirical standards and to a relatively small set of methods, thereby losing insights that can be achieved through cultural and historical studies. The deconstructive approaches can easily become anti-rational and anti-scientific, since science also becomes one of the targets of their deconstructive method. Ironically, *both groups pull back from the concrete examples and situations that are the daily bread of policymakers in local, provincial, and national governments.* How will Marxist ideals be useful to the "art of government" if they become limited by definition to the purely abstract and scientific on the one side, and the purely ideal or deconstructive on the other?

Once again, it appears, the Western thinkers succeed at formulating the extreme possibilities, the excesses on both sides, while failing to find the blended position that would represent a balance between them. They express the dissonance of the present global situation but shy away from addressing the practical issues that policymakers face. How can one govern wisely if the tool in one's hand is a disharmonious Marxism? All agree on the urgency of the task: unrestrained capitalism is like a speeding car heading toward a wall, out of control; where the driver should be hitting the brake, he instead pushes harder on the accelerator pedal. And many agree that Marxist principles can in principle help to guide us through this crisis. But many of the Western theorists seem unable to formulate the updated version of Marxism that leaders need. Only a balanced framework can guide policymakers to wise decisions in the concrete decision-making situations that they face.

NOTES

1. Jacques Derrida, *Positions*, 2nd ed. (London: Continuum, 2004), 38-39.

2. Jacques Derrida, *Of Grammatology*, trans. Gayatri Chakravorty Spivak (Baltimore: Johns Hopkins University Press, 1998), 44.

3. Jacques Derrida, *Specters of Marx: The State of the Debt, the Work of Mourning, and the New International* (New York: Routledge, 1994), 14.

4. Ibid., 100-03.

5. Ibid., 108.

6. Ibid., 39.

7. "It was, on the other hand and indissociably, what we had known or what some of us for quite some time no longer hid from concerning totalitarian terror in all the Eastern countries, all the socio-economic disasters of Soviet bureaucracy, the Stalinism of the past and the neo-Stalinism in process (roughly speaking, from the Moscow trials to the repression in Hungary, to take only these minimal indices). Such was no doubt the element in which what is called deconstruction developed—and one can understand nothing of this period of deconstruction, notably in France, unless one takes this historical entanglement into account." Ibid., 16.

8. See Slavoj Žižek, *The Puppet and the Dwarf: The Perverse Core of Christianity* (Cambridge, MA: MIT Press, 2003), 140.

9. Slavoj Žižek, *In Defense of Lost Causes* (London; New York: Verso, 2008), 453.

10. "No less than Derrida, [Žižek's] own efforts in offering a general description of political act as such retains, as has been seen, an onto-theological trace and a corresponding, problematic privileging of what in itself is ambiguous difference. As such, although he performs a different mode of openness to difference, finally, Žižek ends up repeating a form of that which he finds problematic in Derrida's work." John McSweeney, "Finitude and Violence: Žižek versus Derrida on Politics," *Kritike* 5, no. 2 (2011): 56.

11. Žižek, *In Defense of Lost Causes*, 426–27.

12. "[T]he solution is not to limit the market and private property by direct interventions of the state and state ownership. The domain of the state itself is also in its own way 'private' ... There is nothing more 'private' than a state community which perceives the Excluded as a threat and worries how to keep the Excluded at a proper distance." Ibid., 429.

13. Ibid., 459.

14. Ibid., 459.

15. Ibid., 442.

16. Ibid., 461.

17. See also Slavoj Žižek, *Repeating Lenin* (Zagreb: Bastard Books, 2001), <http://www.marxists.org/reference/subject/philosophy/works/ot/Žižek1.htm>. Here Žižek proposes "authentic historical openness" which would allow one to act without any constraint from current systems.

18. See McSweeney, "Finitude and Violence," 56.

19. "Most Cited Authors of Books in the Humanities, 2007," *Times Higher Education*, March 26, 2009, <http://www.timeshighereducation.co.uk/405956.article>.

20. Especially in his earlier work; see David Harvey, *Explanation in Geography* (London: Edward Arnold, 1969) and David Harvey, *The Limits to Capital* (Chicago: University of Chicago Press, 1982).

21. David Harvey, *The Condition of Postmodernity: An Enquiry into the Origins of Cultural Change* (Oxford: Blackwell, 1989), 132.

22. Harvey, *The Limits to Capital*, 192.

23. Harvey, *The Condition of Postmodernity*, 180.

24. Harvey, *The Limits to Capital*, 324-29.

25. Ibid., 424-31.

26. Ibid., 438. See also Harvey's use of Luxembourg's "accumulation by dispossession." David Harvey, *The New Imperialism* (Oxford: Oxford University Press, 2005), 137-82.

27. Alex Callinicos, "David Harvey and Marxism," in *David Harvey:*

A Critical Reader, ed. Noel Castree and Derek Gregory (Malden, MA: Blackwell Publishing Ltd, 2006), 51.

28. Callinicos, "David Harvey and Marxism," 51.

29. Derek Gregory, "Introduction: Troubling Geographies," in *David Harvey: A Critical Reader*, ed. Noel Castree and Derek Gregory (Malden, MA: Blackwell Publishing Ltd, 2008), 20.

Chapter 7

RETHINKING FREEDOM AND HUMAN RIGHTS AFTER LIBERALISM

Most Americans have been taught that freedom, human rights, democracy, and justice exist only in the liberal tradition—the tradition of John Locke and his followers (see Chapter 2 above). To be a socialist or a Marxist, we are told, is to give up all four.

We call this the great Myth of Liberalism. Probably no statement in political philosophy is more filled with untrue and half-true assumptions. Why would one think that the freedom of John Locke and his modern liberal successors is the only kind of freedom? Such a claim suppresses so much of the history of political theory, and ignores so much counter-evidence, that one is tempted to ask: Whose interests are served by this teaching? Who stands to gain from propagating this Myth?

Although that question is worth pursuing, we will not pause to explore it here. It's more important to trace the roots of the Myth of Liberalism, to lay bare its hidden assumptions, and then to formulate a better alternative.

Why would the Myth seem so compelling to Americans? In part it's because from the very beginning American children are socialized to believe the story of American exceptionalism. Unique among the nations of the earth, we are "the land of the free and the brave." We are the world's oldest democracy, and thus (the story says) we are the best one—perhaps the only *true* democracy. Only our justice system is *really* just, and only our form of government really preserves human rights.

Our teachers and textbooks then add anecdotes about cases in other countries where freedom and justice are absent. Whether explicitly or implicitly, American children are taught how exceptional and unique they are.

The vast majority of Americans continue to believe the story of political liberalism, which locates them in the lineage of John Locke. The story comes in two very different forms, however. The conservative version of the story seeks to "conserve" some set of traditional moral and ethical values that (it says) should guide society, and it advocates for the least possible interference from the government. This is the *libertarian* version of the John Locke story. The *progressive* or *liberal* version consigns such moral and religious values to the private realm, advocating instead for a larger government role in providing welfare and social services for those who need them.

Conservatives will be the most hostile to Organic Marxism. By contrast, liberals sometimes have difficulty seeing how their view is different from it. "We support social democracy, welfare protections, social services, and national health care. 'Liberal' is just our way of saying that we disagree with the conservatives. Aren't liberals already halfway to socialism?"

This view, though widespread, rests on a mistaken assumption. The liberal version of the John Locke story still carries the DNA of its forefathers, John Locke and Adam Smith; thus it remains at base a capitalist solution. Lin Chun writes,

> The welfare state [has] not actually solved problems of poverty and inequality (most significantly manifested in the distribution of wealth and power), and nothing in its policies could be seen as specifically socialist. As Dorothy Wedderburn remarked, the effect of, or the values embodied in, welfare legislation represented no more than an "unstable compromise" between the market and laissez-faire on the one hand, and planned egalitarianism on the other.[1]

Indeed, Western social democracies stand far closer to libertarianism than most liberals realize. Why? On paper, capitalist democracies provide "liberty and justice for all," as American schoolchildren repeat every morning when they salute the flag. But in practice liberty and justice are available to different degrees depending on wealth (and skin color, and other factors).

Marx wanted to extend these benefits to the working classes and the most disenfranchised in society. In his early work, for example, he spoke of the ideal society as a "true democracy"; he later called it "communism" to express the goal of genuine community for all. For Marx, a socialist society will not be opposed to the values of freedom, rights and democracy but will be the fulfillment of these values.[2]

In this and the following chapter we will see that terms like freedom and justice are the focus of heated debate between two competing schools of thought. It's crucial to understand the radically different approaches that are taken toward these terms, so that one can see what is at stake in each case. The dispute is not, as one says, "merely academic." We will find that *significant differences in practice* result, depending on whether one accepts the one perspective or the other.

FREEDOM

The idea of freedom is one of the most emotionally charged ideas in human culture. Whatever the actual limitations and constraints on us, we experience ourselves as free—able to "do what we want," able to change our mind, able to decide freely between multiple options. Perhaps nothing brings more fear than the thought of being held in chains, unable to walk or move our limbs. This fundamental biological drive for freedom of motion, evident in the youngest children, fuels the deeply emotional discussions about freedom in political theory.

Studying the charged debates about freedom over the last four centuries, one quickly discovers that at least two radically different notions of freedom are at work. Put in its most simple form, it concerns

101

the distinction between *freedom from* and *freedom for*. One group of theories emphasizes being free from constraint or outside interference, and thus free to do what one wishes. The other group focuses on the freedom to be able to pursue and achieve goods: better social conditions, better education, more just distribution of resources, higher overall quality of life. Hearing this distinction, one immediately recognizes that *freedom from* and *freedom for* do not need to be in competition. Tragically, however, both sides of the political debate have tended to focus on one at the expense of the other.

FREEDOM FROM CONSTRAINT

In Chapter 2 we traced the influence of John Locke on the origins of the American political system. Following in the tradition of Hobbes and Locke, the American founding fathers believed that the role of government should be minimal. Governments should protect citizens against loss of life, loss of liberty, and loss of property. Here "liberty" (freedom) is meant in the narrower sense of constraints on one's freedom of movement and basic freedoms of choice. A similar understanding of freedom as freedom from constraints underlies the First Amendment to the U.S. Constitution:

> Congress shall make no law respecting an establishment of religion, or prohibiting the free exercise thereof; or abridging the freedom of speech, or of the press; or the right of the people peaceably to assemble, and to petition the government for a redress of grievances.

The fundamental emphasis here is to block or constrain government interference on citizens' behavior. Each citizen should be able to say what he wants, publish what he wants, meet publicly with others when he wants, and petition the government about whatever are his concerns. The first three became known as the rights to freedom of speech, press, and assembly. We will see in the next section that the language of rights has also become divided between "positive" and "negative" rights.

Each item in the First Amendment implies a *freedom from* limitation. For example, freedom of speech means the freedom to express oneself without interference or constraint by the government. The so-called establishment clause, prohibiting the government from establishing a religion, creates a separation between the state and the various religious groups that exist within the country. This means that the government should stay out of the way when religious people pray in their own home or meet in their religious building. The image is that a religion is self-contained and private; all it needs to thrive is that the government not get in the way.

Americans soon learned, however, that things were not this simple. The history of Supreme Court interpretations of the First Amendment shows a constant struggle to find compromises between *freedom from* and *freedom for*. For example, a given member of the Jehovah's Witnesses religion wants freedom from interference, but the government decides that he cannot refuse to authorize a blood transfusion for his child and thereby cause his child to die. The white supremacists who want the freedom to march through the streets of their city cannot create a hate-filled environment that compromises the quality of life of the African-Americans who also live in that city.

Recently lawmakers in the state of Arizona wished to pass a law that would allow business owners to use their religious beliefs as a legal justification to refuse to serve same-sex couples. For example, the restaurant owner could say that a homosexual couple could not eat in his restaurant merely because they are gay. One advocate of this law told the press, "Faith shouldn't be something we have to leave inside our house."[3] He wishes to extend the freedom from constraints on his *private* exercise of religion into a freedom from constraints on how he treats other citizens when he is operating his business.

Imagine, however, that a business provides medical care, or basic social services, or education. Imagine that enough citizens in a city make use of such a law, so that basic health services become unavailable to homosexual couples and their families—or to people with black

103

skin, or to Jews. As Daniel Mach of the American Civil Liberties Union responded, "Religious freedom is a fundamental right, but it's not a blank check to harm others or impose our faith on our neighbors."[4]

Freedom understood exclusively as *freedom from any constraints on what I want to do with my money* has become a major contributor to the global climate crisis. Expressed through the spending habits of wealthy individuals, the unrestrained business practices of multinational corporations, and the lax policies of governments, this mindset has led to abuses of the environment that are now spinning out of control at the global level. The same mindset has created huge injustices across the planet, since poverty, starvation, and pollution in developing nations are byproducts of rich people and governments in developed nations exclusively pursuing their own interests. We need to understand how the two sides of human freedom, which ideally should work together in a harmonious manner, have unraveled into two competing ideologies.

The modern origins of freedom as *freedom from* lie in the social contract tradition of political theory (Hobbes, Locke) and in the French Enlightenment. In her excellent treatment of the Enlightenment, Mary Gregory notes:

> In the eighteenth century liberty referred to the power to either choose or to refrain from choosing; to not being forced to submit to the commands of another human being; to the state of being a free man as opposed to being a slave; to the form of government in which sovereign power resides in the nobility or in the people; *to the ability to be able to do what one wants to do without being restrained from doing it.*[5]

We saw in Chapter 2 that Rousseau expected the government to make positive contributions to the quality of life of its citizens. Gregory notes that "he viewed inequality, luxury and greed not as natural, but rather as evils that resulted when men banded together to form societies" and "opposed the despotic tendencies of unrestrained government."[6] By contrast, Voltaire, sounding rather like Adam Smith, wrote that selfishness, greed, and the desire for luxury were useful features of human nature. Wrapped together under the heading of the profit motive, these desires (Voltaire claimed) are the reasons that humans search and invent. The state should allow these selfish motivations to be manifested, since they drive people to achieve more, which is the cornerstone of human progress.

In his insightful book, *Capitalism and Freedom: The Contradictory Character of Globalisation*, Peter Nolan summarizes the net result of these developments:

> Social Darwinism was a political philosophy that was strongly opposed to any form of state interference with the "natural" workings of society. Laws regulating labour conditions were seen as a form of slavery, since they interfered in the rights of free agents to dispose of their property as they saw fit. The idea that "freedom" essentially meant freedom of contract became the bedrock of "liberal" thinking at the end of the nineteenth century.[7]

These results are not surprising. If an implied social contract is taken as the justification for the state and the basis of its authority, then all the functions of the government need to be channeled through this framework. Freedom is about control of one's property (wealth); government exists to protect propertied individuals; and interference with the dynamics of wealth acquisition are "unnatural." Of even more concern are the dimensions of civic life that cannot be conceived from the neoliberal paradigm—rights such as those emphasized by David Harvey: "the right to life chances ... control over production by the direct producers ... a decent and healthy living environment ... collective control of common property resources."[8]

It was thus the British and French philosophers of the modern period who formed the link between freedom and capitalism. Freedom, understood as non-interference with the pursuit of self-interest, was said to require capitalism as the only system that allows humans to be "genuinely free." And capitalism, the economic system of prefer-ence for the moderns, would only be able to succeed if the capitalists were free from all constraint by governments and other sources. Only if capitalists enjoy a completely "free market" (note how this phrase reduces freedom to a mere adjective modifying "market"!) will they be able to bring the immense benefits to humankind that their wealth can procure. Each term is defined or redefined in terms of the other, not in terms of any broader goals. The capitalists' "freedom from" becomes the central motor of the capitalist economy.

Nowhere is this "Capitalist Manifesto" expressed more clearly than in the classic work by Milton Friedman, *Capitalism and Freedom*:

> Viewed as a means to the end of political freedom, economic arrangements are important because of their effect on the concentration or dispersion of power. The kind of economic organization that provides economic freedom directly, namely, competitive capitalism, also promotes political freedom because it separates economic power from political power and in this way enables the one to offset the other.

> Historical evidence speaks with a single voice on the relation between political freedom and a free market. I know of no example in time or place of a society that has been marked by a large measure of political freedom, and that has not also used something comparable to a free market to organize the bulk of economic activity.[9]

However, the evidence of the last decades undercuts Friedman's claims in multiple ways. Instead of government that "separates eco-nomic power from political power," Americans are seeing govern-ment increasingly serving business interests. Recent court decisions are allowing businesses and extremely wealthy individuals to play an increasing role in financing candidates and thereby influencing the outcome of state and national elections. Since 2008 the phrase "too big to fail" has been added to the national vocabulary. This phrase communicates that banks and other businesses are crucial to national security, so that it becomes the government's responsibility to keep them functioning, no matter how badly they have been managed and no matter what the cost to American taxpayers. By contrast, one never hears the phrase "too poor to be neglected." At the same time that tax laws and bailouts increasingly support the rich, basic social services are being cut for the world's poorest people.

The *reductio ad absurdum* of human freedom is clearly, and painfully, expressed in this statement by former U.S. President George W. Bush:

> The concept of "free trade" arose as a moral principle even before it became a pillar of economics. If you can make something that others value, you should be able to sell it to them. If others make something that you value you should be able to buy it. This is real freedom, the freedom for a person—or nation—to make a living.[10]

FREEDOM FOR COMMUNITY

Marx was very critical of the way that freedom of trade tended to subordinate all other forms of freedom in Western society. In reality, there are multiple types of freedom, each with their own internal logic, which must be encouraged and balanced. Freedom of trade, Marx says, is not a bad thing in itself, but it can become tyrannical if it is allowed to become the measure of all types of social freedom. He writes,

> Freedom of trade, freedom of property, of conscience, of the press, of the courts, are all species of one and the same genus, of freedom without any specific name. But it is quite incorrect to forget the difference because of the unity and to go so far as to make a particular species the measure, the standard, the sphere of other species. This is an intolerance on the part of one species of freedom, which is only prepared to tolerate the existence of others if they renounce themselves and declare themselves to be its vassals.[11]

Marx advocates for a more holistic definition of freedom: "Free activity for the Communists is the creative manifestation of life arising from the free development of all abilities of the whole person."[12] This idea of freedom must be taken up and developed further in an organic, postmodern worldview.

The philosopher of constructive postmodernism, Alfred North Whitehead, offers an antidote to the narrowing of human freedom similar to that of Marx. He links freedom to the open-ended creativity of human civilization and the process of life. The capacity that we call freedom is what lures individuals and societies to move beyond existing, outworn structures:

> The social value of liberty lies in its production of discords. There are perfections beyond perfections ... Thus the contribution to Beauty which can be supplied by Discord—in itself destructive and evil—is the positive feeling of a quick shift of aim from the tameness of outworn perfection to some other ideal with its freshness still upon it.[13]

For the philosophers of ecological civilization, the emphasis falls first on the freedom to actualize the huge potential that beckons to each individual and society. We actualize our potential when we are offered educational and cultural opportunities—and when basic needs for food, shelter, and safety are met. It is not enough merely to offer people the chance to pursue self-interest without interference from other humans and from governments. Criticizing the "freedom from" paradigm, Whitehead writes,

> When we think of freedom, we are apt to confine ourselves to freedom of thought, freedom of the press, freedom for religious opinions. Then the limitations to freedom are conceived as wholly arising from the antagonisms of our fellow men. This is a thorough mistake. The massive habits of physical nature, its iron laws, determine the scene for the sufferings of men ... In modern thought, the expression of this truth has taken the

form of "the economic interpretation of history."[14]

The great Harvard economist and philosopher Amartya Sen has recently proposed that we understand not GDP but *freedom*, understood in terms of social/communal well-being and not solely private protections, as the measure of development:

> It is important to give simultaneous recognition to the centrality of individual freedom *and* to the force of social influences on the extent and reach of individual freedom. To counter the problems that we face, we have to see individual freedom as a social commitment ... Expansion of freedom is viewed, in this approach, both as the primary end and as the principle means of development.[15]

The success of a civilization is measured not just in terms of how quickly it produces capital. Have we really won if we achieve a rapid rise in GDP at the cost of decimating the environment, dropping more and more families below the poverty line, and neglecting education, culture, and quality of life?

HUMAN RIGHTS

We have already seen how the language of freedom naturally expands into the language of rights. The First Amendment of the American Bill of Rights already speaks of the *rights* of freedom of speech, freedom of assembly, and freedom of religion. Rights language has become an indispensable component of international discourse in the global community. Three features of rights language demand our attention.

First, the age is gone when all nations will agree on a list of human rights on the grounds that they are valued by a single religion and its sacred scriptures. International lists of rights, such as the Universal Declaration of Human Rights, reflect increasing agreement across the planet about how humans (and, increasingly, animals and the environment) may and may not be treated. Without a doubt, the core values of each culture and its religions continue to play a significant role in explaining and justifying rights language *for members of that culture.* But local concepts and stories, even if religiously grounded, cannot produce global consensus about universal human rights. This is one reason why the global community speaks increasingly of *natural* rights, not of God-given rights. The power of rights language is not weakened if, globally, they represent nothing more—and nothing less—than the strong consensus of the global community.

Second, agreement on universal human rights is higher and stronger than it has even been before in human history. The category of basic human rights will not go away. The growing strength of rights language is especially notable given that, during the same period, skepticism has grown about traditional ways of grounding rights language.

It is the third point, however, that will demand most of our attention. It is this: the historical narrative shows a distinct progression through three types of human rights. This evolution is so clear, and so important, that one can actually judge political philosophies based on whether they are able to conceive all three types of rights *and* to explain the progression among them. Any political theory that fails this test, we suggest, will not be adequate to today's global situation. Moreover, we will suggest, Organic Marxism is particularly well suited to this task.

We follow Aryeh Neier in describing the three types as "blue," "red," and "green" rights. Roughly, on her model "blue" rights are civil and political rights: the rights to individual liberties, similar to the "freedom from" that we explored above. "Red" rights are economic and social rights, rights that focus more on the quality of life. "Green" rights are collective rights such as the right to peace or the rights of future generations to environmental resources and the biodiversity necessary for human survival. Each of the three types includes the preceding one but also adds to it. The movement through the three types offers an excellent way of understanding rights language.

BLUE RIGHTS

The emergence of the distinctively modern tradition of rights begins with "blue" rights. Modern human rights were initially based on the assumption that societies function best when governments allow citizens to pursue their own self-interest without interference (Adam Smith's "invisible hand"). Neier notes,

> As seen from the perspective of James Madison and those who contributed to the thinking that went into his writing of the American Bill of Rights, the concept of rights referred exclusively to civil and political rights: that is, rights that limit the power of the state to interfere with certain actions of citizens and that empower citizens to influence the actions of the state.[16]

Note that the Universal Declaration of Human Rights (1948), which is the foundational document for the modern human rights movement, also focuses on civil and political rights (the first 21 articles), but does include some recognition of social and economic rights (articles 22-26), such as rights to social security, employment, leisure, and education.

Micheline Ishay's important *History of Human Rights* makes clear what are the consequences of focusing exclusively on blue rights:

> [Adam Smith] observed that a civil government established for the purpose of protecting property rights "is in reality instituted for the defense of the rich against the poor, or of those who have property against those who have none at all." Yet the forces of the market, he explained, constituted a mechanism that would drive the prices of commodities down to their "natural" and most affordable level.[17]

It is no coincidence that "blue" is also a symbol of the aristocracy, as in the expression "blue bloods." In early modern Europe, any positive consequences for persons without property—one could not even speak of them having "rights" at that time—were only byproducts of protecting the property rights of the wealthy. As Ishay shows,

> Independents and Levellers alike equated political freedom with some sort of individual property ownership and independence. Thus they introduced the liberal notion that freedom is first earned through independent economic activity. Although the right to the vote remained limited, the right to property was eventually won, albeit at a high human cost, and feudal land tenures and arbitrary taxation were abolished in England.[18]

If one can speak of rights for the poor, it was only by a kind of secondary application of the rights enjoyed by the wealthy. Thus John Locke wrote in the *Two Treatises* that "everyman has a property in his person; this nobody has a right to but himself. The labor of his body and the work of his hand, we may say, are properly his."[19] The early American leaders took a similar view. They assumed that the right to vote should be contingent on ownership of land and property, because only land ownership shows "sufficient evidence of attachment to the community."[20]

In short, the modern European thinkers saw democracy as a sort of byproduct of property ownership and of the conditions necessary for protecting it. Kant writes that "civil freedom could no longer be infringed without disadvantage to all trades and industries, and especially to commerce." As Neier correctly notes, "That view, essentially unchanged since its eighteenth-century origins, would find expression in the post-cold war foreign policy doctrine of the world's only superpower, which linked world peace to the synergetic expansion of markets and democracy."[21]

RED AND GREEN RIGHTS

We have seen that, in the beginning, individual human rights in Western Europe were extensions of property rights. Classical liberalism eventually extended these initial rights into other kinds of blue rights, that is, other rights of individual choice. But the grounding of these new rights continued to follow the logic of individualism and property ownership out of which they were born.

Red rights are not primarily concerned with the ability of individuals to freely pursue self-interest, but with securing basic needs for each individual while pursuing the good of the community. The concept of red rights began to play a role as philosophers realized that individual choices rely in various ways on communal values and community cooperation. If individual property owners act only to acquire more wealth for themselves, the society will not actually continue to function. Socialists, Communists, Marxists, and their allies attempted to move the conversation beyond the rights of individual choice to include the economic and social rights that are necessary for a well-ordered society. Central to the international human rights movement have been documents such as the International Covenant on Economic, Social and Cultural Rights, proposed for ratification by the United Nations in 1966. In addition to the right to "just and favourable conditions of work" (Article 7) and the right to form trade unions (Art. 8), the International Covenant includes a variety of social and cultural rights that go significantly beyond the limitations of blue rights thinking:

> The States Parties to the present Covenant recognize the right of everyone to education. They agree that education shall be directed to the full development of the human personality and the sense of its dignity, and shall strengthen the respect for human rights and fundamental freedoms. They further agree that education shall enable all persons to participate effectively in a free society, promote understanding, tolerance and friendship among all nations and all racial, ethnic or religious groups, and further the activities of the United Nations for the maintenance of peace.[22]

To include rights to employment, health care, and education, as well as the right to participate in cultural life, is to move into the heart of red rights. It is to take a perspective on what all human beings need if they are to thrive. To conceive rights in this way is to see society organically, as an interconnected system. Unlike the blue rights paradigm, organic thinking recognizes that it is neither just nor healthy when many live a truncated existence so that a small proportion of citizens can thrive. On this view, the blue right "not to be interfered with" is seen as a fungible right: when free market profits for some come at great cost for many others, the national and international community is justified to rebalance society so that all can enjoy a basic quality of life. Freedom from interference is a good, but it is not the only good.

Green rights represent the final step toward an organic worldview. Here it is not only the quality of life of all humans that is taken into account, but also the survival of nonhuman animals and ecosystems. Just as economic, social and cultural rights can't be established on the basis of freedom from interference alone, so also the right to a healthy environment goes beyond the perspective of both blue and red thinking.

One of the founding fathers of socialist and communist thought, Pierre-Joseph Proudhon, began to develop the framework for this extended view of rights in 1840. Proudhon pointed to the existence of a third category, a "right outside of society." He wrote that a property

> is a right outside of society; for it is clear that if the wealth of each was social wealth, the conditions would be equal for all, and it would be a contradiction to say: Property is a man's right to dispose at will of social property. Then if we are associated for the sake of liberty, equality and security, we are not associated for the sake of property; then if property is a natural right, this natural right is not social.[23]

Proudhon challenged the inclusion of property in the list of natural rights set forth in the French Declaration of the Rights of Man and of the Citizen, preferring social ownership of the means of production. The early socialist resistance to all private property turned out to be unworkable, however, and most Marxists today combine socialist principles with some private ownership. Thus for Deng Xiaoping, socialism has to be open to all human civilizations, including the capitalist systems, in order to show its advantage. It must "absorb and learn from all advanced business models and management methods of all countries including developed capitalist countries, which reflected the law of modern socialized production."[24]

But Proudhon also included proto-ecological reasons for his conclusion. He argued that one's labor does not entitle one to property because the material for production already existed before the laborer began: "He argues that labour alone is the basis of value, but that this nevertheless does not give the labourer a right to property, since his labour does not create the material out of which the product is made."[25]

It is this insight on which the language of green rights is built. Land and other natural resources are neither matters of purely private interest, nor are they purely social. The resources on which the entire society—indeed, human civilization as a whole—rests are the foundations for both personal and social well-being. We call them green rights to draw attention to this third category.

"Eco-justice" is the more popular term to describe this same conclusion. As Li Huibin, a leading Marxist scholar states, "We need to protect the legally-established ecological rights of individuals, families, communities, and nations, and to defend ecological equality and ecological justice. I think this is not only the intrinsic component of ecological civilization, but also the ideal and goal that Marxists and Constructive Postmodernists are struggling for."[26]

One sees in this short section that organic philosophy represents a radically different way of thinking. (Perhaps this helps explain the opposition of capitalists and libertarian thinkers to the international environmental movement.) "For the common good" is not just a minor modification of the individualistic perspective. Even more than red (social) rights, green rights lift our eyes above and beyond personal gain to the vision of an interconnected society and planet. On a small planet, no man is an island. What you own and how you live impacts the quality of life within the whole web of life, both human and non-human. "Green" thinking, the foundation for ecological civilization, is thus a revolutionary transformation of human thought. We suggest that it represents the next stage in the evolution of human social thought.

CONCLUSION

It is unfortunate that many scholars and politicians still treat the discussion of human rights as a single topic. We have discovered instead that no less than three different frameworks are at work. Rights language based on *freedom from interference* is only the beginning, since it is motivated by the individual's wish not to be restrained or constrained. For example, the first 20 articles of the Universal Declaration of Human Rights begin with rights such as the right to life, security of person, fair trial, not to be held in slavery, not to be arrested arbitrarily, and so forth. One should not ignore these rights, but neither should one limit the discourse to them alone.

Social theorists helped humanity extend from one-dimensional to two-dimensional thinking. Marx spoke for the heart of socialism when he included the good of society as a basic goal and not merely as a byproduct of property owners' pursuit of wealth. Societies are stronger when they acknowledge economic, social, and cultural rights. The global community has gradually accepted its responsibility to support educational and cultural activities that raise the quality of life of all citizens.

With the awareness of green rights, social theory is now moving to a full three-dimensional way of thinking. Ecological civilization supplements economic and social rights with core organic values such as the right to a healthy environment and the right to peace.[27] Green rights are very clearly collective rather than individual rights. As one adopts this framework, one moves beyond modern individualism to constructive postmodern, community-based thinking. Alfred North Whitehead recognized the radical nature of this move:

The whole concept of absolute individuals with absolute rights, and with a contractual power of forming fully defined external relations, has broken down. The human being is inseparable from its environment in each occasion of its existence. The environment which the occasion inherits is immanent in it, and conversely it is immanent in the environment which it helps to transmit.[28]

NOTES

1. Lin Chun, *The British New Left* (Edinburgh: Edinburgh University Press, 1993), 78.

2. See Karl Marx, *Critique of Hegel's Philosophy of Right*, trans. Joseph O'Malley and Annette Jolin (Cambridge: Cambridge University Press, 1970). This text can be read online at <http://www.marxists.org/archive/marx/works/1843/critique-hpr/>. Marx's discussion of "true democracy" appears in chapter 2.

3. Michael Paulson and Fernanda Santos, "Religious Right in Arizona Cheers Bill Allowing Businesses to Refuse to Serve Gays," *New York Times,* February 21, 2014, <http://www.nytimes.com/2014/02/22/us/religious-right-in-arizona-cheers-bill-allowing-businesses-to-refuse-to-serve-gays.html?_r=0>. The quotation is from Joseph E. La Rue, the legal counsel at Alliance Defending Freedom, a Christian legal organization in Scottsdale, Ariz., that advocates for religious liberty.

4. Ibid.

5. Mary Efrosini Gregory, *Freedom in French Enlightenment Thought* (New York: Peter Lang, 2010), 3, italics added.

6. Ibid., 2-3. Gregory points out that Rousseau was a republican who praised the freedoms given to the citizens of Switzerland and encouraged France to follow the Swiss example.

7. Peter Nolan, *Capitalism and Freedom: The Contradictory Character of Globalisation* (New York: Anthem Press, 2008), 13.

8. David Harvey, *A Brief History of Neoliberalism* (Oxford: Oxford University Press, 2005), 204.

9. Milton Friedman, *Capitalism and Freedom*, 40th Anniversary ed. (University of Chicago Press, 2009), 9.

10. Quoted in Nolan, *Capitalism and Freedom*, 17, quoting from Bush's Security Strategy of 2002.

11. Karl Marx, *On the Freedom of the Press and Censorship*, trans. Saul Padover (New York: McGraw-Hill, 1974), 39. Marx adds, "Freedom of trade is precisely freedom of trade and no other freedom because within it the nature of the trade develops unhindered according to the inner rules of its life. Freedom of the courts is freedom of the courts if they follow their own inherent laws of right and not those of some other sphere, such as religion. Every particular sphere of freedom is the freedom of a particular sphere, just as every particular mode of life is the mode of life of a particular nature. How wrong it would be to demand that the lion should adapt himself to the laws of life of the polyp!"

12. In *The German Ideology*, abstract of Chapter 3. Available online at <https://www.marxists.org/archive/marx/works/1845/german-ideology/ch03abs.htm>.

13. Alfred North Whitehead, *Adventures of Ideas* (New York: Free Press, 1967), 257.

14. Ibid., 66.

15. Amartya Sen, *Development as Freedom* (New York: Random House, 2001), xii.

16. Aryeh Neier, *The International Human Rights Movement: A History* (Princeton University Press, 2012), 59.

17. Micheline R. Ishay, *The History of Human Rights: From Ancient Times to the Globalization Era* (Berkeley: University of California Press, 2008), 102.

18. Ibid., 93.

19. Ibid., 93.

20. Ibid., 96. This language is drawn from a state constitution.

21. Ibid., 103. As the early American theorist Thomas Paine wrote, "If commerce were permitted to act to the universal extent it is capable, it would extirpate the system of war, and produce a revolution in the uncivilized state of Governments. The invention of commerce has arisen since those Governments began, and it is the greatest approach towards universal civilization that has been made by any means not immediately flowing from moral principles" (quoted in Neier, *International Human Rights Movement*, 103).

22. Article 13 of the International Covenant on Economic, Social and Cultural Rights, adopted and opened for signature, ratification and accession by General Assembly resolution 2200A (XXI) of 16 December 1966, entry into force 3 January 1976, in accordance with article 27; <http://www.ohchr.org/EN/ProfessionalInterest/Pages/CESCR.aspx>. Like the majority of the world, China has already signed and ratified this document. The United States signed the document under the Carter administration, but it was never ratified by Congress, and subsequent presidents have not found it politically expedient to ask Congress to do so. Some see the treaty as antithetical to American and capitalist values. See the excellent analysis by Barbara Stark, "At Last? Ratification of the Economic Covenant as a Congressional-Executive Agreement," *Transnational Law & Contemporary Problems* 20, no. 1 (Spring 2011): 107–42.

23. Quoted in Neier, *The International Human Rights Movement*, 60. Also see Ishay, *The History of Human Rights*, 152. "[N]ineteenth-century socialists regarded themselves as heirs of eighteenth-century ideals

of human rights and world peace. Yet they opposed the Enlightenment belief that peace could be secured in the competitive jungle of a free market society. If anything, wars were perceived as the end game of the economically advantaged class, which sought to promote its political and economic power worldwide. Inequities of property generated by laissez-faire economic policies . . . were not only at the root of social injustice, but . . . the source of wars between nations."

24. Deng Xiaoping, *Selected Writings*, vol. 3 (Beijing: The People Press, 1993), 373.

25. George Woodcock, *Pierre-Joseph Proudhon* (London: Routledge, 1956), 47. On the other hand, John Bellamy Foster writes of "The Mechanistic 'Prometheanism' of Proudhon" in Chapter 4, "The Materialist Conception of History," *Marx's Ecology: Materialism and Nature* (New York: Monthly Review Press, 2000).

26. Li Huibin, "Ecological Rights and Ecological Justice," in *Ecological Civilization and Marxism*, Li Huibin, Xue Xiaoyuan & Wang Zhihe, eds. (Beijing: Central Compilation and Translation Press, 2008), 66.

27. See Neier, *The International Human Rights Movement*, 62-63.

28. Whitehead, *Adventures of Ideas*, 63.

Chapter 8

DEMOCRACY AND JUSTICE: A POST-LIBERAL PERSPECTIVE

What holds for freedom holds even more clearly in discussions of democracy and justice. When American schoolchildren pledge allegiance to the flag of the United States of America, I think they hear it as "[we are the only] nation…with liberty and justice for all." Perhaps a few people know that Marx was striving to create a more just form of society and that he viewed socialism as the most consistent form of democracy. But few Americans have paused to do a comparative study of liberal and socialist approaches to these topics. (Few have an accurate understanding of what "socialist approaches" means.)

Justice means fairness. Since the ancient Greeks, justice has been pictured as a blindfolded woman holding a scale in her hands. Unswayed by personal gain, blind to fame or wealth of the disputing parties, she distributes the resources fairly between all parties.

Some years back Alisdair MacIntyre wrote a now-classic work, *Whose Justice? Which Rationality?*[1] Of course, MacIntyre was not the first to recognize that the Western traditions include multiple notions of justice and that they are worlds apart. Has the liberal tradition launched by John Locke resulted in a fair (just) distribution of resources across the population? Or has it produced rules that favor the wealthiest and mete out disproportionate punishments on those who have the least? If the kind of wealth-based democracy that the U.S. and many Western nations have embraced is *not* just, what other options exist that might help to correct the injustices? How much have wealth-based notions of justice influenced the way we have constructed our particular form of democracy?

DEMOCRACY

The word *democracy* simply means rule by the people (*demos*). Perhaps no political arrangement has seemed as obviously desirable as this one. And yet this simple term raises a variety of probing questions: who are the "people" who get to rule? Does the smaller group of people in direct positions of power within a democracy in fact rule in the interests of all of the people within the country? To what extent does our system focus us on the good of all human beings—present and future, citizens and non-citizens—and, indeed, on the good of all living beings? And to what extent does it operate more for the short-term gain of its own citizens and them alone?

DEMOCRACY IN SERVICE OF THE MARKET

For Francis Fukuyama, whose *The End of History* a few years ago proudly proclaimed the final victory of capitalistic democracy over all competitors, the answer is simple: liberal democracy is the best system because it protects property-owners from outside interference:

> For Hobbes and Locke, and for their followers who wrote the American Constitution and Declaration of Independence, liberal society was a social contract between individuals who possessed certain natural rights, chief among which were the right to life—that is, self-preservation—and to the pursuit of happiness, which was generally understood as the right to private property. Liberal society is thus a reciprocal and equal agreement among citizens not to interfere with each other's lives and property.[2]

In short, Fukuyama still employs the defense of democracy developed by the early modern American and European philosophers. The route to happiness comes through owning private property; thus the government needs to keep others from interfering with your property. When this approach leads Fukuyama and his allies to use the language of rights, the rights they name first are the rights to life and property.

As we saw in the previous chapter, Organic Marxists are not opposed to the language of human rights. We do however recognize that the focus must extend beyond individual or "blue" rights, such as the right to individual freedom and property, so that it includes "red" and "green" rights as well. The same corrective is needed in discussing democracy. One can affirm with Fukuyama that "Democracy...is the right held universally by all citizens to have a share of political power, that is, the right of all citizens to vote and participate in politics."[3] But what we oppose (together with other supporters of the International Covenant on Economic, Social and Cultural Rights of the United Nations) is the view that democratic government requires *nothing more than* the individual rights of liberalism. Fukuyama represents this view:

> The right to participate in political power can be thought of as yet another liberal right—indeed, the most important one— and it is for this reason that liberalism has been closely associated historically with democracy.[4]

True, classical liberalism is one framework, one ideology, for approaching "rule by the people." But it is not the only framework, and neither is it the best one. The unique contribution of any "rule by the people" should be that the needs of all the people are taken fully into consideration. But, unfortunately, capitalist democracy has tended to become "rule by the individual, for his own gain."

A word on terminology: those who hold Fukuyama's view are increasingly calling themselves "libertarians," in order to distinguish themselves from present-day liberals, whom they mistakenly confuse with socialists. David Boaz, Executive Vice President of the Cato Institute in Washington, DC, correctly understands the link between Locke's liberal tradition and free-market libertarians:

Libertarianism may be regarded as a political philosophy that applies the ideas of classical liberalism consistently, following liberal arguments to conclusions that would limit the role of government more strictly and protect individual freedom more fully than other classical liberals would.[5]

Boaz—as much as we disagree with his politics—has grasped the trajectory of Western liberalism much more clearly than the American moderate Left. Today's libertarians have worked out the implications of the classical liberal starting point (Locke, Adam Smith, John Stuart Mill) more consistently than have present-day liberals. If liberals want to avoid the libertarian conclusions, they need to incorporate another tradition within political philosophy. Only when the rampant individualism of liberalism is tempered by socialist assumptions (Marx) can the *reductio ad absurdum* be avoided.

What then distinguishes these two major approaches: libertarian democracy and the version of democracy that we are calling Organic Marxism? Europeans in the early modern period invented the concept of an implicit social contract (see Chapter 2), which became a defining feature of libertarianism. There is, they believed, an implicit agreement among the voting citizens of a country that government should serve one central role. You agree not to interfere with the life and property (wealth) of other property-owners, in return for their agreement in return not to take your property. The rulers of the democracy are allowed to stay in power as long as they pass and enforce laws of non-interference. Everything else should be left to market competition to decide.[6] Each property owner can and should increase his own wealth. As long as he doesn't directly harm others, all other matters belong in the "private sphere" and are up to him to decide.

To approach political theory in this way gives markets the central role in defining democracy. The evidence is overwhelming that this arrangement has proved to be a momentous mistake, producing gross injustices among humans and devastating the planet. It also forsakes our obligation to formulate the central values of a nation, of human civilization, and of life on earth. It is far better, we suggest, to define democracies in terms of the common good—what they can offer their citizens and the planet—rather than in terms of what they are forbidden from doing.

One should fault capitalism-based democracies not only for the unjust consequences that they have wrought on the poor and the planet. One should fault them as well for their unduly negative view of human nature, a view that has served to justify morally unacceptable treatment of (non-wealthy) humans and animals. Recall that the liberal tradition predicts that, left to themselves, humans will act in selfish, even anti-social ways. Thus, they argue, one needs a political system that will transform selfish motivations into outcomes that are good for others. Adam Smith "discovered" that if society allows each person to be selfish in the ways that he wants to be and to amass as much wealth as he can (as long as he doesn't directly steal it from others), society as a whole will benefit.

Readers may notice, of course, that it's rather self-serving for the already-wealthy to give themselves *carte blanche* to amass more wealth. After all, when it comes to wealth, the world is hardly a level playing field. Some are rich enough to own multinational businesses such as Microsoft, whereas others do not have the money even to open a small storefront shop; and clearly the income between the people on the two ends of the spectrum will be massively different. Isn't this clearly a recipe for the rich to get richer?

IS EUROPEAN-STYLE SOCIAL DEMOCRACY ENOUGH?

So are "social democracies" the answer? At various times since the Second World War, the democracies of Northern Europe have increased the social services that the government offers to the citizens and have strengthened the social safety net for the poor and unemployed. The social reforms in these nations are certainly a step forward from the "small government" slogan of libertarian capitalism, which opposes social health care and cancels government programs that support those in need. Amartya Sen calls this "positive democracy." In his view, it is the byproduct of reasoned debate when access is given to all citizens, and not just to the wealthy:

> If the above analysis is correct, then democracy's claim to be valuable does not rest on just one particular merit. There is a plurality of virtues here, including, first, the intrinsic importance of political participation and freedom in human life; second, the instrumental importance of political incentives in keeping governments responsible and accountable; and third, the constructive role of democracy in the formation of values and in the understanding of needs, rights, and duties. In the light of this diagnosis, we may now address the motivating question of this essay, namely the case for seeing democracy as a universal value.[7]

Sen's work shows that it's not necessary to leave behind the ideal of "rule by the people" in order to introduce social services and to protect the most vulnerable citizens. Democracy is not incompatible with community-based thinking.

What Sen fails to recognize, however, are the inherent limits of systems that are based on Western liberal capitalism. He seeks to blend individual and social rights in his conception of social democracy. But political and economic systems that retain the individual pursuit of wealth (capitalism) as their ruling ideology can only graft on social values and "green rights" as a sort of afterthought. In these systems citizens are understood first as individual consumers who vote their own economic interests. The last decades have shown that, whenever there is an economic downturn or the fear of immigration from their poorer (and darker) neighbors to the south, voters begin to dismantle the social services and to support protectionist policies.

The European social democracies have therefore in the end not turned out to be a sort of beachhead for socialism. Individual socially-oriented policies mitigate a few of the most painful byprod-ucts of capitalism, but without bringing the sort of systemic reforms that are necessary. The big picture is still controlled by the class of the wealthiest companies and individuals, who continue to act in and to vote their own interests. Social reforms depend on excess wealth; they are expanded only when there is a sense of relative stability and the absence of threat. As long as the basic economic structure of these nations remains unchanged, social policies remain vulnerable. This is not the foundation that is required for long-term ecological sustainability and a global community oriented toward long-term peace and cooperation.

ORGANIC MARXISM FOR THE COMMON GOOD

From the standpoint of Organic Marxism, more fundamental changes are necessary within Western capitalist democracies if they are going to overcome unsustainable economic practices and domination by the wealthiest one percent. We name three in particular, without which the current system will continue to work against genuine reform. First and foremost, there has to be a change in power relations. Currently the owners (the wealthy) control the reins of government; most legislation furthers their interests. The voices of the working class and the poor are heard dimly, when at all. No true "rule by the people" (democracy) exists as long as power is not really shared with the people.

Second, social values (the so-called red and green rights) must become foundational to the political and economic systems, rather than allowing the individual pursuit of wealth and comfort to be the driving motor of the state. Only when blue rights are not the sole *raison d'être* of the state will social and environmental interests begin to play a significant role in government decision-making.

Accompanying the first two changes must be the establishment of community structures and community-based thinking. There simply is no way to achieve a truly democratic society, society "for the common good," without local groups with decision-making powers that meet the human need for community. Environmental collapse, scientists tell us, will bring the collapse of broader social and economic systems. National governments will not be able to address all the crises that arise. Communities will find themselves forced to become more self-reliant, which is possible only when we develop effective communal structures.

It's also true that, in the absence of significant community involvement, people feel depersonalized. Depersonalization produces apathy, and apathy produces a power vacuum. Inevitably, non-community-based power structures move in to fill the vacuum: bureaucracy in socialist systems, and profit-driven corporations in capitalist systems. In turning away from this direction, Organic Marxism shifts the focus from an individualistic to a communitarian perspective. Communitarianism has been growing in response to the weaknesses in the liberal system, and we predict that it will play an increasingly significant role as the environmental crisis looms ever larger.[8]

Community-based economics thus lies at the heart of a vibrant, democratic socialism. The classic expression of this economic theory, Cobb and Daly's *For the Common Good: Redirecting the Economy toward Community, the Environment, and a Sustainable Future*, remains the manifesto for the economics of Organic Marxism. Cobb and Daly write,

> The alternative is to think of the larger community normatively as a community of communities. One's local community would then become a primary basis for self-identification, and participation in its affairs would take on greater importance for two reasons. First, there would be some increase in the significance of local decisions. Second, the representatives chosen locally would participate in important decisions at higher levels and in the selection of representatives to still higher levels. Personal identification would continue to operate at several levels to varying degrees.[9]

Cobb and Daly remain true to the heritage of classical Marxism. Their vision extends all the way from their critique of unsustainable "growth-based" economic models to their proposal of a radically new economic order. Like Marx before them, they realize that a post-capitalist economy will bring with it a "withering away of the state," as Engels put it.[10] They recognize that nationalist competition inevitably conflicts with global ecological thinking:

> The proposal of conceiving the world normatively as a community of communities is an attenuation of the idea of sovereignty. There should be no sovereign states, nations, or global government. The presently sovereign nation-states would retain important roles but devolve others on smaller units and surrender still others to the United Nations. All communities would exercise some "sovereignty," but none would be sovereign in the sense of modern political theory. The myths of social contract on which these modern theories of political sovereignty were based are obviously false historically. They also distort both theory and practice.[11]

Of course, nations will not easily give up their controlling power on the global stage, and the myopia that accompanies this power. Even the most enlightened of the Northern European social democracies still assume that the nation-state should be able to define and pursue its own self-interests. Much therefore depends on how rapidly global climate change causes the collapse of individual nation-states and of the economic structures that currently control global trade. In one sense, we hope the collapse will proceed slowly, since in that case the costs to human life and biodiversity will be lower. Also, if the collapse is slow, the world will see a period when independent states are run according to social democratic principles. By contrast, if the collapse of the global infrastructure is rapid, as Cobb and Daly believe, then economic interactions among the survivors will of necessity occur only within some communities and regions. In this case, one can only hope that the gradual rebuilding of global trade will function according to Cobb and Daly's model of a "community of communities," rather than on the model of "sovereign nations" that has wreaked so much havoc on this planet.

JUSTICE

We saw that Organic Marxism accepts a higher mandate: to work for the common good of all persons; it challenges the privileging of the wealthy that dominates Western democracies today. Only government "of the people, by the people, for the people" (President Lincoln, Gettysburg Address) is truly democratic government; a nation run "by the wealthy, for the wealthy" is democracy in name alone. We will now discover that, of the four central concepts explored in this and the preceding chapter, the concept of justice sheds perhaps the clearest light on the transition that is required.

Unfortunately, our discussion of the various models of democracy was still a bit formal; it accomplished the move from individual to communal, but it didn't communicate enough about the specific values by which these communities live. By contrast, a probing discussion of justice issues, and of specific injustices, brings a greater degree of concreteness. In the process, one learns more about the actual policies of societies that are built around the central principles of Organic Marxism.

The most urgent justice issue raised in politics and economics is the question of distributive justice: within a society, what methods of distributing economic burdens and benefits are unjust, and what practices maximize justice? The positions discussed by philosophers fall along a clear continuum. Furthest to the right is the "desert" theory of justice (as in "to get your just deserts"): those who work hard deserve the riches that they acquire; hence it's unjust to use any of their wealth in order to help people in poverty. [12] In the middle are "egalitarian" positions, which insist that distribution of resources should be equal across the population. (The famous Harvard philosopher John Rawls is often associated with this position, though some believe he fits more naturally under the next heading.) Next to the left are those positions that seek to maximize some value across the society, such as overall welfare, access to education, quality of life, the capacity to succeed, etc. In this case, the principle of distribution is not conceived at the individual level but across the whole society. Finally, at the far end of the spectrum from the "desert" theory is the Marxist answer: maximize contributions from those who are most able to give them, and prioritize distributions to those who need them most.

It will come as no surprise to hear that the early modern European philosophers advocated the positions on the far right end of this continuum. Consider just two examples. For the eighteenth-century British philosopher David Hume, morality consists of just two parts: "natural" morality, which includes benevolence to those close to us, and "artificial" justice, which, when it is achieved, is unintentionally produced by human actions. "For Hume justice concerned three artificial extensions of the natural person, namely relations to things, other persons and events (property, promises and contracts)."[13] This thoroughgoing individualist approach to justice makes it a derivative concern or an unintended byproduct rather than a "natural" principle.

Adam Smith tied his theory of morality to how an impartial spectator would respond: "The moral life of the species can be seen as the search for . . . common standpoints from which the propriety or suitability of actions to their situations can be judged. Over time certain regularities can be discerned in this search and these are commonly specified in terms of the qualities of character that lie behind [them], that is, in terms of the virtues, including justice."[14] Not surprisingly, this rather unusual view of morality is similar to Adam Smith's idea of the "invisible hand" of capitalism, which transforms the selfish actions of the capitalists into the greatest possible benefit for society as a whole.

In discussing human rights above, we noted that it's hard to avoid the conclusion that the libertarian position is self-serving: those who have the most wealth somehow "discover" that the only human right that matters is the right to their own property—and, when it comes to acquiring possessions, the right to freedom from outside interference. The early modern European position on justice is similar. It maintains that the only kind of justice the state should uphold is the justice of strict equality: the wealthy should not be taxed at a higher rate than the poor, and they should receive equal distributions of government support. The rich work hard; hence they are entitled to whatever profits come their way. If the poor person does not earn enough to support his family, it must be because he is lazy.

On this view, systemic injustices are excluded from consideration. Because libertarians assume that capitalist economics establishes a level playing field, they want to conclude that wealth is evidence of hard work and strong character, whereas poverty implies laziness and lack of character. The kinds of injustice that arise from factors outside the control of the individual worker—disadvantages that come from one's class, gender, skin color, educational opportunities, or access to capital—are generally excluded from consideration under the libertarian theory of justice.

How then can we move toward a more pluralistic concept of justice, one that takes into account the full range of factors that are relevant to evaluating just and unjust acts? Sheer numerical equality is simply not complex enough to capture all the factors relevant to just decision making; we need to strive for a far more systemic and long-term point of view. It does not suffice to consider only the given, the status quo; we need an imaginative, ethically sensitive exploration of *how society could be restructured today.*

Amartya Sen does not go far enough, but his discussion of justice does offer a starting point. In *The Idea of Justice,* he notes that it is "central to the idea of justice…that we can have a strong sense of injustice on many different grounds, and yet not agree on one particular ground as being *the* dominant reason for the diagnosis of injustice."[15] Injustices are multi-factorial; there's rarely just one failure of justice at work. Moreover, justice includes considerations of myriad social relations and processes; it depends on how an action is realized in social relationships. The outcomes, Sen notes, cannot be captured by any simple account of objective duties:

> An appropriate understanding of social realization—central to justice as *nyaya* [realized as opposed to merely ideal justice]— has to take the comprehensive form of a process-inclusive broad account. It would be hard to dismiss the perspective of social realizations on the grounds that it is narrowly consequentialist and ignores the reasoning underlying deontological concerns.[16]

A theory of justice that lives up to these requirements must include at least three major features. (1) One needs to avoid any "arbitrary reduction of multiple and potentially conflicting principles to one solitary survivor, guillotining all the other evaluative criteria." Narrowing the field, as libertarians do, "is not, in fact, a prerequisite for getting useful and robust conclusions on what should be done."[17] This implies the need for a pluralistic approach. Rather than limiting one's attention to a single notion of distributive justice, one needs a multi-faceted theory of justice that encompasses the whole continuum.

(2) One can achieve a sufficiently broad and multi-faceted picture only if one begins with the analysis of injustices and derives one's theory of justice from there. It takes both intellectual work and intuitive practice to deepen awareness of the whole range of injustices. Cultural, economic, social, and historical research is required, as well as philosophical analysis.

(3) In particular, justice has to do with how different communities interact. An individual may be treated unjustly, but usually the full analysis of the situation includes patterns of mistreatment. In most countries these patterns calcify into inequalities between the classes. Rectifying injustices thus requires readjusting the relations between the communities involved, whether by removing systemic oppression,

increasing political representation, improving economic or educational opportunities, or redistributing resources.

A communitarian approach to injustices that employs these three-features begins to make concrete what is implied by the ideal of justice. Marx may have been suspicious of the term "justice" because it is often used by the wealthy to justify their behaviors and policies. But he has powerfully expressed what a just system would look like:

> In a higher phase of communist society, after the enslaving sub-ordination of the individual to the division of labor, and there-with also the antithesis between mental and physical labor, has vanished; after labor has become not only a means of life but life's prime want; after the productive forces have also increased with the all-around development of the individual, and all the springs of co-operative wealth flow more abundantly—only then then can the narrow horizon of bourgeois right be crossed in its entirety and society inscribe on its banners: *From each according to his ability, to each according to his needs!*[18]

The ideal of justice that we are uncovering here will look to Marx's outcome as its goal: "From each according to his ability, to each according to his needs." At the same time, a postmodern, organic Marxism will recognize that injustices are complex and multi-faceted; that cultures and ecologies are intertwined nondeterministic systems where small changes have unpredictable outcomes; and that interventions therefore call for careful study and great sensitivity. Marx's determinism is left behind, and his belief that utopia is imminent is set aside. Nonetheless, the ideal of justice Marx formulated remains as powerful as ever.

The Marxian goal, translated into constructive postmodern terms, is described by the political theorist Franklin Gamwell. Gamwell draws from the resources of Whitehead's process philosophy:

> An actuality realizes greater good because it realizes greater creativity, and the greater good of all realizations together is

the greater realization of unity-in-diversity. With Whitehead, we can say that concrete good is defined aesthetically.[19]

In this sense, injustices represent imbalances—disharmonies—between subsystems, and only from the perspective of the whole can justice emerge. Justice seeks the dialectical goal of a harmonious unity-in-diversity.

In the end, justice is about the redistribution of power. Power-interests are deeply ingrained, and those with power rarely give up their privileges voluntarily. If it were not for the clouds of global crisis that are already forming on the horizon, we would have to conclude that change is unlikely. But the planetary changes that humans have wrought on this planet are coming; the only question is whether they will produce increased brutality and viciousness, or a more enlightened civilization after the fall of the present one. It behooves us to formulate visions of a more harmonious and just society, in the hope that the next chapter will be an improvement over the one that is now coming to an end.

CONCLUSION

The period of human civilization known as modernism has brought more change than any other era in human history. Unfortunately, this particular era also narrowed its horizon, identifying the universal human goals—freedom, justice, democracy, human rights—with a narrowly capitalist and individualistic worldview. Later modern movements—Marxism, socialism, European and Russian communism—sought to correct this mistake. But in the context of the modernist competition, they became enmeshed within the same limitations of either/or thinking that had infected their opponents.

Only with the advent of the postmodern era has it become possible to begin speaking of these four ideals again without the dominance of capitalist principles and either/or thinking. The so-called First

Enlightenment in early modern Europe may have intertwined freedom, human rights, democracy, and justice with capitalist assumptions. But a Second Enlightenment is now under way, one that seeks to purify these basic human aspirations from the mistakes of the modern era.[20] Organic Marxism seeks to honor the higher ideals of one of the great European reformers, Karl Marx, while transplanting his program of reform into the context of a postmodern, ecological world.

As the starting point for this postmodern rethinking, we have advocated the process economics of Cobb and Daly's *For the Common Good*. Cobb and Daly focus on an Earth-centered global order, understood as a "community of communities." They acknowledge that, under modern assumptions, individuals gain their rights to personal happiness and wealth within the context of their particular nation-state. Nations compete against other nations, just as individuals compete for limited wealth against other individuals. And, just as individuals ask for the freedom not to be interfered with, so nations have also turned to the United Nations—or to the armies of the most powerful nations— for protection of their sovereignty against aggressors.

Like Franklin Gamwell, quoted above, Cobb and Daly envision an era when the competition between individuals and between nations does not get the last word. They share the central ideal of an Organic Marxism: an ecological world order, understood as a community of communities that is relational all the way down. In such a world, every world citizen is accountable to the communities of others, as he or she is also accountable to a particular home community. And all of us are, together, accountable to the global community of life, without which we cannot survive.

NOTES

1. Alasdair C. MacIntyre, *Whose Justice? Which Rationality?* (Notre Dame, IN: University of Notre Dame Press, 1988).

2. Francis Fukuyama, *The End of History and the Last Man* (New York: Free Press, 2006), 200.

3. Ibid., 43.

4. Ibid.

5. David Boaz, *Libertarianism*, Chapter 1, "A Note on Labels: Why 'Libertarian'?," <http://www.libertarianism.org/ex-3.html>.

6. A few authors have argued that libertarian principles can be combined with socialist form of governments. See, e.g., Nicholas Vrousalis, "Libertarian Socialism: A Better Reconciliation between Self-Ownership and Equality," *Social Theory and Practice*, 37 (2011): 211-26.

7. Amartya Sen, "Democracy as a Universal Value," *Journal of Democracy* 10.3 (1999): 3-17, quote p. 11.

8. See the *Encyclopedia Britannica* article on Communitarianism, now online at <http://www.britannica.com/EBchecked/topic/1366457/communitarianism>, and the excellent presentation by the philosopher Daniel Bell, "Communitarianism," *The Stanford Encyclopedia of Philosophy* (Fall 2013 Edition), ed. Edward N. Zalta, at <http://plato.stanford.edu/archives/fall2013/entries/communitarianism/>. William Davies describes recent work in this field as "neo-communitarianism" in his "The Emerging Neocommunitarianism," *The Political Quarterly* 83/4 (2012): 767-76.

9. Herman E. Daly and John B. Cobb, Jr., *For the Common Good: Redirecting the Economy Toward Community, the Environment, and a Sustainable Future*, 2nd ed (Boston: Beacon Press, 1994), 177.

10. Engels wrote, "The interference of the state power in social relations becomes superfluous in one sphere after another, and then ceases of itself. The government of persons is replaced by the administration of things and the direction of the processes of production. The state is not 'abolished,' it withers away." See Engels, *Anti-Dühring*, Pt. 3, Chap. 2; cf. "Withering Away of the State," in *The Encyclopedia of*

Political Science, ed. George Thomas Kurian (Washington, DC: CQ Press, 2011), *loc. cit.*

11. Daly and Cobb, 178-79.

12. See Section 6, 6, "Desert-Based Principles," in Julian Lamont and Christi Favor, "Distributive Justice," *The Stanford Encyclopedia of Philosophy* (Spring 2013 Edition), ed. Edward N. Zalta, <http://plato. stanford.edu/archives/spr2013/entries/justice-distributive/>, and the literature cited in this section.

13. Alexander Broadie, ed., *The Cambridge Companion to the Scottish Enlightenment* (Cambridge, UK: Cambridge University Press, 2003), 211-12.

14. Broadie, 212. See also Samuel Fleischacker, "Adam Smith's Moral and Political Philosophy," *The Stanford Encyclopedia of Philosophy* (Spring 2013 Edition), ed. Edward N. Zalta, <http://plato.stanford.edu/ archives/spr2013/entries/smith-moral-political/>.

15. Amartya Sen, *The Idea of Justice* (Cambridge, MA: Belknap Press of Harvard University Press, 2009), 2.

16. Ibid., 24.

17. Ibid., 4.

18. Karl Marx, *Critique of the Gotha Programme* (1875), Chapter 1, in Marx and Engels, *Selected Works* (Moscow: Progress Publishers, 1970), III: 13-30, emphasis added; now online at<https://www.marxists.org/ archive/marx/works/1875/gotha/ch01.htm>.

19. Franklin Gamwell, *Existence and the Good: Metaphysical Necessity in Morals and Politics* (Albany: State University of New York Press, 2011), 171-72.

20. See Wang Zhihe and Fan Meijun, *The Second Enlightenment* (Beijing: Peking University Press, 2011).

Part Three

Organic Marxism

Chapter 9

MARXISM AND THE ECOLOGICAL SCIENCES: THE SCIENCE OF ORGANIC SYSTEMS

ORGANIC AND CONTEXTUALIZED KNOWLEDGE

Over the course of this study, we have repeatedly observed the diverse ways that Marxism has been embodied and embedded in particular historical and cultural contexts. Marx may have originally presented his analysis as a timeless apprehension of the dialectic of human history and the class struggle, and many of his insights do still speak powerfully to our time. Today, however, we see even more clearly that the dynamics of socialism and capitalism, of wealth and poverty, always come woven into a particular time, place, and society. The scalpel in the hand of a great surgeon brings health and saves lives; the same scalpel in the hands of a violent person can bring death. Previous chapters have revealed how differently Marxism is understood in the context of modernist thought and of constructive or deconstructive postmodernism. Building on those results, we now explore the development of Marxism in the context of organic thinking.

Knowledge is *organic* when it grows in a system constituted by living, interconnected relationships both among its parts and with its surrounding environment. What constitutes an "environment" in this sense depends on what kind of entity one is talking about. The environment for a cell consists of the cells that surround it and the medium in which it lives (earth, water, or air). The environment for an organism consists of the other organisms with which it interacts and the non-living characteristics of its ecological niche (temperature, mineral resources, food sources and toxins). The environment for a person consists of other persons, both present and past, and the social values and conventions that they embody, together with the other environmental features already named. Finally, the environment for a state or society encompasses all of these factors, *as well as* its unique history, culture, language, beliefs, geography, and aspirations for the future.

These observations might seem obvious, except for the fact that they are so frequently ignored or overlooked. Philosophers create theories based on their experience of a particular country, culture, or age; and they write *for* their context. Frequently the theories are then transported to completely different countries and cultures, presupposing that the features of the original context will still apply at the new destination. Experience shows that this assumption is often false.

There is a second reason why the organic nature of all living philosophies, Marxism included, is so frequently overlooked. It is this: when the modern European philosophers encountered the claim that philosophies are not simply universal but are organically connected to a particular culture, they tended to equate that view with relativism. Many of them claimed that if theories are *not* objective and universal—if they do not apply to all people at all times—then they must be purely subjective. But in that case, they warned, humans will have no criteria for deciding between political and ethical systems. One will have no way of knowing which statements are true and which false, which actions are good and which evil; complete chaos will result, because now "anything goes."

This kind of either/or thinking was widespread in Europe in the modern period. Among its harmful effects was the alleged forced choice between "knowledge is objective and universal" on the one side and "all is relative" on the other. *Tertium non datur*, they said; there is no third alternative, no middle way.

Numerous Marxist authors in the postmodern West have sought to undercut this false dichotomy. In his classic early work, *Knowledge and Human Interests,* the great philosopher of the Frankfurt School, Jürgen Habermas, showed that human interests affect all knowledge claims; the idea of purely objective knowledge is a myth.[1] There is an organic relationship between what we know and the needs and interests that we bring. Richard Bernstein's *Beyond Objectivism and Relativism* likewise made a comprehensive case that the vast majority of human claims to knowledge fall in the space between sheer relativism and objectively justified claims.[2] These early opponents of modernism relied on primarily negative arguments in order to weaken the hold of a centuries-old prejudice. Because their work was successful, we are now in a position to develop a *positive* account.

Fortunately, during the same years the sciences of life have been developing as well. The paradigm for much of modern science was reductionism. As Steven Weinberg famously wrote, "All explanatory arrows point downward"[3]—living systems must ultimately be explained in terms of the laws of pre-living systems, such as chemistry and physics. The rapid growth of systems biology is helping to change that paradigm, however. Today when scientists study a particular system—say, the system of all protein interactions in an *E. coli* bacterium—they study both the lower-level systems that influence protein interactions, and the higher-order systems that constrain their behaviors as well. The arrows of explanation, it turns out, point both downward and upward.

The best example of this more organic approach to the study of living systems is one that emerges out of the environmental sciences: the organic relationship between an organism and its ecosystem. For too long, biologists sought to explain interactions between organisms in purely mechanistic terms. Today, the organic model allows us to move "beyond mechanism," as the title of an important recent book describes it.[4] Just as the social sciences need to describe and explain the personal dimension of human existence, including the complex worlds of meaning that humans create and live within, so also the biological sciences can now describe organisms as organisms, that is, as agents acting within their particular ecosystems.

THE SCIENCES OF INTERCONNECTED SYSTEMS

A quick survey of a few of the contemporary sciences provides a good introduction to the details of the emerging organic world view. If it were not for these developments in the natural sciences, the science of organisms would not be possible.

Interconnection in the physical sciences. Physics and physical chemistry cannot directly teach about organic relationships, since they study the pre-organic physical world. However, several developments in physics over the last 120 years offer support for the organic model in the biological sciences. They also provide some helpful analogies to organic models in biology. (It goes without saying that disanalogies also exist.)

The physical world turned out to be far more interconnected then scientists had thought before the twentieth century. In Newtonian physics, one calculates the trajectories of independently existing physical objects in a rigid Cartesian space, with time as a separate type of dimension. It was Albert Einstein's theory of special relativity that first revealed the interconnection of space and time. His theory of general relativity then linked the geometry of space to the mass of objects; extremely massive objects, such as black holes, actually "bend" space.

Quantum physics, the physics of the very small, brought an even greater level of interconnectedness. The first surprise was the interconnectedness of the observer with the object observed. Many physics students learn about the "collapse" of the wave function, represented by the Schrödinger wave equation, through an experiment known as the double-slit experiment. In this experiment, a beam of light, which is divided and sent through two separate slits simultaneously, impacts a screen differently depending on whether or not the beam of light is measured as it passes through one of the two slits. If unmeasured before the screen, the light apparently passes through *both* slits, since when it hits the screen it shows the kind of interference effects that one would expect from a wave. If measured at one slit, however, the interference effects disappear; the light now strikes the screen as individual photons of light. The act of observation apparently suffices to transform the light from waves to particles.

According to the standard or "Copenhagen" interpretation of quantum mechanics, the act of observation or measurement brings about a "collapse" of the quantum probabilities into a specific state of affairs. Before observation, many physicists said, the subatomic state existed merely as a potential-to-be-observed. Thus in Carl Friedrich von Weizsäcker's famous thought experiment, a single electron inside a vacuum-sealed box would be described mathematically as being in all parts of the box simultaneously, based on its probability distribution. If a divider is then placed in the middle of the box and the physicist measures, he will find the electron either 100 percent present or 0 percent present on one side of the box, as one would expect from a particle.[5]

The connection between the observer and what is observed has had some rather radical implications. For example, it would mean that a photon of light traveling for 300 million light years from a distant star remained a mere potential-to-be-observed until the moment that you perceive it, at which point it is retroactively resolved into a particular photon of light, which we now say (retrospectively) has been traveling through space for those hundreds of millions of years. Following the logic of this supposition, the famous Princeton physicist John Wheeler suggested that the universe as a whole might have existed in a sort of potential state until agents evolved who could observe it, at which point it become actual for the first time.[6]

The discovery of entangled particles by Alain Aspect in 1982 offered yet another dramatic example of universal interconnection. Aspect's experiments have since been replicated at distances above 300 kilometers. The experiment involves two prepared particles issuing from a single source and traveling in opposite directions. The physics says that their spin is indeterminate until the moment of measurement. If one measures just one of the particles at a particular instant and discovers it to be (for example) spin up, the other particle instantly resolves into its complement, in this case spin down. Because there is not time for a message to travel between the particles even at the speed of light, no information could have passed from the one to the other. Most physicists conclude that the two particles constitute a single physical system, even when separated by 300 km or more. Given that entangled particles emerge in very many different places in the universe, we must now conclude that the universe manifests profound interconnections across vast distances. Again, these are not yet organic, but they lay the foundation for organic interconnections at the level of life.

The scientific description of interconnections at the microphysical level is further deepened in quantum field theory. The equations of quantum field theory presuppose that these fields are physically more fundamental than particles. The quantum field manifests itself as particles under certain conditions and at certain times; particles arise out of the field as a sort of distillate.[7] It would be false to say that only fields exist; after all, the physical world is described by both discrete and continuous functions. Still, it's clear that the interconnectedness at the microphysical level (waves, fields, plasma clouds, etc.) is far greater than classical physics ever imagined.

Systems biology. In 1953 Crick and Watson discovered the double helix structure of DNA, which transmits genetic information from parent to offspring. Not surprisingly, in the few decades that followed, the primary focus fell on these newly discovered biochemical units that are involved in cell reproduction: DNA molecules and their chemical structure, genes and chromosomes, amino acids and proteins, the biochemistry of cells, and intercellular communication. Unfortunately, environmental factors received less attention during those years. In the first excitement about the genetic breakthroughs, scientists tended to overstate their ability to explain most biological phenomena in genetic terms: cell functioning, disease, macroevolution, even psychological characteristics such as intelligence.[8]

In recent years, however, scientific attention has turned to the study of more systemic influences. Both epigenetics and systems biology focus on interactions between genetic information and environmental factors. Systems biology studies individual cells, or groups of cells, viewing them as systems. Because of the rapid growth of microbiology, systems biologists are now able to explain how cells function in terms of specific subsystems within a single cell, such as the system of all proteins (proteomics) or the system of all metabolites (metabolomics). Predictions of broader developments within the body, such as the probability of suffering from breast cancer, are far more accurate when systems of proteins are considered rather than just individual genes. Indeed, biologists now recognize that groups of genes switching on and off in a coordinated fashion, rather than individual genes, are responsible for most of the body's developmental processes.

BEYOND MECHANISM: THE NEW SCIENCE OF ORGANISMS

Returning organisms to biology. A growing movement within the biological sciences has challenged the mechanistic and reductionist assumptions that ruled biology since the advent of Neo-Darwinism, the "new synthesis" of Darwin and genetics of the 1930s and 1940s. In the past, those who defended explanations at the level of organisms were considered to be anti-naturalist and anti-empirical. The reductionist methods of science, it was said, require that living organisms be explained primarily at the biochemical, chemical, and physical levels. Explanations given in terms of organisms were said to be "holistic" in a negative sense; talk of organisms as beings with perceptions and purposes was considered to be too vague to be scientific. The reductionists challenged whether one could ever provide rigorous scientific analysis and testing of organism-based theories.

But advances in the biological sciences have changed the situation dramatically. We are now able to provide testable accounts of how unicellular organisms "perceive" their environments through chemical osmosis. We can study the evolution of the first nerve cells and the formation of rudimentary nervous systems. We can identify specific structures that perform specific organismic functions. "Teleology"—the study of structures and behaviors that enable organisms to carry out purposive actions—is no longer supernatural or God-inspired; it is now an accepted part of the scientific study of the natural world. Biologists recognize organisms as teleological in the harmless sense that the evolutionary process defines goals for *all* organisms. As theoretical biologist Stuart Kauffman recently described it in a conversation, each organism is "out to earn a living in the world." When a micro-organism swims up a glucose gradient toward a food source, or when it recoils from a toxin, Kauffman argued, it is acting teleologically, with purpose. These are examples of actions that it performs *as an organism, engaging in organic relations with its surroundings.* The organism as a unit is an emergent agent, constituted by sub-processes but not reducible to them.[9]

Ecosystems theory. In the late twentieth century biologists began putting together the conclusions they had acquired through the new advances in genetics and microbiology. In recent years this explosion of detailed knowledge has produced a far deeper understanding of how organisms interact with each other and with their environments. The new biology does not *reduce* organisms to the subsystems and chemical components of which they are composed; rather, it draws on the knowledge of subsystems in order to produce more accurate descriptions of how organisms are able to function as agents in the world. We are as interested in telling the story of the emergence of structures as we are in breaking the emergent structures down into their component parts. As biologists began to turn their more detailed knowledge to the study of agents in interaction, the new ecological sciences were born.

We now know that much of the biosphere consists of reciprocal organic relationships. (Marxists might view this as a particular kind of dialectical materialism). The one-way deterministic relationships of the older biology, by contrast, only tell part of the story. So, for example, we have long understood how genes code for proteins and how proteins carry out programmed functions within the cell. More recently, biologists have learned how influences from outside the cell affect the timing of gene expression, even altering the order of bits of chemical information (transposons). Genetic and environmental information continually interact, in both directions, with both influencing how organisms exercise their agency.

Evolutionary developmental biology ("evo devo") studies the complex mechanisms for intercellular communication. We now know that behaviors of individual cells are strongly influenced by systems of cells. Nobel-prize laureate Gerald Edelman describes the brain as a whole as an evolving, interconnected system, responding to its surrounding environment.[10]

The body of each organism can thus be conceived as a sort of ecosystem, with the body's subsystems (such as the immune system and the mechanisms that preserve homeostasis) linking its parts into an interconnected and self-regulating whole. Just as no one would analyze the economy of a village apart from its interactions with other towns and with the province, so also no one would study a subsystem of a body without including its relationships with other subsystems and with the body as a whole.

Nor are environments merely static backdrops or containers, determining the fates of the organisms that live there. Of course, external events can impact an ecosystem from outside, as when a tsunami carries ocean water into a forest far inland from the ocean. More typically, however, an ecosystem is co-constituted by its member species. Biologists once treated each ecological niche as a pre-given environment, within which organisms had to fight for survival against their competitors. Today we understand that the inhabitants are agents who are continually making and transforming their own niche, at the same time that they are adapting to changes in climate, in resources, and in the behavior of other organisms.[11]

In sum, the new biology is about emergent organic relationships between living beings and their environments, mediated through the subsystems of cells, organs, and subsystems. Instead of defining the process only in competitive terms, biologists today such as Martin Nowak at the Harvard University Program for Evolutionary Dynamics interpret it in a cooperative manner, as a kind of symbiosis (literally, "living together").[12]

The contemporary study of consciousness. We close with a brief word on the neurosciences, where similar kinds of changes are also taking place. The "brain determinists" held that to reconstruct the electrochemical processes in the brain is to understand thought; no separate analysis of subjective experiences or mental influences is required.[13] Ideas are merely "epiphenomena," they argued; they arise from neuronal firings but do not play any causative role. As one researcher from a University of California medical center told us, "Wires and chemicals, that's all we are; wires and chemicals."

By contrast, several decades ago neuroscientists such as Roger Sperry, the Nobel laureate in Medicine, begin to challenge this unidirectional analysis of thought. According to Sperry, mind is an emergent property of the brain, one that reveals its own unique types of causal influence.[14] Studying the *interaction* of brains with cultural systems, using a correlational model, has led to a richer understanding of how brains and mental awareness are related. One can learn about the neural correlates of consciousness without having to eliminate consciousness, ideas, and culture as natural realities in their own right.

The school of "embodied, embedded cognition," for example, considers the brain in relation to the whole body, and both in relation to the surrounding environment—including thoughts, ideas, and culture.[15] Far more knowledge of the mind-body relationship can be achieved when one studies them in a systemic, bidirectional manner than if one treats brains only as causes and ideas only as byproducts.

CONCLUSION

In this chapter we have explored just a few examples of developments in contemporary science. Physics and chemistry are not organic sciences, though they too are revealing types of interconnection that were inconceivable in the context of modern, Newtonian science. But the physical sciences have played a role in the emergence of the new organic sciences. We considered systems biology, organism-centered approaches in biology, ecosystems theory, and the contemporary study of consciousness. These advances, taken together, shed important new light on what an "organic" approach means. When the insights of organicism are applied to social, political, and economic questions, Organic Marxism is the result.

As an important recent book describes it, one can now do biological science "beyond mechanism" by "putting life back into biology."[16] For much of the modern period, scientists were forced to choose between a non-scientific holism and a complete reduction of living beings to their physical and chemical components. (This is similar to the choice between objectivism and relativism that characterized modern philosophy.) Today this is no longer a forced choice. Thanks to advances in the life sciences, and to a change of theoretical perspective, biologists can now study the biosphere organically, giving the agency of organisms a central role. Detailed knowledge about subsystems, drawn from biochemistry and microbiology, does not compete with organic biology; it contributes to the complete picture.

Organic Marxism is grounded, in part, in this newly emerging understanding of organisms, ecosystems, and the earth's biosphere as a whole. Like the new biology, it is organic and bidirectional rather than deterministic and unidirectional. This is not a case of choosing one's science based on one's political beliefs; Russian Marxists once attempted that strategy, to the great detriment of both science and politics.[17] Instead it's a matter of recognizing an important paradigm change in the biological sciences and drawing out its implications for the study of human social systems. The recent developments have helped move scientists beyond the idea that only a strictly reductionist science could count as good biology.

Unfortunately, political theorists have been slow to recognize the implications of this shift to an organic paradigm for traditional political theories such as Marxism. The implications are revolutionary. Isn't it inconsistent to view the biosphere as built up out of living, evolving, organic relationships, while maintaining that political and economic systems function in a mechanistic, deterministic fashion? Isn't it strange to say that "brain" and "mind" exist in dynamic interaction, while conceiving of culture and ideas as a mere "superstructure" that is carried along by socio-economic forces as its real causes? Postmodern Marxists should let Marx's nineteenth-century version of deterministic materialism "wither away," replacing it with an updated organic model, so that the enduring insights of his work can continue to guide political theory today.

The famous theoretical biologist Stuart Kauffman has recognized the promise that the new organic biology holds out for revisioning human societies in the twenty-first century. He writes:

> [The] rather fixed world is not how real life is: we live a life of ever-unfolding, often unprestatable opportunities that we partially create and co-create, with and without intent. I am thus falling in love with "Living the Well Discovered Life." Then my own dream for "Beyond Modernity" starts to become our thirty civilizations around the globe, woven gently together to protect the roots of each, yet firmly enough to generate ever new cultural forms by which we can be human in increasingly diverse, creative ways, each helping himself or herself and the other to live a well-discovered life, and ameliorating our deep

shadow side. We need an enlarged vision of ourselves and of what we can become.[18]

Notes

1. Jürgen Habermas, *Knowledge and Human Interests*, trans. Jeremy Shapiro (Boston: Beacon Press, 1971).

2. Richard Bernstein, *Beyond Objectivism and Relativism: Science, Hermeneutics, and Praxis* (Philadelphia: University of Pennsylvania Press, 1983).

3. Steven Weinberg, *Dreams of a Final Theory* (New York: Pantheon, 1992).

4. Brian G. Henning and Adam C. Scarfe, eds., *Beyond Mechanism: Putting Life Back into Biology* (New York: Lexington Books, 2013).

5. Carl Friedrich von Weizsäcker, *The World View of Physics*, trans. Marjorie Grene (Chicago: University of Chicago Press, 1952).

6. John Archibald Wheeler with Kenneth Ford, *Geons, Black Holes, and Quantum Foam: A Life in Physics* (New York: Norton, 1998).

7. Bernard d'Espagnat, *In Search of Reality* (Berlin: Springer, 1983).

8. Richard Dawkins, *The Selfish Gene* (New York: Oxford University Press, 1976).

9. Philip Clayton and Paul Davies, eds., *The Reemergence of Emergence* (Oxford: Oxford University Press, 2006); Clayton, *Mind and Emergence: From Quantum to Consciousness* (Oxford: Oxford University Press, 2004).

10. Gerald M. Edelman, *Neural Darwinism: The Theory of Neuronal Group Selection* (New York: Basic Books, 1987).

11. F. John Odling-Smee, Kevin N. Laland, and Marcus W. Feldman,

Niche Construction: The Neglected Process in Evolution (Princeton, NJ: Princeton University Press, 2003).

12. Martin Nowak, "Five Rules for the Evolution of Cooperation," *Science* 314, no. 5805 (2006 December 8): 1560-63. For an excellent overview of the new ecosystems theory, see Robert E. Ulanowicz, *A Third Window: Natural Life beyond Newton and Darwin* (West Conshohocken, PA: Templeton Foundation Press, 2009).

13. For the classic expression of this view see Patricia Smith Churchland, *Neurophilosophy: Toward a Unified Science of the Mind-Brain* (Cambridge, MA: MIT Press, 1986); Churchland, *Brain-wise: Studies in Neurophilosophy* (Cambridge, MA: MIT Press, 2002); Jaegwon Kim, *Mind in a Physical World: An Essay on the Mind-Body Problem and Mental Causation* (Cambridge, MA: MIT Press, 1998).

14. Roger Wolcott Sperry, *Science and Moral Priority: Merging Mind, Brain, and Human Values* (New York: Columbia University Press, 1983). For an overview of this debate, see Philip Clayton, *Mind and Emergence* (note 9 above).

15. Francisco Varela, Evan Thompson, and Eleanor Rosch, *The Embodied Mind: Cognitive Science and Human Experience* (Cambridge, MA: MIT Press, 1991); Evan Thompson, *Mind in Life: Biology, Phenomenology, and the Sciences of Mind* (Cambridge, MA: Belknap Press of Harvard University Press, 2007).

16. Brian G. Henning and Adam C. Scarfe, eds., *Beyond Mechanism* (see note 4 above).

17 See David Joravsky, *The Lysenko Affair* (Cambridge, MA: Harvard University Press, 1970).

18 Stuart Kauffman, "Evolution beyond Newton, Darwin, and Entailing Law," in Henning and Scarfe, *Beyond Mechanism*, 22.

Chapter 10

ORGANIC MARXISM, PROCESS PHILOSOPHY, AND CHINESE THOUGHT

ORGANIC MARXISM AS AN OPEN MARXISM

In this chapter we turn to the significant parallels between Organic Marxism, process philosophy, and traditional Chinese thought. Establishing the interconnections between these three different traditions is a crucial step in developing any social philosophy that serves the common good rather than the wishes of the few.

Engaging in comparative discussions like this one is a central feature of a growing group of Marxist schools of thought. We here use the common label "Open Marxism" in order to draw attention to what these emerging schools share in common.[1] Open Marxisms flourish in the constructive postmodern context, rejecting the rationalism and determinism that dominated the modern European period. They acknowledge that all of life is an open-ended process and that leaders manage at the local, national, and international levels always "at the edge of chaos."[2] Scientific thinking has moved from the study of closed systems to open, non-static, organic systems (Chapter 9). In response, economic and political theories have likewise begun to shift from the old orthodox and doctrinaire schools of thought to much more fluid, dynamic, and responsive approaches. For scholars and leaders today who are interested in structuring society for the good of humanity and the planet, these new embedded and contextualized Marxisms are bringing new life to Marxist critiques of wealth and power in the West.

The tendency for the wealthiest class to assume power, and to utilize that power to its own advantage at the expense of the non-wealthy, is pervasive across capitalist systems; it's why such systems exist in the first place. Yet the details of how the injustices are overcome, and what society looks like afterwards, are not uniform. Open Marxisms recognize how greatly cultures vary and how deeply cultural systems affect the way a given society is organized and experienced. These differences crop up even when analyzing such central Marxian themes as work, production, and class relations.

What about the distinctive features of the Chinese context? Many scholars today, both in China and in the West, are working in the spirit of the new open Marxisms. We include among them the "Return to Marx" movement, which represents an important Marxist school in China today. This movement emphasizes the importance of turning back to the original Marx and reading his works, without being dominated by the interpretations of Lenin and the later Russian Marxists. The "Return to Marx" school offers an important corrective to a certain tendency in the early phase of Chinese Marxism, which sometimes let Russian Marxists define the form that Marxism should take in China. At the same time, recent scholarship has also uncovered the dissimilarities between nineteenth-century German Marxism and our present context. The differences invite one to update Marx and to engage in a constructive rethinking of Marxism. As Professor Wang Zhihe writes:

> Unlike orthodox Marxism or dogmatic Marxism, Chinese Marxism is an open Marxism which changes form according to the current situation. From Mao Zedong's thought and Deng's theory to Jiang's "three represents theory" and Hu's "Scientific Outlook on Development," all point to such an open orientation.[3]

Numerous publications on constructive postmodernism in China have already shown how deeply process thought connects with the ancient philosophical traditions of China. (In this respect, postmodern thought contrasts strongly with modernism, which usually defines itself *in opposition to* the traditions that precede it.) Organic Marxism is a form of process thinking; both affirm that reality is an open, evolving process. Each time categories of thought are planted in a new context— be it a new culture, historical period, region, or political movement— they sprout and grow in new ways. Consequently, open process thinkers do not expect Marxism to be a static thing but to evolve continually, just as human social systems are constantly evolving.

These are the reasons it is crucial to explore the connections between the three terms in the title to this chapter. Regarding the first relation, the links between traditional Chinese thought and process philosophy have long been recognized. Concerning the second, we have been attempting to show in these chapters how process philosophy helps to transform modernist Marxism into Organic Marxism. It remains only to show, third, how Chinese traditional wisdom can play an important role in Organic Marxism. For example, we have been disappointed to see that Ecological Marxism rarely mentions the Chinese traditions. We hope that our constructive proposal will help to overcome that limitation.

MARX AND WHITEHEAD

Alfred North Whitehead is as central to process thought as Marx is to socialism. We believe that Whitehead is important for Organic Marxism in two ways. On the one hand, he helped to convince Western thinkers in the twentieth century that process is central to both science and human experience, in the way that the *I Jing* convinced Chinese philosophers of the same conclusion. On the other hand, Whitehead's challenge to either/or thinking in politics helped to open the door for postmodern Marxism.

Especially since the Second World War, many people in the West believe that every nation is either capitalist (which they believe is good) or Communist (which they believe is bad). Either a country allows market forces to operate, which makes it libertarian and capitalist; or it bans markets in favor of state ownership, which makes it Marxist and Communist. Worse, during the Cold War people in the West argued that freedom, democracy, justice, and human rights are only present in capitalist countries.

When one encounters a false dichotomy, the wisest thing to do is to challenge the claim that the two sides are incompatible. One should look instead for both/and solutions that are more adequate than either of the alternatives alone. This is the core of dialectical thinking, which was central to Hegel and Marx. (It's ironic that Western critics identify dialectical thinkers like Hegel and Marx with only one side of a forced choice, since their central contention was that the dialectical advance of history will over time incorporate *both* sides of each opposition.) It seems clear that there are times where market forces bring benefits within a nation and between nations; and there are other cases in which unrestrained markets produce injustices that neither local communities nor the global community should accept. A major contribution of Organic Marxism lies in its ability to blend elements from both of these two socioeconomic systems. We challenge the claim that democracy and socialism are inherently opposed to one another. Marx was right to view socialism as the most consistent form of democracy.

Alfred North Whitehead clearly saw the advantages of this both/ and approach:

> "It begins to look as though the one thing democracy has that
> is worth saving is the freedom of the individual. [But] I would
> say," remarked Whitehead, "two. The freedom of the individual
> is one. But your knowledge of history will remind you that
> there has always been misery at the bottom of society ... Our
> own age is the first time when ... there need be no material
> want. Russia has relieved the suffering of the masses at the

price of the individual's liberty; the Fascists have destroyed personal liberties without really alleviating the condition of the masses; the task of democracy is to relieve mass misery and yet preserve the freedom of the individual."[4]

In a recent book, Anne Fairchild Pomeroy has argued that Marx and Whitehead can supplement each other: "Marx needs Whitehead to ground his claims regarding the proper ethos and telos of human life and its productive-processive interaction with, for, and as a part of the world as a relational unity; Whitehead needs Marx to focus on the destructive aspects of capitalism as a form of world productive-process."[5]

It's surprising that one finds such resistance to this both/and solution. Instead of thinking in dialectical (or Daoist) fashion, nations have remained locked into one option or the other. Sadly, North Americans have been particularly resistant to blending in the resources of socially oriented thinking. Whitehead saw this clearly:

We English and Americans ... are singularly unimaginative in our interpretations of the term "democracy"; we seem unable to admit under our definition any form of society which does not conform closely to our own ... I believe that the two great powers which will emerge from this war [World War II] will be Russia and America, and the principles which animate them will be antithetical: that of Russia will be cohesion; that of America will be individualism.[6]

Certainly the last decades have shown an increasing turn toward individualism among Americans—at exactly the time that global climate disruption calls for community-based thinking and integrated international action to reduce pollution levels (to which the United States is a major contributor), thereby taking steps toward becoming a more ecological civilization. Both Marx and Whitehead challenge individualism and encourage a more social thinking.

WHAT IS PROCESS THOUGHT?

One can identify four central features of process thinking. Each one has deep resonance with traditional Chinese philosophy. When combined, they provide the conceptual foundation for Organic Marxism.

(1) *A relational view of reality.* Every event is constituted by its relationships to other events. There is therefore no such thing as a discrete individual, existing by itself. The features of one event affect all other events.

Alfred North Whitehead expressed this insight by translating the Western language of things or entities into the language of events. Actual entities, he explained, are really events; he also spoke of them as "actual occasions." Thus, as Whitehead wrote in his great work *Process and Reality*, "to 'function' means to contribute determination to the actual entities in the nexus of some actual world. Thus the determinateness and self-identity of one entity cannot be abstracted from the community of the diverse functionings of *all* entities."[7]

Like the ancient Chinese philosophical work, the *I Jing*, Whitehead's philosophy understands processes as more basic than things. Things can only be *externally related* to each other. For example, two billiard balls can collide, but the effects will only be superficial; the billiard balls themselves remain the same. By contrast, Whitehead affirmed that humans and other living events are actually *internally related* to each other. Since we all exist in relationship (whether we admit it or not), he spoke of the principle of *universal relativity*:

> The principle of universal relativity directly traverses Aristotle's dictum, "A substance is not present in a subject." On the contrary, according to this principle an actual entity *is* present in other actual entities. In fact if we allow for degrees of relevance, and for negligible relevance, we must say that every actual entity is present *in* every other actual entity.[8]

160

Process philosophy is thus at its heart an ecological philosophy—which explains why process philosophy plays such a foundational role for Organic Marxism. As the process eco-philosopher Jay McDaniel recognizes:

> all living beings have their existence and identities in relation to, not apart from, all other living beings. This means that the very identity of a living being, including each plant and animal, is partly determined by the material and cultural environment in which it is situated . . . This means that all entities are thoroughly ecological in nature and that human beings are themselves ecological in being persons-in-community, not persons-in-isolation.[9]

Process philosophy takes this basic ecological insight and develops it into a comprehensive philosophical view of the world. On this view, every event is constituted by the events of its past. Each event takes in and synthesizes these past events to a greater or lesser degree. More complex events don't just repeat the past; they integrate and transform earlier events in a novel way. To deny our relatedness to other events, or merely to repeat them, results in less beauty and harmony. The great process philosophers John Cobb and David Griffin expand this insight into a comprehensive principle for all living things:

> There is no moment that is not constituted by its synthesis of elements from the past. If to be free from the past were to exclude the past, the present would be entirely vacuous. The power of the new is that it makes possible a greater inclusion of elements from the past that otherwise would prove incompatible and exclude each other from their potential contribution. Where the existentialist seems to see an antithesis between having the moment controlled by the past and allowing the future to be determinative, Whitehead says that the more effective the future is, the more fully the potential contribution of the past is realized.[10]

Political theory over the centuries has fought an endless battle between approaches centered on the individual (liberalism, libertarianism) and those centered on the community or society (socialism, communism, communitarianism). In Organic Marxism, which weds Marxist thought and process thought, this battle is circumvented. Following Whitehead, we prefer the middle way, whereby the two perspectives are synthesized. According to Whitehead's solution, "We reduce [our entire] past to a perspective, and yet retain it as the basis of our present moment of realization. We are different from it, and yet we retain our individual identity with it. This is the mystery of personal identity, the mystery of the immanence of the past in the present, the mystery of transcendence."[11]

(2) *Influence without determinism.* Each event is constituted by the past and deeply informed by the past, *but none is completely determined by its past.* Process philosophy does not imply "top-down" or past-to-future control. Indeed, as events and systems of events become more complex, this indeterminacy becomes more pronounced:

> I]n each concrescence whatever is determinable is determined, but ... there is always a remainder [and hence an element of freedom] for the decision of the subject-superject of that concrescence ... This final decision is the reaction of the unity of the whole *to its own internal determination.* This reaction is the final modification of emotion, appreciation, and purpose. But the decision of the whole arises out of the determination of the parts, so as to be strictly relevant to it.[12]

In contrast to determinism, indeterminacy is a source of novelty. After all, only in open systems can new and creative developments occur. Novelty is therefore a key ingredient in process aesthetics, because it is only through creative experimentation that humans find new solutions to global challenges.

Whitehead thus provides grounds for hope in history. As Cobb and Griffin note, "First, the future is fully and radically open. It must take account of all that has been, but the past never settles just how the future will take account of it. Its freedom in relation to the present is not merely that it can readjust the elements in the present world with differing emphases. It can also introduce wholly new elements that change the weight and meaning of those it inherits from the present."[13]

With this new focus on open systems, a major objection to Marxism is answered. The class struggle is not overcome through an inexorable process of change; that picture makes of us mere objects in a tide that no one can stem. Instead, political and economic actors consciously form and foster communities of reform—justice-based communities that bond their members together in working for the greater good:

> The vision that is needed is of new communities that are not experienced as restrictive of freedom. They must be voluntary communities, but that is not enough. Voluntarily to accept the oppression that was felt in involuntary communities is not improvement... The voluntary community must be bound by different kinds of ties, ties that are experienced as fulfillment rather than limitation.[14]

(3) *Aesthetic value.* The process view of reality is not value-free. *Every* event has intrinsic value, which is measured by its capacity for relationship and creativity: "Every unit of process, whether at the level of human or of electronic events, has enjoyment... To be, to actualize oneself, to act upon others, to share in a wider community, is to enjoy being an experiencing subject quite apart from any accompanying pain or pleasure."[15]

For process thinkers, value is defined as cooperative and communal rather than competitive and individual. In Whitehead's words, experience is the "self-enjoyment of being one among many, and of being one arising out of the composition of many."[16] Or, as he writes earlier in *Process and Reality*, "experience is nothing other than what the actual entity is in itself, for itself."[17]

163

This theory of value has deep parallels with traditional Chinese thought. Value cannot be understood without discerning beauty; beauty cannot be understood without discerning harmony; and harmony cannot be understood without considering the perspective of the whole. In the Chinese philosophical classic *Dao de Jing* of Laozi, the word *Dao* is used to express this underlying unity of all things. Whitehead links beauty, harmony, and unity in a very similar way:

> There is a unity in the universe, enjoying value and (by its immanence) sharing value. For example, take the subtle beauty of a flower in some isolated glade of a primeval forest. No animal has ever had the subtlety of experience to enjoy its full beauty. And yet this beauty is a grand fact in the universe. When we survey nature and think however flitting and superficial has been the animal enjoyment of its wonders, and when we realize how incapable the separate cells and pulsations of each flower are of enjoying the total effect—then our sense of the value of the details for the totality dawns upon our consciousness.[18]

Those political theorists who define values only in terms of the individual are not just being selfish; they are actually making a philosophical mistake. They neglect the holistic dimension of value, which intrinsically extends beyond the individual: "Everything has some value *for itself, for others, and for the whole.* This characterizes the meaning of actuality. By reason of this character, constituting reality, the conception of morals arises. We have no right to deface the value experience which is the essence of the universe."[19]

(4) *Balance between private and public.* It follows directly that events are characterized by a balance between private and public identities. Events—and therefore all persons—are constituted by their relationships with others. We are constituted by the ways that we influence and are influenced by our environment. In short, *process philosophy is inherently an ecological philosophy.*

At the same time, as we have seen, each event, organism, or person is also free to decide how it will react to the past and move into the future. Value is an achievement, one that requires the continual use of one's freedom in ways that benefit the community. It may be true that "An entity is actual, when it has significance for itself." By this Whitehead means, "an actual entity functions in respect to its own determination. Thus an actual entity combines self-identity with self-diversity."[20] This idea of "self-diversity" means that each one has *being from* its predecessors (its ancestors), which have provided the data for its own becoming, and *being for* those who follow after it, who will be affected by the decisions it has made. This organic connection of all things means that *freedom from* various constraints must always be *freedom for* the good of others (see Chapter 7 above). For process thinkers, freedom and responsibility are just two sides of the same coin:

> As the human capacity for freedom is promoted, so is the human capacity to attain greater achievements of beauty, but also to achieve greater evil...From a process perspective, sheer freedom is not freedom at all. If there were only novelty, we would not have harmonization and unity of experience, only pure discord. Rather, true freedom is always, in the root sense, *responsible* freedom, i.e., freedom in responsibility.[21]

CHINESE PROCESS THOUGHT

The Chinese contributions to process thought over the last two decades have been very significant. Although it has supporters in many parts of the world, process philosophy has grown more quickly in China than any other nation. More than twenty research centers focusing on Constructive Postmodernism and process thought have been established at Chinese universities, including Zhejiang University, Peking Normal University, and Harbin Institute of Technology. According to Professor Yang Fubin's research, as of 2010 "no other school of contemporary Western philosophy, such as analytical philosophy or phenomenology, has yet established so many special centers of study in China."[22]

The American process philosopher, Jay McDaniel, who has frequently taught process philosophy in China, has recently listed ten important comparisons between Chinese thought and process thought.[23] We know of no list of parallels that is as insightful and helpful as Prof. McDaniel's list. With his kind permission, we reproduce his text here:

> Whitehead's philosophy has been studied in China since the 1930's, and many scholars inside and outside of China believe that his thought resembles Chinese ways of thinking more than Western ways in many ways. Indeed, Whitehead himself believed that in certain ways his philosophy was more Chinese in tone. Here is a small sampling of the comparisons that various scholars have made over the past thirty years.
>
> 1. *The Book of Changes* (*I Jing*) gives us the image of a universe filled with events that interact in spontaneous and creative ways, giving rise to patterns of connection that have myriad meanings amid the inevitability of change. Whitehead pictures the universe in much the same way. He pictures the building blocks of the universe as events rather than substances, and says that these events reveal various patterns of connection which he calls pure potentialities or eternal objects. He offers a philosophy of events in process.
>
> 2. Confucianism sees the human being as a person-in-community whose fulfillment lies in responsiveness to a web of social relations and adds that an ideal form of social interaction is *ren* (benevolence). Again process philosophers will agree. They emphasize that humans are social in nature; there cannot be one human being unless there are others, and that human beings

become whole in and through their interactions with one another. Whitehead offers a philosophy of social relations.

3. Philosophical Daoism speaks of the universe as a flowing process of which humans are an integral part and encourages them to dwell in harmony with the larger whole. If these scholars are right, then Whiteheadian philosophy is indeed Chinese in tone and substance. Whiteheadian philosophy, like Chinese philosophy, pictures human beings as within, not outside of, the realm of Ten Thousand Things (*wanwu*) and believes that human well-being lies in living in harmony with the greater whole.

4. Chinese Buddhism in the Hua Yen tradition gives us the image of a universe in which every entity is present in every other entity in a network of inter-existence or inter-being. Hua Yen Buddhists imagine the universe on the analogy of a network of jewels, each of which has an infinite number of facets, and all of which are mirrored in the others. Again process philosophy will agree. In *Process and Reality*, Whitehead claims that the whole purpose of his philosophy is to show how one being can be present *in* another; he proposes that all entities are present within all others even as they are distinct from one another.

5. Chinese Buddhism in the Chan tradition emphasizes the primacy of each present moment of experience, as the place where enlightenment occurs. For Whitehead, too, there is a primacy to the present moment of experience—the here-and-now—because it is only in the present moment that there is subjective immediacy. The immediacy of the past has perished and the immediacy of the future does not yet exist.

6. Traditional Chinese Medicine is built upon the assumption that the human body is not simply an isolated entity,

cut off from the world, but a place where the whole universe enters into human life, such that the body is a microcosm of the universe. Scholars also suggest that the body consists of centers of energy that are connected to one another in myriad ways, amid which balance can be achieved with help from herbs, acupuncture, movement, and other forms of non-Western medicine. If this is true of Chinese medicine, then there are indeed areas of overlap with process philosophy, because process philosophy, too, sees each pulsation of energy within the human body, and thus the body as a whole, as a subjective unification—a concrescence—of the entire universe, and it sees each moment of human experience as arising out of deep and pre-verbal experiences of the body, which are called experiences in the mode of causal efficacy.

It is parallels such as these that lead some scholars to suggest that Whitehead's philosophy is a Western way of catching up with Chinese ways of thinking and adding science to the mix. And it is parallels such as these that lead many to wonder if Whitehead's philosophy cannot be a bridge between China and the West.

This bridge is being crossed by many scholars on both sides of the ocean, and there is now a very large corpus of scholarly work, written in Chinese and in English, for more advanced study. Readers are encouraged to visit the website of the Institute for Constructive Postmodern Development of China for further resources.[24]

Of course, some Chinese readers are also shaped by Chinese Marxism. There are also parallels between process thought and Chinese Marxism, which to Western readers may not seem more "Chinese" than "Western," but which will nevertheless be important to both readers. Four are especially worthy of mention here.

7. Chinese Marxism emphasizes a scientific approach to life; and so does process thought. A distinguishing feature of the process tradition is that it draws heavily on insights from early quantum theory and relativity theory and, more importantly, embraces the scientific method as an essential source of wisdom for modern life.

8. Chinese Marxism says that it is important for people to consider the vulnerable and poor in society, and not simply be concerned with more selfish motives; and so does process thought. Process thinkers are especially interested in building a world in which communities exist, in rural and urban settings, that are creative, compassionate, participatory, equitable, ecologically wise and spiritually satisfying—with no one left behind.

9. Chinese Marxism decries an overly abstract form of philosophy that gets lost in theory and neglects practice; and so does process thought. Process thought criticizes the fallacy of misplaced concreteness, emphasizing that, when we consider reality, we must recognize that elucidating immediate experience, as suffered and enjoyed by human beings and other living beings, is the primary justification for human thought.

10. Chinese Marxism is evolving into a way of thinking that takes the earth itself not simply as a backdrop for human industry, but as a web of life in which all life unfolds. It is becoming an organic Marxism. Whitehead's philosophy emphasizes and encourages this organic way of thinking, offering a cosmology that can support and enrich Marxist social analysis.

An interesting feature of the process perspective is that it believes these four emphases can be combined with the emphases above into a single approach to life. Thus Whitehead's philosophy may offer a way for Marxism itself to develop in ways that are enriched by traditional Chinese thinking and, for that matter, by more appreciative approaches to religion than is characteristic of orthodox, Western Marxism.[25]

In these ten points, Jay McDaniel shows deep insight into process philosophy, traditional Chinese thought, and Marxist thought; we are indebted to his presentation. We agree with Professor McDaniel that deep organic connections exist between these three schools of thought. It is indeed possible to graft them together into a single living whole—not merely as an abstract philosophy, but as a new form of eco-praxis.

CONCLUSION

We have found that these three philosophies—traditional Chinese philosophy, process philosophy, and Organic Marxism—are beginning to grow together in the postmodern world. Of course, other scholars have already begun to recognize the connections. From the beginning, process philosophers acknowledged that their views were closer to traditional Chinese thought then to modern Western thinking. Likewise, the significant affinities between constructive postmodernism (process philosophy) and Chinese Marxism have been frequently discussed. For example, in a recent paper, Professor Wang Zhihe identifies four important parallels between Chinese Marxism and process philosophies:

(1) Both regard process as a central notion of their philosophies;

(2) Both reject the fallacy of misplaced concreteness;

(3) Both have a strong consciousness of social responsibility and pursue the common good of the individual, the community, and nature;

(4) Both hold a comprehensive and organic stance to the world.[26]

The interest of Chinese scholars in process philosophy and the rapid increase in the number of Chinese-language publications on this topic provide further evidence of the deep connections. In a recent survey conducted by People's Forum Poll Research Center on "The Most Valuable Theoretical Point of View in 2012," the statement by Professor Tang Yijie of Peking University, a leading specialist in Chinese philosophy, was selected as the most significant analysis:

> At the end of the last century, Constructive Postmodernism based on process philosophy proposed integrating the achievements of the first Enlightenment and postmodernism, and called for the Second Enlightenment. The two broadly influential movements in China today are (1) "the zeal for traditional culture" and (2) "Constructive Postmodernism." If these two trends can be combined organically under the guidance of Marxism, [they will] not only take root in China, but further develop so that, with comparative ease, China can complete its "First Enlightenment," realizing its modernization, and also very quickly enter into the "Second Enlightenment" and become the standard-bearer of a postmodern society.[27]

It is important for thinkers and leaders in the West to understand what these developments—in China, in Marxism, and in process thought—mean and what positive changes they are likely to produce. Dr. Wang Zhihe suggests that part of the reason for the harmony between them is that "China is a nation of process thinking that understands the universe 'in terms of processes rather than things, in modes of change rather than fixed stabilities.' The Chinese not only have faith in the dynamic harmony of nature and humankind, but also have faith in change and transformation."[28] In the same article Dr. Wang notes that, in ancient Chinese, the opposite of the word "poor" is not rich, but "change." And in the *I Jing (The Book of Changes)* we read, "Poor leads to changes, changes in turn lead to finding a way out, and in turn *enable sustainability.*"

Clearly, then, there are natural connections and deep affinities between these three schools of thought. We therefore recognize that Organic Marxism is not the invention of something new; it is the naming of an intellectual development that is already well underway.

Our primary task in the few remaining chapters, then, is to understand *why* it is attractive to let these three currents flow together into a single stream, and *what implications* it will have—for the environmental movement, and for the future of Marxism—if this stream becomes a major river, flowing across national boundaries and traditions. It may be that, for the first time, the world has produced a school of socially oriented thinking that is strong enough and attractive enough to undercut the liberal philosophies that have dominated the West, and from there most of the planet, over the last four centuries.

NOTES

1. The book edited by Jacques Bidet and Stathis Kouvelakis, *Critical Companion to Contemporary Marxism* (Leiden: Brill, 2008), provides some sense of the range of Marxisms.

2. The phrase "at the edge of chaos" is used by my friend and co-author Stuart Kauffman in *Investigations* and numerous publications. On management principles in the context of so-called chaotic systems see David Parker and Ralph Stacey, *Chaos, Management and Economics: The Implications of Non-linear Thinking* (London: Institute of Economic Affairs, 1994) and Tony J. Watson, *In Search of Management: Culture, Chaos and Control in Managerial Work* (London and New York: Routledge, 1994). See also Chapter 7, "Process Philosophy and Systems Management," in Philip Clayton, *Science and Ecological Civilization: A Constructive Postmodern Approach* (forthcoming in Chinese translation).

3. Wang Zhihe, "Constructive Postmodernism, Chinese Marxism, and Ecological Civilization," paper presented at the 9th International Whitehead Conference in Krakow, Poland, September 2013.

4. Alfred North Whitehead, *Dialogues of Alfred North Whitehead*, ed. Lucien Price (Boston: David R. Godine, 2001), 91.

5. Anne Fairchild Pomeroy, *Marx and Whitehead: Process, Dialectics,*

and the Critique of Capitalism (Albany: SUNY Press, 2004), 9, quoted in Wang Zhihe, "Constructive Postmodernism, Chinese Marxism, and Ecological Civilization."

6. Whitehead, *Dialogues*, 268.

7. Alfred North Whitehead, *Process and Reality,* corrected edition (New York: Free Press, 1978), 25, emphasis added.

8. Ibid., 50, emphasis added.

9. Jay B. McDaniel, "A Process Approach to Ecology," in *Handbook of Process Theology*, ed. Jay McDaniel and Donna Bowman (St. Louis: Chalice Press, 2006), 243.

10. John B. Cobb and David Ray Griffin, *Process Theology: An Introductory Exposition* (Philadelphia: Westminster Press, 1976), 83-84.

11. Alfred North Whitehead, *Adventures of Ideas* (New York: Free Press, 1967), 163.

12. Whitehead, *Process and Reality*, 27-28, emphasis added.

13. Cobb and Griffin, *Process Theology*, 112.

14. Ibid., 113.

15. Ibid., 16-17.

16. Whitehead, *Process and Reality*, 220.

17. Ibid., 51.

18. Whitehead, *Modes of Thought* (New York: Free Press, 1968), 119-20.

19. Ibid., 111, emphasis added.

20. Whitehead, *Process and Reality*, 25. Whitehead provides a technical description of this process: "The individual immediacy of an occasion is the final unity of subjective form, which is the occasion as an absolute

reality. This immediacy is its moment of sheer individuality, bounded on either side by essential relativity. The occasion arises from relevant objects, and perishes into the status of an object for other occasions. But it enjoys its decisive moment of absolute self-attainment as emotional unity" (Whitehead, *Adventures of Ideas*, 177).

21. Paul Custodio Bube, "Process Theological Ethics," in *Handbook of Process Theology*, ed. Jay McDaniel and Donna Bowman (St. Louis: Chalice Press, 2006), 152.

22. Fubin Yang, "The Influence of Whitehead's Thought on the Chinese Academy," *Process Studies* 39 (Fall/Winter 2010): 34-49, quote p. 342.

23. Jay McDaniel, "Ten Comparisons between Chinese Thought and Process Thought," on his "Jesus, Jazz, and Buddhism" website, posted July 7, 2013, <http://www.jesusjazzbuddhism.org/>. We are grateful to Professor McDaniel for his permission to cite the text here.

24. The Institute for Constructive Postmodern Development of China can be found on the web at <http://www.postmodernchina.org/cgi/index.php>.

25. This text is reproduced from Prof. McDaniel's website with his permission; <http://www.jesusjazzbuddhism.org/comparing-whitehead-and-chinese-thought.html>.

26. Wang Zhihe, "Constructive Postmodernism, Chinese Marxism, and Ecological Civilization."

27. Tang Yijie, "The Enlightenment and its Difficult Journey in China," *Wen Hui Bao*, November 14, 2011, <http://theory.people.com.cn/n/2013/0110/c49165-20158762.html>. Prof. Tang is Professor at PekingUniversity and Director of the Research Institute of Confucianism at Peking University, as well as Director of the Research Institute of Chinese Culture.

28. Wang Zhihe, "Constructive Postmodernism, Chinese Marxism, and Ecological Civilization." The quotation is taken from Jan B.F.N.

Engberts, "Immanent Transcendence in Chinese and Western Process Thinking," *Philosophy Study* 6 (2012): 377-83.

Chapter 11

RETHINKING MARXISM
IN A TIME OF ECOLOGICAL CRISIS

In earlier chapters we traced some of the ways in which capitalism has become a major cause of the global economic crisis. This connection is not surprising: if over-consuming the world's resources is a problem, then one should be wary of a system that needs to encourage ever-greater consumption in order to fuel its need for ever-growing output. Similarly, if injustice in the distribution of wealth is a problem, one should avoid a system that helps the wealthy to become wealthier at the expense of the poor becoming poorer. One should prefer a system that, in contrast to capitalism, includes a concern for the common good right at the roots of its social, political, and economic philosophy.

What is more controversial is the extent to which Marx was actually concerned with ecological principles. This brief chapter must therefore take on two important tasks: first, to show the compatibility of Marx's thinking with the ecological perspective; and, second, to outline the ways in which Marxism may need to be revised and extended, so that it can offer leadership as humanity struggles for the first time with a humanly produced global ecological crisis.

Marx, Marxism, and Ecology

Interpreters of Marxism have long believed that Marx himself had little to say about ecology. Some have held that Marx was concerned only for the conditions of human existence, and that he assumed unlimited industrialization was the only way to improve these conditions.

Although in recent years many scholars have reevaluated Marx's ecological contributions, most still see these contributions as marginal to his work, or as too insubstantial to make a difference in current ecological discussions. As John Bellamy Foster has noted, "A great many analysts, including some self-styled ecosocialists, persist in arguing that such insights were marginal to [Marx's] work, that he never freed himself from 'Prometheanism' (a term usually meant to refer to an extreme commitment to industrialization at any cost), and that he did not leave a significant ecological legacy that carried forward into later socialist thought or that had any relation to the subsequent development of ecology."[1] Finally, some have even argued that ecological thinking is anachronistic when applied to Marxism: if Marx wrote many years before the emergence of threats such as toxic waste, nuclear technology, or climate change, how can there be important insights in his work that remain relevant to the current ecological crisis?

We disagree with these judgments. The evidence suggests that Marx took relations to nature seriously as a fundamental part of his critique of capitalism. We will have to extend Marx's thought a bit beyond where he took his own philosophy, a task we undertake in the next section. To this extent, we disagree with those Marxists who have claimed that "everything is already in Marx," so that no such adaptation and extension is necessary. Extending the work of Karl Marx is possible and plausible, however, only because he builds into his original work a basic understanding of humans' embeddedness in nature.

More generally, though, why should one think that Marxism is an important resource for those who are concerned about ecological destruction? There are direct and indirect reasons to take this connection very seriously. The *indirect* argument is simple and, we think, overwhelming: there is a fundamental relationship between capitalism and environmental destruction. For one, capitalism requires continued growth, both in local markets and in the GDP of every successful nation. But the precarious ecological situation of our planet requires either steady-state or downsizing economies. Unbridled capitalism is not capable of meeting this need.

Equally as important, the "free market" is not able to accurately value natural resources or environmental risk. That natural resources are limited, and that the long-term effects of certain products and forms of production will devastate the planet—these facts are outside the purview of market valuations, which tend to be based on rather more local and short-term concerns. If resources were infinite, and if the earth could absorb unlimited amounts of pollution, this blindness on the part of the markets would not matter. But as resources begin to run out, and as pollutants begin to overwhelm planetary ecosystems, these market miscalculations will have devastating consequences for most life forms on this planet. If your compass is broken, you won't be able to steer your boat successfully.

It is this realization of the inherent limitations of capitalism that is fueling the growing movement to redefine socialism as *ecosocialism*. Ecosocialism shares our view that capitalism has been "a deadly detour for humanity." Its growth is motivated by "a vision of a transformed society in harmony with nature, and the development of practices that can attain it. It is directed toward alternatives to all socially and ecologically destructive systems ... It is based on a perspective that regards other species and natural ecosystems as valuable in themselves and as partners in a common destiny."[2]

MARX AS AN ENVIRONMENTALIST?

The direct argument for the connection of Marxism and ecology has been developed primarily by the Ecological Marxists. One of the leaders in this school, John Bellamy Foster, has done important work to demonstrate ecological thinking in Marx's writings. We agree with his assessment of Marx's writings:

Some environmental commentators of course persist in claiming that Marx believed one-sidedly in the struggle of human beings against nature, and was thus anthropocentric and anti-ecological, and that Marxism as a whole carried forth this original ecological sin. But there is mounting evidence . . . of Marx's very deep ecological penetration and of the pioneering insights of socialist ecologists, which has conclusively pulled the rug out from under such criticisms.[3]

The main piece of evidence comes from Marx's concept of a "metabolic rift" between humans and the earth. Specifically, Foster argues that capitalism inevitably produces a break in what would otherwise be a single natural metabolism that includes humans and all the other organisms and ecosystems that constitute the biosphere of our planet. He writes:

> Marx's concept of the metabolic rift was the core element of this ecological critique. The human labor process itself was defined in *Capital* as "the universal condition for the metabolic interaction between man and nature." It followed that the rift in this metabolism meant nothing less than the undermining of the "everlasting nature-imposed condition of human existence."[4]

By linking capitalism to this rift in the very fabric of the earth's metabolism, Marx was able to criticize not only the ways that city-dwellers exploited the agricultural countryside, but also "deforestation, desertification, climate change, the elimination of deer from the forests, the commodification of species, pollution, industrial wastes, toxic contamination, recycling, the exhaustion of coal mines, disease, overpopulation and the evolution (and co-evolution) of species."[5]

With this argument Marx is not just making a rhetorical point; he is drawing attention to a fundamental component of his theory of capital. In one of the central passages in *The Grundrisse* he writes:

> It is not the *unity* of living and active humanity with the natural, inorganic condition of their metabolic exchange with

nature, and hence their appropriation of nature, which requires explanation or is the result of a historic process, but rather the *separation* between these inorganic conditions of human existence and this active existence, a separation which is completely posited only in the relation of wage labor and capital.[6]

This crucial passage helps to explain how the economic theory that became the basis for modernism and globalization is flawed. As Marx rightly notes, any naturalistic account of human life presupposes a deep unity between three realms: human life, other life forms, and the physical and chemical conditions for life on this planet. What is *unnatural* is to separate these three realms. In separating wage labor and capital, the capitalists ended up separating workers from the conditions of their own production. Over time, capitalism progressively obscured the very preconditions for life and work that had been excluded from its analysis, until the earth itself began to cry out in protest.

John Bellamy Foster offers a rich account not only of Marx's nonreductive materialism, but also of his fascination with Darwin and with Leibig's agricultural chemistry. Marx's excitement about the discovery of the first prehistoric human remains, for example, shows the growing influence of evolutionary theory on his thought—quite in contrast to the traditional view that Marx relied chiefly on Hegel and Feuerbach in constructing his historical analysis.[7]

In short, it is not surprising that nature's contributions played such a central role in Marx's thinking. Both Marx and Engels were deeply engaged with the natural sciences. Marx was a materialist and an evolutionist. What's crucial is that his background led him to associate materialism less with *physical determinism* than with the emergence of ever new social structures and forms of organization (as the "New Materialists" of our own postmodern age are also doing[8]):

It is important to understand that the materialist conception of nature as Marx understood it—and as it was frequently understood in his day—did not necessarily imply a rigid, mechanical determinism, as in mechanism (that is, mechanistic materialism). Marx's own approach to materialism was inspired to a considerable extent by the work of the ancient Greek philosopher Epicurus, the subject of his doctoral thesis ... His philosophy was devoted to showing how a materialist view of the nature of things provided the essential basis for a conception of human freedom.[9]

Early humans differentiated themselves from other animals primarily in their use of tools and labor, through which they began transforming natural means to assist them in meeting their needs. Engel's proposal, which deeply influenced Marx, provided a naturalistic account of how humanity evolved to be *homo faber*, the animal that works and constructs: "[W]hen the primates, who constituted the ancestors of human beings, descended from the trees, erect posture developed first (prior to the evolution of the human brain), freeing the hands for tool-making."[10] This natural evolution enhanced humans' ability in the struggle for survival: "As a result, early human beings (hominids) were able to alter their relation to their local environment, radically improving their adaptability."[11] But this evolution came with a cost, because it opened up the possibility of a rupture or "rift" with the very natural world on which we depend for our survival.

These insights from Marx and Engels were largely lost in the subsequent history of Marxism. The "emergentist" view of evolution that they defended was the "middle way" between scientific positivists on the one side and non-materialists (such as conservative Christians) on the other. With a few exceptions, such as the British Emergentists of the 1920s, the battle between those two extremes grew in volume and prominence, gradually eclipsing the middle way. The positivists (then and now) deny any dialectical patterns in nature, and the religious conservatives deny Darwinian evolution. Only in the last few decades have the insights of natural emergence again been recognized.[12] "In the East," Foster adds, "Stalin purged the ecological elements from Russian communism, largely because these individuals (Bukhalin, Vavilov) tended to criticize the government's exploitation of natural resources."[13]

ORGANIC MARXISM: WITH MARX BEYOND MARX

With John Bellamy Foster, we share the conviction that contemporary ecological thought is caught in a stalemate between constructionists (culturalists) and anti-constructionists (deep ecologists). In his view, "the attempt to transcend this dualism has merely produced the notion of a 'cautious constructionism'—an important result but lacking any substantive content or clear theoretical orientation."[14] Analysts have assumed that Marxism has nothing to say to contemporary ecologists, and have therefore neglected the potential benefits of the dialectical tradition. "Marxism has an enormous potential advantage in dealing with all these issues," Foster argues, "precisely because it rests on a theory of society which is materialist not only in the sense of empha-sizing the antecedent material-productive conditions of society, and how they served to delimit human possibilities and freedom, but also because, in Marx and Engels at least, it never lost sight of the neces-sary relation of these material conditions to natural history, that is, to a materialist conception of nature."[15]

Foster published these words in *Marx's Ecology* in 2000. Events in the years since then, we believe, have changed the situation in some important ways. Natural science had made significant advances—in the study of emergent phenomena, in systems biology, and in eco-systems theory. Awareness of the environmental crisis is now global, and the urgency of the situation has moved ecologists beyond many of the stalemates of 2000. Finally, the evolution of Marxism in China, the world's most populous Marxist nation, has revealed how deeply cultural and historical factors influence the interpretation and practice of Marxist ideas.

Given these new data, we conclude that the revisions to Marxist thought need to be more extensive than Foster suggested in 2000. His three central terms—materialist, historical, and dialectical—should be retained in order to reconstruct an ecological, realist social theory. And yet each one must now be nuanced and extended in new ways:

- Materialist in the sense of *emergentist naturalism*. One looks for natural, not supernatural, explanations; but one also recognizes that new dynamics and agents emerge continually in natural history, including human agents in all their cultural and ideational complexity.

- Historical in a sense that includes *cultural history* as well. One studies not only the history of capital, class, and the means of production, but also cultural and intellectual history—*all* the causal factors that contribute to the evolution of societies.

- Dialectical in a sense that includes *all dialectical relations*— every form of conflict that gives rise to new and unexpected solutions.

In the past, Marxism was unfairly neglected because it was assumed to be anti-ecological; it was caught in the battle between positivists and religious conservatives. Environmental Marxism, we suggest, has been caught in a similar battle that is raging around the term "environmental." The narrower interpretation of this term is held hostage to an older, more reductive model of science. Unfortunately, many Marxists still believe this is the only viable understanding of science. The "new environmentalism" is much broader, however. It embraces the insights of emergent evolution and cultural studies, thereby opening a "third window" for studying the natural world, as Robert Ulanowicz has powerfully expressed it.[16] It is not necessary to reject the fields of social ecology and cultural studies as inconsistent with Marxist commitments.

Organic Marxism represents an expanded understanding of materialism, one that some philosophers today are calling "broad naturalism."[17] Broad naturalists understand natural evolution to include not only biological but also intellectual, cultural, and even worldview-level dimensions. As the Harvard biologist E.O. Wilson likes to say, Darwinian evolution holds cultural evolution "on a leash"; it can't break natural laws. Nor can a starving man write great philosophy. At the same time, the natural evolutionary process includes the full range of human experience—cultural, artistic, philosophical, aesthetic, religious, and spiritual.

For Marxists, the most difficult dimension is often religion. Since Marx described religion as the "opiate of the people," Marxists have tended to view it with a higher level of suspicion. It's now possible, we believe, to nuance that suspicion. The Marxist critique of religion usually focuses on conservative Christianity, which affirms supernatural events and is therefore indeed anti-materialist. But remember that Marx was himself a Jew. Many Jews and Christians have felt that Marx's socialism actually stands closer to the core values of their own tradition than does the capitalism that rules the West. In his authoritative history, John Cort traces the Christian socialist movement back to the early church and forward into the present.[18] The fusion of Marx and radical Christian principles, for example in the work of Gustavo Gutiérrez and his followers in Latin America, gave birth to liberation theology,[19] which in turn influenced a large group of liberation movements in North America, Europe, and Korea (*minjung* theology); it also helped to establish the liberation movements of post-colonialism. Many Leftist thinkers, such as Joerg Rieger, are both Marxists and theologians.[20]

Moreover, many religions are consistent with scientific naturalism. The process theologian David Griffin defends a naturalistic view of religion, for example.[21] Likewise, the "wisdom traditions" of China—one can dispute whether they should even be called "religions"—do not affirm a supernatural God. Chinese traditional thought is not a "world-denying" tradition, which means that it's easier to reconcile with Marxist commitments. Today postmodern Marxists are incorporating central insights from Confucianism and Daoism in their analyses.

The pluralism of sources has also led to a pluralism of applications. For example, unique features in the cultures of Asia, Africa, and South America allow one to extend Marxist principles in new ways. Complex differences in language, cultural practices, and religions can lead to far-reaching reforms, as in "socialism with Chinese characteristics." The evolution of late capitalism requires new forms of Marxist critique, as does the growing ecological crisis. As Marxists acknowledge cultural variability, it becomes easier to build specific constructive programs for the good of society and the planet, even in highly specific contexts.

CONCLUSION

In this chapter we have highlighted the contributions of the school known as Ecological Marxism. *Marx's Ecology* by John Bellamy Foster identifies the deep ecological themes in Marx's materialism. In a recent article, he shows that in Engels's *Condition of the Working Class in England* (1844) "environmental conditions were presented as of even greater importance to the overall material conditions of the working class than factory conditions."[22] Similarly, his *Ecology against Capitalism* correctly describes the wealthy, the capitalist elite, as representing a "higher immorality" and condemns capitalism for its perversion of humanity and degradation of nature.[23]

The improvements in technology from Marx's time to our own cannot overcome the fundamental relationship between capitalism and environmental destruction. To recognize this connection is to become aware that all socialism today must be ecosocialism. As Michael Löwy writes, ecosocialism is the attempt "to provide a radical, civilizational alternative to capitalism, rooted in the basic arguments of the ecological movement, and in the Marxist critique of political economy. It opposes to capitalism's *destructive progress* (Marx) an economic policy founded on non-monetary and extra-economic criteria: social needs and ecological equilibrium."[24]

Given the urgency of ecosocialist reforms, it is discouraging to find frontal attacks on John Bellamy Foster being made in the name of orthodox Marxism, as if his research expressed nothing more than left-liberal bourgeois discomfort with consumerism. "This focus on opulent consumer faddism is above all a petty-bourgeois critique of capitalism," writes the *Workers Vanguard*. "For children of suburbia who turn to individual lifestyle changes to find meaning, the problem might be having too much. But 'doing more with less' is not an option for the vast bulk of the population struggling each month to pay the bills and make ends meet."[25]

It is true that Marx wrote first of all about the class struggle and socialism; the environmental crisis did not motivate his call for revolutionary socio-economic changes. But economic growth today faces global limits that it had not yet reached in Marx's day. It is utopian to write only about raising the standard of living for lower-class workers when the planet is reaching the limits of consumption. The unjust distribution of resources in a capital-driven economy remains as urgent as it was in Marx's day. But to hold out the prospect of unlimited growth in the name of Marxism is to deny todays' reality:

> For young radical activists, it might seem a natural to try to fuse eco-radicalism with socialism. *But environmentalist ideology and socialism are entirely irreconcilable. All variants of environmentalism are an expression of bourgeois ideology,* offering fixes predicated on class-divided society and the reinforcement of scarcity. Marxists fight for a society that will provide more for the toiling and impoverished masses and ultimately eliminate material scarcity altogether. To this end, it will take a series of workers revolutions across the globe to rip the mines, factories and other means of production from the grip of their private owners, paving the way for an internationally planned, collectivized economy . . . *Progress in human development, i.e., ending misery and want, will not result from curtailing production but from raising it to unparalleled heights.*

> *By lifting the dead hands of private profit and property rights,*
> *the proletarian seizure of power would give great impetus to*
> *economic growth.*[26]

Such responses reflect a Marxism locked in the past, not a Marxist blueprint for the future. Injustices cry out to be addressed. But they must be addressed in that scientific spirit with which Marx approached his historical analysis, which in today's world requires recognition of quickly diminishing resources and human-induced global climate disruption. Of course, the primary burden must be borne by those persons and nations who have caused the crisis, whose consumption is the highest, and who can most afford to pay the clean-up costs. But this does not mean that workers can therefore enjoy consumption at "unparalleled heights."

If Organic Marxism must part ways with Ecological Marxism at some point, it will come with our call to include the specifics of cultural location as an organic part of applied Marxism. Marxist social theory never exists in disembodied form; it exists authentically only when it is effectively embodied in a culture and organically tied to the lived experience of its people. Organic Marxism—effective Marxism—embraces a people's historical traditions, their cultural mores, and their deeper ethical insights as contained in their own wisdom traditions. How will Marxist ecology take root in the hearts of men and women if it is not connected to the cultural and spiritual resources of a particular people and its culture?

NOTES

1. John Bellamy Foster, "Marx's Ecology and Its Historical Significance," in *International Handbook of Environmental Sociology*, ed. Michael Redclift and Graham Woodgate, 2nd ed. (Northampton, MA: Edward Elgar, 2010), 106.

2. See: <http://ecosocialisthorizons.com/ecosocialism/>. See also David

Pepper, *Eco-Socialism: From Deep Ecology to Social Justice* (London: Routledge, 1993). On Marx and eco-socialism, see especially Pepper's Chapter 3. An index of ten online articles on eco-socialism and five important books is given at: <http://climateandcapitalism.com/ecosocialism-ten-essential-articles-and-five-essential-books/>.

3. Foster, "Marx's Ecology and Its Historical Significance," 118.

4. Ibid., 109.

5. Ibid., documented in John Bellamy Foster, *Marx's Ecology: Materialism and Nature* (New York: Monthly Review Press, 2000).

6. Karl Marx, *The Grundrisse* (New York: Vintage, 1973), 489, quoted in Foster, "Marx's Ecology and Its Historical Significance," 118.

7. Foster, "Marx's Ecology and Its Historical Significance," 110.

8. Diana Coole and Samantha Frost, eds., *New Materialisms: Ontology, Agency, and Politics* (Durham, NC: Duke University Press, 2010); Jane Bennett, *Vibrant Matter: A Political Ecology of Things* (Durham, NC: Duke University Press, 2010). Clayton Crockett, *Religion, Politics, and the Earth: The New Materialism* (New York: Palgrave Macmillan, 2012).

9. Foster, *Marx's Ecology,* 2.

10. Foster, "Marx's Ecology and Its Historical Significance," 112.

11. Ibid.

12. See Philip Clayton and Paul Davies, eds., *The Re-emergence of Emergence* (Oxford: Oxford University Press, 2006).

13. Foster, "Marx's Ecology and Its Historical Significance," 113.

14. Foster, *Marx's Ecology,* 17.

15. Ibid., 19.

16. Robert E. Ulanowicz, *A Third Window: Natural Life beyond Newton*

and Darwin (West Conshohocken, PA: Templeton Foundation Press, 2009).

17. See Mario DeCaro and David Macarthur, eds., *Naturalism in Question* (Cambridge, MA: Harvard University Press, 2004). See also Philip Clayton, "Mediating Between Physicalism and Dualism: 'Broad Naturalism' and the Study of Consciousness," in Melville Y. Stewart, ed., *Science and Religion in Dialogue*, 2 vols. (Oxford: Blackwell, 2010), chapter 67, II: 999-1010. (This book was also published in Chinese.)

18. John C. Cort, *Christian Socialism: An Informal History* (Maryknoll, NY: Orbis Books, 1988).

19. Gustavo Gutiérrez, *A Theology of Liberation: History, Politics and Salvation,* translated and edited by Caridad Inda and John Eagleson (London: SCM Press, 1973).

20. See Joerg Rieger, *Christ and Empire: From Paul to Postcolonial Times* (Minneapolis, MN : Fortress Press, 2007); Rieger (with Néstor Míguez and Jung Mo Sung), *Beyond the Spirit of Empire: Theology and Politics in a New Key* (London: SCM press, 2009); Rieger (with Kwok Pui-lan), *Occupy Religion: Theology of the Multitude* (Lanham, MD: Rowman & Littlefield Publishers, 2012). See also Rieger, ed., *Opting for the Margins: Postmodernity and Liberation in Christian Theology* (Oxford: Oxford University Press, 2003); Rieger, ed. *Religion, Theology, and Class: Fresh Engagements after Long Silence* (New York: Palgrave Macmillan, 2013).

21. David Ray Griffin, *Two Great Truths: A New Synthesis of Scientific Naturalism and Christian Faith* (Louisville, KY: Westminster John Knox Press, 2004); Griffin, *Panentheism and Scientific Naturalism: Rethinking Evil, Morality, Religious Experience, Religious Pluralism, and the Academic Study of Religion* (Claremont, CA: Process Century Press, 2014). See also A.R. Peacocke, *All That Is: A Naturalistic Faith for the Twenty-First Century,* ed. Philip Clayton (Minneapolis: Fortress Press, 2007).

22. John Bellamy Foster, "The Fossil Fuels War," *Monthly Review* 65/4 (Sept. 2013): 1-14, quote p. 12.

23. John Bellamy Foster, *Ecology against Capitalism* (New York: Monthly Review Press, 2002).

24. Michael Löwy, "Ecosocialism: Putting on the Brakes Before Going Over the Cliff," published in *New Politics,* republished online in *Critical Thinking* # 56, vol. 14/4 (Winter 2014), <http://socialistworker.org/blog/critical-reading/2014/02/09/michael-l%C3%B6wy-ecosocialism>.

25. "John Bellamy Foster & Co.: 'Ecosocialism' Against Marxism, Part One," *Workers Vanguard* No. 1032 (18 October 2013), <http://www.icl-fi.org/english/wv/1032/ecosocialism.html>.

26. "John Bellamy Foster & Co.," emphasis added.

Chapter 12

THE ECOLOGY OF ORGANIC MARXISM

Exploding the Myth of Unlimited Growth

During most of the five thousand years since the first great human civilizations emerged, the human drive toward expansion and domination was not a problem for the earth itself. Although humans gradually dominated other species, our power to disturb the planet was relatively limited. Even a hundred years ago, the resources of the planet seemed almost infinite in comparison to human needs.

But in the last few decades things have changed radically. Of course, nature remains powerful, even frightening, in her ability to overwhelm and destroy. The earthquake and tsunami in Japan just a few years ago, which decimated the defenses of a nation that proudly thought it was ready for anything, offer an unforgettable reminder of this fact. Events from space, such as a major asteroid, remain out of our control. Nevertheless, in our lifetimes something has happened that is unique in the history of this planet. For the first time ever, humanity has encountered absolute limits on growth.

You find these limits wherever you look. Humanity has made itself fundamentally dependent on hydrocarbons, yet we now know that the global hydrocarbon reserves are limited—and the environmental cost of burning them all would be disastrous. As a species we are fundamentally dependent on drinking water. Yet across the planet the amount of usable fresh water is decreasing below the population's needs, threatening the lives of hundreds of millions of people. The only thing we need more than water is clean air, yet we have transformed the atmosphere of the entire planet. And the list could be extended on and on and on. There is virtually no part of the planet where the hand of humankind cannot now be measured: the deserts of the Sahara, the highest mountain peaks of the Himalayas, the depths of the oceans.

The trouble is that the foundations of the Western economic system are based on the (fictional) assumption of continuous economic growth, which implies the further assumption that natural resources and raw materials are unlimited. As we have just seen, however, the natural resources of this planet are most definitely *not* unlimited. In fact, most major multinational corporations, including the oil companies, are already calculating backwards from the depletion of the natural resources on which they depend. As growth-based economics increasingly reaches the planetary limits on growth, the chaotic cascades and collapses will only increase in frequency and violence. The social and political consequences of this growing instability are unspeakably grave.

With these facts in mind, it's not difficult to see why economic theory may well be the most important topic in discussions of ecological civilization today. Around the planet, the vast majority of economic theories that are influencing world leaders are based on the demand for growth. The whole set of economic arrangements on which current societies and their citizens' lifestyles depend will continue to function only if the global economy continues to expand at something like the current rate. This fundamental axiom of the current system applies to virtually every economic unit—from the macro-economic patterns of the G20 nations, to the economic models on which the multinational corporations depend, to mid-sized companies doing business within a single country, to the budgets of cities and states in a given country, and even down to (for example) the shop owner in a small town.

And now you see the problem: the entire economic system of the twenty-first-century civilization that humanity has built depends on growth—the very kind of growth that the planet can no longer sustain. There is no simple way around this contradiction; it is as fundamental as any that humans have ever faced. No little tweaks, no minor changes in economic models, no soft touches of government regulation will suffice to abolish the contradiction between our current models of economic success and the planet's limits, which we are now reaching. Only a radically new theoretical framework, like the one we are calling Organic Marxism, can bring economic planning back into line with planetary reality.

SEEKING CIVILIZATIONAL CHANGE: THE PHILOSOPHY OF ORGANISM

As we have seen in previous chapters, Organic Marxism augments the way Marxism used to be taught. It encourages the updating of Marxian principles as they are grafted with individual cultures. While maintaining the basic values of Marx, Organic Marxism insists that the specific categories of his thought need to be adapted as they are transmitted today.

The organic sciences are important allies, of course (Chapter 9). But traditional values, cultures, and even religious beliefs can *also* serve as allies in building a postmodern philosophy of organism. If we are to win support for economic alternatives robust enough to counteract the destructive force of global petrocapitalism, we will need to build alliances with *all* traditions of thought and practice, new and old, that support the movement toward a more just and sustainable society.[1]

To embrace a philosophy of organism requires one to make the transition from modern to postmodern categories. Most modern philosophies worked with a logic of exclusion rather than with a logic of organic inclusion. For example, one of the most basic assumptions was that Marxists and religious persons could never work together in harmony. After all, Marx said, religion was an "opiate" that deadened workers' awareness of their real condition. Modernist European

195

Marxism therefore sought to overcome religion in order to revolutionize economic conditions, transform politics, and improve social conditions. Religion in the era of modernism was indeed often guilty of supporting colonialism and unjust hierarchies of power. The majority religion of North America, Christianity, tended to transform Jesus' concern for the poor and marginalized into a cultural imperialism. Christendom's intolerance of other religions and ways of life contributed to nationalism, militarism, and xenophobia. Instead of focusing on personal transformation and justice for the poor, as its founder taught, modern Christianity tended to seek power and domination.

In a postmodern civilization, by contrast, these oppositions are being reexamined. For example, scholars from China now learn about Western religions, asking whether they can help support the values of an ecological worldview. Many postmodern religious people in America now believe that communitarian philosophies stand closer to the values of the Jewish prophets, and to the prophetic teachings of Jesus, than the capitalist free market ever did.

This is only one example of the new alliances that are possible for organic thinking. As a postmodern worldview devoted to pursuing economic alternatives to global capitalism, Organic Marxism builds on the insights of intellectual allies—whether ancient or postmodern, Eastern or Western, religious or philosophical. Many of these allies are challenging the dominant assumptions of Western modernism and deconstructive postmodernism.

The most important ally, in our opinion, is process thought. In the West, process philosophy refers to a major school within philosophy that was originated by Alfred North Whitehead (1861-1947). As we saw in Chapter 10, the core idea of this school is that all life, all existence, and all experience are constituted as, and by, a never-ending process:

> It is fundamental to . . . the philosophy of organism that the notion of an actual entity as the unchanging subject of change is completely abandoned. An actual entity is at once

the subject experiencing and the superject of its experiences
... The ancient doctrine that "no one crosses a river twice" is
extended. No thinker thinks twice; and, to put the matter more
generally, no subject experiences twice.[2]

For Whitehead, this philosophy of organism has three central
implications:

(1) Interconnection. Human beings are not isolated units, mere
individual atoms. We are always "internally related" to one another.
As Whitehead writes, "This internal relatedness is the reason why an
event can be found only just where it is and how it is ... For each relationship enters into the essence of the event; so that, apart from that
relationship, the event would not be itself."[3] It is more true to say that a
society or culture or nation constitutes its members than it is to say that
a group of separate, discrete individuals comes together to constitute
a society, culture, or nation. This view that *we are constituted by our
relationships* is the opposite of *individualism*, the dominant modern
view that each individual is an isolated unit. The West has exported
many bad ideas, but perhaps none of these has been as damaging as
the idea of individualism.

(2) Ever-changing process. The second central idea of process philosophy is that nothing is identical across time. Imagine my friend Lin
as a child, a teenager, and an adult. The teenage Lin is of course related
to the young girl who she was 15 years ago. But we must not say that
the two are identical; the changes in her appearance, her thinking, and
her surroundings have been so significant that we can only speak of
a *resemblance* between the earlier and the later state of a person. The
same is true for the relationship between Lin as a teenager and as an
adult. Certain patterns of her personality continue to be expressed over
time, for example, her intelligence, her graciousness, and her devotion
to her family. Still, the process of her life brings constant changes; nothing stays still. The same is true for you and me. To put it paradoxically,
the only thing that remains constant is the process itself.

We mentioned at the beginning that process philosophy may be a more natural way of thinking for Chinese people than for Western people. In traditional Western thought, the emphasis was always on *unity over time*. The Greek philosophers who first established the patterns of Western thought proclaimed that *what is real is unchanging*. As a result, as Plato concluded in his famous dialogue *The Republic*, anything that undergoes change is not truly real; it is in part an illusion.[4]

The early Christian thinkers made a similar move. They identified the individual with having an eternal and unchanging soul. The soul constituted the essence of the person. All the things about a person that change—her appearance, her culture, and the ever-changing thoughts and feelings that she experiences—are not part of what she *really* is. Of course, there is a problem here: these changing features of ourselves are what we most value in ourselves and those around us! Process philosophy, by contrast, puts the emphasis back on what is more important to us: the never-ending journey of experience, fresh insights and the maturation of previous thinking, new and deepening friendships, and the growth of character.

(3) Holism. In addition to interconnection and ever-changing process, process thinking emphasizes holism. The whole is greater than the sum of the parts. This, too, is a deep insight of traditional Chinese thought. In the *Dao De Jing*, Laozi writes:

The Master views the parts with compassion,
because he understands the whole. (Laozi, *Dao De Jing*, 39)

The Master understands the parts because he sees them from the perspective of the whole. Not only does he bring understanding, however; he also brings compassion. We feel compassion for the small child because we understand the adventure that lies before her; we understand this moment in her life from the perspective of the many years of experience that we have acquired. Likewise, the Master has compassion for the poor man, the confused person, and even the person who has made a terrible mistake. Why? He can have compassion because he understands the whole range of experience and influences that have brought about the tragedy or the mistake.

Wisdom grows out of the perspective of the whole. By contrast, the foolish man can see only the individual moments—his wishes, his momentary desires, his goals at this particular time. Western thought has not been holistic thought. It has often tried to *build up* to an understanding of the whole, piece by piece. But how can you build the whole if you only know the parts? If you don't understand the shape of the whole that you are trying to actualize, you are like the builder who begins putting together the bricks in front of him without any plan. Soon he gives up in despair because without a plan only chaos emerges. The student without a clear plan for her education as a whole has difficulty in organizing her studies. The city officials without a long-term plan for their city cannot create a beautiful space for the residents to live in. The nation that does not have a clear vision of the values by which it will live can construct attractive buildings and powerful industries, but it cannot make a lasting, positive impact upon the world.

Too often Western leaders have been myopic, managing their cities and countries one step at a time. They have built some impressive technologies, factories, universities, and scientific achievements. But without a vision for the whole, the individual achievements do not come together into a coherent civilization. The process philosophy of Alfred North Whitehead calls us back to the ancient Chinese wisdom traditions and concepts such as *tien, qi,* and *li,* which encourage a holistic perspective. Remember the words from the *Dao De Jing* that I quoted above: "The Master views the parts with compassion, because he understands the whole." Enlightened leaders hold before themselves a more complete vision of the entire system or civilization that they are attempting to actualize. Only from that perspective are they able to choose their individual steps wisely.

The Manifesto of Organic Marxism

Ecological Civilization represents both a theory and a practice. It has very practical implications for government policies, organizations, and the design of society. These practices are rooted in the philosophy of organism, on the one hand, and in Marxist analyses of the dynamics of class and capital, on the other.

Ecological Thinking. According to ecological thinking, reality is made up of interrelated events rather than individual, isolated substances. These events, which make up the lives of all living beings and of nature as a whole, have intrinsic value. As a result, one must treat the other always also as an end in itself, and never merely as a means.[5] Genuine value lies in each event, in each organic relationship, not in extrinsic factors such as what products can be used for or how much money they fetch in the free market.

In ecological thinking, living things are constituted by their relationships with each other and with their ecosystems and social systems. Each participant in these relationships has its own purposes, which must not be disregarded. But even our individual features are developed through interactions with communities. Relations among communities deeply affect the nature of each, which then affects the lives of its members. In this sense (see Chapter 9 above), ecosystem studies tend to converge with the Marxian analysis of class, just as atomism in physics converges with liberal individualism.

The universe is more than blind chance unfolding through physical laws; all things have value, and all seek to maximize their value. For living beings, this drive takes the form of the struggle to survive and to thrive. For humans, that drive is also expressed in more complex ways: the desire for beauty, the fear of death, the search for meaning, the quest for love. Knowing this, humans become responsible to actively seek inclusive values, offering to others what we wish for ourselves. Equally, humanity becomes responsible to consider not only human interests but also the interests of other species as inherently valuable as well.

The Manifesto of Organic Marxism. At the heart of the Manifesto stand three central claims: capitalist justice is not just; the "free market" is not free; and the costs of global climate disruption will be most severe among the poor. Recognizing these truths, we call on global leaders to reorganize human civilization according to ecological and socialist principles.

(1) *Capitalist justice is not just.* Justice is conceived very differently in capitalist and Marxist theory. Marx writes, *"From each according to his ability, to each according to his need."* This famous phrase reflects Marx's society-based understanding of what is just. By contrast, the capitalist theory of justice says, "From each according to his wishes, to each according to the market." That is, each person decides which part of the market to invest his time and money in, and how hard to work. Whatever the market then pays him—or doesn't pay—counts as just.

As Organic Marxists, we blame this capitalist view of justice both for worker inequities and for the growing environmental catastrophe. We now know that the planet itself cannot sustain the payouts that the capitalist system provides to the world's wealthiest one percent, nor the lifestyle of consumption and waste that they buy with their wealth. With Marx, we advocate a system that brings the distribution of resources into harmony with *what people actually need to survive, not with their unlimited desires.* All the evidence shows that, within capitalist systems, the wealthy do not freely redistribute their wealth to the poor. Across virtually every culture, when the wealthiest are able to pocket high profits and decide how to spend their money, they choose luxurious lifestyles and high personal consumption. Only a postmodern socialist order will limit these excesses.

(2) *The "free market" is not free.* The "father of capitalism," Adam Smith, believed that markets are the most rational and moral way to regulate human interactions. According to *laissez-faire* capitalism

(Chapter 2), governments are required not to intervene in the markets in any way. Smith even used the metaphor of God: markets are so good at rewarding the virtuous and punishing the lazy that it is *as if* an "invisible hand" were guiding capitalist society.

Ironically, Adam Smith's doctrine came to be known as the "free market" doctrine. As a result, generations of people have confused the "freedom" of human rights and basic human liberties—a freedom that humans care much about—with the alleged freedom of the wealthy to accumulate as much wealth as they can.

Anyone who looks at the world in 2014 with open eyes will recognize that Adam Smith was wrong. Capitalism has created a massive underclass of people whose work is not rewarded with wealth and comfort. The unrestrained pursuit of wealth on the part of those with economic power has left approximately half the world's population—*over three billion people*—living on less than $2.50 a day.[6] The richest 400 families in America possess more wealth than the bottom 155 million Americans combined.[7] The evidence is overwhelming that the wealthiest nations have designed the world economic system to bring maximum gains to themselves. This is not a "free" market; it is a market of virtual slavery for the increasingly impoverished classes around the globe. It is time for us to rise up and require markets to play the role of servant, not of master. Henceforth we expect markets to serve a subordinate role, fostering the goal of the "common good" for the planet as a whole.

(3) *The costs of global climate disruption will be most severe among the poor.* Unless we intervene, climate change will wreak untold suffering on the world's poorest citizens and on a third to a half of animal species.

In the *Communist Manifesto*, Karl Marx writes that workers "have nothing to lose but their chains" and calls them to "Unite!"[8] Marx's call to action has not been without response, as the history of socialism over the last 165 years shows. But Marx's call by itself has until now been insufficient. People in power have enjoyed their physical comfort and the toys that technology provides. By contrast, those stuck in poverty, despite their numbers, have not had the power or the education to overthrow unjust economic and social systems. Multinational corporations have been able to unduly influence governments and world leaders, blocking reforms. Unless something significant changes on this planet, it's unlikely that the deadly grasp of global capitalism will be loosened.

But significant changes *are* taking place on this planet. Scientists agree that the effects of climate disruption are becoming increasingly severe. Social and economic systems as we know them are coming under increasing pressure. Many will collapse, along with the governments that are based upon them. The future will not be "business as usual."

Much can be done. To choose the common good over a wealth-driven economy means implementing the socialist principles that are implied by Organic Marxism. It's time for governments to rule for the people, rather than for the wealthy. It's time for transnational agreements to limit the power of multinational corporations, allowing the people to rebuild our societies on the basis of sustainable "steady state" economics.[9]

Humanity has two choices. We can begin now to turn away from the myth that it is best for the planet is to let wealthy people rule in their own interest. Or we can wait until the collapse of capital-based civilization in order to initiate structures that serve the common good. Now, not later, is the time to act.

CONCLUSIONS

Both ecology and Marxism remind us at every moment to think of the broader web of life to which we belong and on which we depend. Ecologists study how life-sustaining actions work harmoniously within particular ecosystems. Social sustainability is also a matter of balanced webs of interaction. Socialism is the philosophy that aims to foster and preserve this balance.

In these last chapters we have summarized the philosophies of process and relationship that combine ecology and Marxism. One process philosopher, John Cobb, has managed to summarize the resulting worldview in only ten sentences. He calls it "Ten Ideas for Saving the Planet":[10]

1. Reality is composed of interrelated events.

2. There are gradations of intrinsic value.

3. God [understood as the unifying feature of the process] aims at maximizing value.

4. Humans are uniquely (but by no means exclusively) valuable and uniquely responsible.

5. Education is for wisdom.

6. The economy should be directed toward the flourishing of the biosphere.

7. Agriculture should regenerate the soil.

8. Comfortable habitat should make minimal demands on resources.

9. Most manufacturing should be local.

10. Every community should be part of a community of communities.

Above all, this worldview emphasizes process. Philosophers have been too quick to abstract from the natural processes of life, reifying instead the individual, the effects of his actions, and the intellectual constructs that he creates. But these are abstractions; *the deepest reality is the process itself.* What living beings do in their communities at every moment in the process of life—breathing, relating, working, thinking, understanding, giving, participating—is what counts. Abstractions make for beautiful books, filled with lofty ideals; too often, however, the ideas remain unapplied and inapplicable (even the authors don't try to live them out). *Ideas that matter make a difference in concrete lived reality*, affecting the interactions of people in communities, face to face and eye to eye; the partnerships that they form; and the work they do together.

Ecological civilization is not an abstract philosophy, a mere set of theoretical principles. Marxist thinking has always been focused on moving beyond abstract debates and keeping societal reform at the center of attention. It is about living in the world in a different way. This worldview, which we have labeled Organic Marxism, is compelling. Readers across multiple nations and cultures recognize when policies are just and life-giving and when they are not. It's to the praxis of Organic Marxism that we now turn.

Notes

1. Recall the words of Chinese professor Tang Yijie: "Two broadly intellectual trends are seen as influential in China today: 1) The zeal for 'national essence' or 'national character,' and 2) 'Constructive Postmodernism.' These two trends can, if under the guidance of Marxism, not only take root in China, but further develop so that with comparative ease, China can complete its 'First Enlightenment'—realizing its modernization; and also very quickly enter into the 'Second Enlightenment'—becoming the standard-bearer of a postmodern society." See Tang Yijie, "The Enlightenment and Its Difficult Journey in China," trans. Franklin J. Woo, *Process Perspectives* 34. 2 (Spring 2012), <http://www.ctr4process.org/publications/ProcessPerspectives/archive/PP-34.2-Spring2012.pdf>.

2. Alfred North Whitehead, *Process and Reality*, corrected ed. (New York: Free Press, 1978), 29.

3. Alfred North Whitehead, *Science and the Modern World* (New York: Free Press, 1967), 123.

4. "And do you not know also that although they make use of the visible forms and reason about them, they are thinking not of these, but of the

ideals which they resemble; not of the figures which they draw, but of the absolute square and the absolute diameter, and so on—the forms which they draw or make, and which have shadows and reflections in water of their own, are converted by them into images, but they are really seeking to behold the things themselves, which can only be seen with the eye of the mind?" Plato, *The Republic*, trans. Benjamin Jowett (Hoboken, NJ: Capstone, 2012), 157.

5. Immanuel Kant calls this the Categorical Imperative in *The Groundwork of the Metaphysics of Morals*, trans. Allen Wood (New Haven, CT: Yale University Press, 2002), 31.

6. <http://www.globalissues.org/article/26/poverty-facts -and -stats#src1>.

7. Eric Liu, "How America is Rigged for the Rich," <http://www.cnn.com/2014/04/09/opinion/liu-income-inequality/>.

8. Marx, *Manifesto of the Communist Party* (1848), Chapter 4, online at <https://www.marxists.org/archive/marx/works/1848/communist-manifesto/ch04.htm>.

9. See the materials of the Center for the Advancement of the Steady State Economy: <www.steadystate.org>.

10. John B. Cobb, "Ten Ideas for Saving the Planet," <http://www.jesusjazzbuddhism.org/ten-ideas-for-saving-the-planet.html>.

Chapter 13

THE PRAXIS OF ORGANIC MARXISM

Some try to argue that Marxism fails as a matter of principle. Thus, critics complain, socialists cannot use Marx to formulate social and economic solutions at the global level, because countries are so different from one another that no universal analysis can be valid. When Marxist concepts are adapted to fit the specific features of a given culture, they respond that Marx's principles are no longer really guiding the economic analysis and the proposals for change—it's no longer really Marxist. This double-edged criticism is one of the two that one hears most often in the West. (The other one is that Marxism was "already tried and proven false.")

Throughout this book we have been challenging the false dilemma that fuels this complaint. Either Marxist theory is completely universal, our critics say, and thus too abstract to be helpful; or it is so modified from Marx that it's not really Marxist anymore. We reject the either/or thinking that underlies this charge. European thinkers in the early modern period were preoccupied with the tensions between universal theories and theories that adapt to the ever-changing contexts of action in the world, which they called relativism. It's part of our "postmodern condition," however, to live with the interweaving of general ideas and specific contexts, as messy as this interweaving may be (see Chapter 10).[1]

For a parallel, think of postcolonial theory. Clearly the nature of colonization and the manifestations of colonial rule varied greatly between

Africa, India, China, Latin America, and other countries, which means the struggles around the globe to recover from colonialism are not identical. But common features of our postcolonial condition exist nonetheless. As Childs and Williams write, "post-colonialism has an inescapable global dimension, but it does not mean that post-colonial *theories* are inevitably totalizing in an overweening effort to master and explain everything (totalizing in its 'bad' sense)."[2] Explanatory breadth does not exclude highly adapted forms of micro-analysis at the local level.

So also with Marxist analysis. We have contended that power is increasingly held and exercised by the wealthiest segment of society (individuals and corporations). Power is not distributed merely through "the luck of the draw," person by person; the power hierarchy expresses differential relations between classes. We have also shown that capitalist economics, philosophy, and practice have produced vast inequities and injustices as a byproduct, and that only when societies break the hold of these assumptions can the injustices be overcome. These are general claims. They are in no way weakened when specific socialist reforms are adapted and implemented—"organically"—to meet the needs of specific cities, countries, or cultures. That multiple "Open Marxisms" are evolving to address the specific context of late capitalism and the growing environmental catastrophe does not falsify Marxism. To the contrary, it demonstrates its continuing usefulness as a social and economic alternative to the capitalist treatment of society and the environment.

This chapter moves from the general to the specific. In order to spell out the praxis of Organic Marxism, we must first to formulate its four central guiding principles, and then its specific policy guidelines. Only then can we recommend a series of concrete practices in the closing section.

GUIDING PRINCIPLES

Four general principles have run like red threads through the preceding chapters. It is now possible to state them clearly and succinctly:

208

(1) *For the common good*. Most commentators take it as axiomatic that a democracy exists for the sake of the people. After all, the word "democracy" *means* "rule by the people." And yet the evidence is overwhelming that most democracies in the world today primarily serve to increase the wealth of their richest members. A recent *Harvard Magazine* article shows how unaware even educated Americans are of the actual wealth disparities in their own country. Few know that over 80% of the wealth in the United States is in the hands of only 20% of the population. By contrast, the poorest 40% of the population possesses, between them, a mere 0.3% of the wealth. Members of this group have an average net worth of $2,200.[3] By the end of 2011, according to the *Wall Street Journal,* the net worth of the richest 7% of Americans had risen nearly 30% above what it was before the Wall Street crisis of 2008. "By contrast, the average wealth of America's remaining 93%, some 111 million households, actually dropped by 4%."[4] It is contradictions such as these that lead David Harvey to write of "the end of capitalism" in his most recent book.[5] Political renewal begins with reforms that serve the *common* good.

(2) *Organic, ecological framework*. Understanding the human situation on this planet means grasping a simple principle: the human species will succeed only as long as we retain a harmony and balance between the human species, the global ecosystem, and the other species with whom we share the biosphere. Scholars use the term "human exceptionalism" for those ideologies that treat humanity as an exception to the natural principles that govern all other life forms on the planet. For centuries our species derived its values primarily from its own interests, treating other life forms as "resources" for human gain. Today, however—for the first time in planetary history—these policies have brought about a man-made climate disruption that threatens human civilization as a whole, together with the very biodiversity on which our survival depends.

(3) *Class matters.* The wealthy created, and now profit from, a global economic system that keeps billions of humans below or near the poverty line. Climate change is caused in the first place by the consumption patterns of the wealthy classes, not by the poor. Individual rich people may be nice or mean. Some may even contribute a portion of their wealth toward ecological causes. But as a *class*, they are the ones who are perpetuating the broken and destructive economic systems. Hence the solutions will also be class-based rather than class-blind. Corrective policies must move beyond the decisions of individual persons to address class inequalities, putting the responsibility for change where it belongs.

(4) *Long-term, holistic perspective.* Today we recognize that unregulated capitalist corporations will pursue the goal of short-term profits for their stockholders, often at great expense to other humans and the environment. We have learned to expect that, when a given market or a country's resources are depleted, multi-national corporations will move on to other markets where they can win a higher rate of return for their stockholders. Sometimes, of course, the stockholders of companies vote on behalf of socially responsible policies in small and symbolic ways, which the managers then implement. By and large, however, owners and managers will act to maximize profits for their business; this is the nature of the system. Recall Adam Smith's promise to capitalists that their efforts to maximize profits will always benefit society in the long run—an empty promise that the wealthy continue to make to the poor, as in Ronald Reagan's "trickle-down economics."

In short, one cannot expect a business to exist for the good of the nation's population as a whole; this is simply not its mandate. Business decision-makers seek to ensure high rates of return on their investments, year after year. As conditions change or resources are depleted, the business will switch markets or diversify its portfolio to retain "competitive" profits for its owners or shareholders. One of the clearest examples in recent years has been the oil industry. The trends hold as much for North American firms such as ExxonMobil, with $400 billion in sales in 2012 (according to Forbes), as they do for British Petroleum or Royal Dutch Shell. Educated people in all countries are aware that global petroleum resources will eventually run dry and that conservation, not overproduction, is necessary if the planet is to wean itself from its addiction to oil and petroleum byproducts. Yet the oil companies, racing to increase production in the final years of their industry, are enjoying profits rarely seen in any branch of business. They are also spending huge amounts of money in lobbying Western governments, and especially the United States, to open up new oil fields, to build pipelines, and to overturn regulations and restrictions.

One should not be surprised by the behavior of the oil companies and their managers; it's what one should expect. By contrast, one *does* expect a well-run government to act in the people's interest. The mission of governments is to take a much longer-term perspective because depleting all the resources—agricultural land, rivers and forests, clean air, mineral resources—will leave the next generation of citizens without the ability to survive and thrive. Long-term planning of this sort requires policies for conserving and protecting resources that are based upon an extremely long-term perspective. It is said that the average family can plan for its grandchildren but has trouble thinking ahead to the needs of *their* children, the fourth generation. The Native peoples of North America, by contrast, have traditionally utilized "The Seventh Generation Rule": act in such a way that the net effect of your decisions will be positive for the seventh generation after you—your great great great great grandchildren.[6]

Taking the long-term perspective requires holistic thinking. We do not help even the third-generation when our investments in industrialization or in urbanization leave the world so polluted that the cities become uninhabitable, the air unbreathable, and the countryside barren. Profit-based policies are incapable of taking the required long-term perspective.

Long-term planning is systemic planning. One views the nation as a whole as a system built out of sub-systems. Planning for growth in any one area is done in light of its effects on all other areas that are impacted by that growth. Expectations for profit-taking in the present are reduced, in order that more investment can be made in the future. At this point, the government often comes into conflict with business-people and business interests within the nation. Their interest in quick profits leads businesspeople to be critical of long-term investments in infrastructure—investments whose payoff may lie many decades in the future. To resist their influence requires firm resolve on the part of leaders who work on behalf of the people and the Earth. Their long-term vision will lead them to oppose demands for high personal and business profits in the short term. There are times when short-term GDP growth comes at too great a long-term cost.

Yet the reason for these limits is overwhelming: only a global civilization built on organic principles is sustainable. The cracks and fissures of unsustainable practices and policies are now visible to observers around the world. Increasingly the damage is reflected in our weather patterns, documented openly in our newspapers, and discussed in the streets. Even the United States, where the "carbon footprint" per person is among the highest in the world, is now establishing regional centers to prepare for the increasing effects of climate change on agriculture and forests.[7]

POLICY GUIDELINES

The previous chapters suggest three overarching guidelines, which in turn provide the framework for more specific policy initiatives:

(1) National interests are no longer the only defining context for government decision making.

In the days when planetary resources appeared to be unlimited, it was rational (if not ethical) for each nation state to consume as many resources as it possessed or could take through conquest and control. Today we know that the planet's resources are dwindling rapidly and must be divided between all nations, as well as between human and nonhuman populations. In the past, governments negotiated with other nations primarily in order to regulate human commerce, to resolve disputes, and to end wars. In the coming years, by contrast, *environmental diplomacy will of necessity rise to the highest priority.* Sharing resources, reducing waste, and negotiating international treaties to limit greenhouse gases and other kinds of pollution will become the most important goals for successful statesmanship. For example, water shortages are expected to be the most inflammatory area of environmental dispute in the coming fifteen years. Air pollution, fishing rights, and energy policy will also play increasingly urgent roles in international diplomacy.

Marx already realized that the fundamental socio-economic issues transcend national boundaries. The global flow of capital may well prop up national governments as long as they serve its needs, but the dynamics of capital transcend any given nation. The solutions, Marx realized, will therefore need to be transnational. By and large, national governments have not seen the plight of farmers, underpaid workers, and the chronically unemployed as urgent enough for them to work together to find solutions. They have also not ceded sufficient power to the United Nations, or to any other transnational organization, to make significant changes. Initiatives to help the middle class and the poor have therefore been limited to small-scale reforms within the context of current power structures.

That era is coming to an end. As climate change brings chronic food and water shortages, the deteriorating situation will bring social unrest that is too dangerous to ignore. Throughout history, masses of hungry and displaced persons have been the most potent source of social instability and revolution, even civilizational collapse. It's idealistic to think that the rich and powerful, governments and multinational corporations, will suddenly feel compassion for the poor and freely choose to redistribute their wealth. More likely, the falling standard of living for the middle classes and their increasing vulnerability will prompt demands for change that are too powerful to ignore. In the best case, systemic changes will come about through treaties and democratic processes. In the worst case, overthrowing the new dynasties of wealth (or what Thomas Piketty calls "patrimonial capitalism"[8]) will come through violent revolutions and a protracted period of social chaos and economic collapse. Efforts by individual nations will not be sufficient to bring about the global systemic changes that are needed.

(2) It becomes increasingly urgent for policies to address the reality that power now falls in the hands of an ever smaller number of people, who control more and more of the world's wealth.

We have not written this book merely to score academic points. Volumes have been written about why Marx's analyses failed to convince governments, intellectuals, and workers. Some critics cite inadequacies in Marx's historical and empirical work, or theories that they dislike such as his utopianism or his theory of value. Others attack the doctrines of later Marxist schools (Leninist, Stalinist, Maoist, and many others), which they allege created confusion about the core principles of Marxism. Yet others cite shortcomings in the implementation of Marx's principles by socialist governments, which produced a popular backlash against Marxist political and economic philosophies.

Many of these academic discussions miss the point. Marxism criticizes the world's dominant economic system, which allows people to amass as much wealth as they can and to spend it as they wish. Should we be surprised that this critique generates backlash? To acquire things and to use them selfishly is a big part of human nature. Technological advances—the new smartphone, the new app, the new car—make each new toy more enticing and addictive. Today technology, more than religion, has become the opium of the people. In developed and developing countries alike, people long to acquire more and consume more.

The natural drive to produce and to own is not in itself the problem. For most of human history, it served the species well. Consider, for example, the periods when settlers were first moving into "virgin" territories and needed to rapidly develop farms, cities, and industries. (Even in these times, however, governments were necessary to provide restraints, stability, and infrastructure.) But the industrialization and technologization of the planet have fundamentally changed the situation. We now recognize that the unrestrained drive to possess and consume has become the motor that is driving an out-of-control global economy toward planetary limits (and beyond) at an unsustainable tempo. In this new context, steady state economics, regulatory agreements, reduced consumption, and international collaborations have become essential for the survival of the planet. The days of "take what you can get" have passed, and capitalism without brakes has become dysfunctional.

In today's situation, over-acquisition and over-consumption are a class problem. Class-based analyses became unpopular in the 1950s, when the middle class grew rapidly and reduced the wealth differential with the upper classes. (The cold war mentality did not help either.) In the last decades, however, the classes have again been moving rapidly apart. For the world's poor, who are located predominantly in the global South, a middle-class existence has fallen hopelessly out of reach. Likewise, the level of wealth and power of the upper class now dwarfs that of the middle class, and the gap is growing more and more rapidly.[9]

Effective policies will need to address the vast discrepancies in power, wealth, and consumption of the upper, middle, and lower classes. We cannot begin to address an economy spiraling out of control until we make visible the power sources that are controlling it. Thanks to the internet, the data are available as never before. An educated and increasingly disenfranchised middle class will become increasingly vocal about systems that are tilted in favor of large corporations and wealthy families. Again, it is far better for policymakers to begin to address the inequalities now than to wait until social unrest begins to arise.

(3) "From each according to his ability, to each according to his need."

Marx's famous phrase reflects his distributive theory of justice. We saw in Chapter 8 how differently justice is conceived in capitalist and Marxist systems. In the ideal capitalist system, each person decides in what branch of the market to work and how hard. The market will (allegedly) distribute rewards with complete justice according to the person's own intelligence and hard work.

If the planet were of infinite size and its resources were unlimited (as Adam Smith assumed), governments would not need to restrain individual consumption. That's why Smith claimed that the capitalism system is just and fair for all: the high profits of your neighbor do not mean that you (or anyone else) will get less. If everyone works hard, everyone will reap more and more from the planet. But Adam Smith was wrong. For virtually every natural resource—water, minerals, agricultural land, forests, even the air we breathe and the average temperature of the planet—scientists can now calculate the approaching limits. Limits produce what economists call a zero-sum game: higher consumption for your neighbor means lower consumption for you. When the rich grow richer, the poor must grow poorer.

Humans do not like to be restrained in how much they can acquire and consume. This explains the preference for limited government restrictions in most societies. But in a zero-sum game governments are necessary to curb excesses. That's even truer when available resources are approaching their limits. In times of war, famine, drought, and national emergency, people have been willing to submit to limitations for the survival of society. Now, for the first time in history, it is a *global* emergency that justifies this role of government. Hence the need for policies built on the Marxian principle, "to each according to his need."

THE PRACTICES OF ORGANIC MARXISM

How can a more organic Marxism provide specific guidance for responding wisely and appropriately to these challenges? Because governments and economies are structured differently across countries and cultures, policies will vary; concrete proposals need to be written by those who are experts about the situation in each individual country. Nevertheless, the principles of Organic Marxism that we have been examining do offer some serious guidance to policymaking. The sections that follow offer a first outline of these implications. In consultations with policy experts in each field, they could easily be expanded into broad programs for action.

Economic benchmarks and GDP. Organic Marxism suggests radical changes in the way that human societies interact with the environment. It calls for a restructuring of global economies so that they are focused first on the "flourishing of the biosphere," as John Cobb writes above. Moreover, scholars are recognizing that material growth often doesn't contribute to the happiness of a nation's citizens.[10] Currently the Kingdom of Bhutan is the only country to measure its economic progress in terms of "Gross National Happiness," a holistic indicator of citizens' wellbeing.[11] In 2013, as another step toward holism in economic thinking, Singapore indicated a desire to build its "social reserves" as well as its financial reserves.[12] Even using happiness as an economic indicator is not radical enough, however, unless one also takes into account the costs to the class of disenfranchised people and the ecosystems upon which humans depend.

Organic Marxism suggests an economic theory that measures progress in terms of social goods. Chinese policymakers, who have focused heavily on Gross Domestic Product (GDP) for many years, are beginning to express concerns about the many crucial indicators of success that are not considered, and in some cases adversely affected, by the standard measures of GDP. Unfortunately, the United States does not offer a good model of calculating the impact of policies on *all* of its citizens. Lacking holistic measures of whether the society as a whole is thriving, current measures tend to reflect only gains among the wealthiest of citizens.

Agriculture. One area that requires particularly urgent attention is agriculture. Just as Mao focused on rural farmers as the backbone of his movement for reform in China, Organic Marxism encourages the combination of ancient wisdom and new agricultural techniques in order to achieve social and environmental justice. Some techniques, for example, such as family farms, organic farming and local food production, have been the norm for millennia. The overuse of pesticides and the transportation of food across long distances have only become dominant practices in the past century. Also, only since the Industrial Revolution have capitalists thought to apply industrial patterns to farming—with disastrous results for soil preservation, crop rotation, symbiosis between plants and, above all, for the cultural traditions around the planet that depend on small farming communities.

The problems created by these practices will be lessened as we begin turning back to more traditional patterns as models for the agricultural sector. Organizations such as the Agricultural Sustainability Institute, the Land Institute, and the Sustainable Agriculture, Biodiversity and Livelihoods Programme of the International Institute for Environment and Development (IIED) have brought major advancements in the science of sustainable agriculture.[13]

One of the pioneers in this field is Wes Jackson. Books such as *New Roots for Agriculture, Rooted in the Land: Essays on Community and Place*, and *Nature as Measure* lay the foundations for sustainable agricultural practices, explaining traditional methods of medium-scale farming such as crop rotation and biological methods of pest control.[14] They resonate with the deep wisdom that was common sense for human beings until the Industrial Age. For example, Jackson shows readers how to "consult the genius of the place," learning from the land and the ecosystems and working with them in a harmonious manner rather than by domination.[15] Other authors have followed the equally specific suggestions of Dean Freudenberger,[16] offering concrete policy suggestions that include the rotation of crops, no-till farming, and the use of plants that fix nitrogen in the soil.

Some agriculture-related challenges will require new research. For example, the Yunnan Academy of Agricultural Sciences has been working on developing a variety of perennial rice that would allow farmers to harvest from a single plot for multiple years. Currently, annual varieties of rice allow rain to erode soil and wash away nutrients.[17] While perennial rice is not yet available for wide-scale agricultural use, it represents a promising development that needs to be supported and encouraged with appropriate policies. Technical advances alone are not enough, however, as long as agribusiness continues to disempower farmers, separating them from the results of their labor. Traditional farming villages and practices offer concrete options for postmodern, sustainable agriculture.

Manufacturing. Organic Marxism might also suggest new methods of manufacturing. The ancient way that human societies produced things was for an artisan to create each individual thing by hand. With the onset of industrialization, artisans were replaced by assembly line workers, which, as Marx realized, meant that the workers did not own the means of production and were alienated from their labor. It is impossible, of course, to return to a pre-industrial society. Yet there are things that a postmodern society could learn by considering features of an artisan's relation to his work, including techniques for reinstilling skill and pride, identification with one's work, regional distinctives, and even individual uniqueness in producing products.

Increasingly, it will become necessary for more and more manufacturing to be done locally in order to reduce the reliance on fossil fuels to transport goods. This shift will mean that a more limited range of products will be available. This is already true in many countries in the world, and it is not clear that having fewer purchasing options reduces the quality of life for the average citizen. As John Cobb writes,

> Most of us Americans have far more goods than we need. Our problem is to store them or clear out our closets to make room for new ones. This flood of goods replaced a situation in which

most of the things people really needed were produced by hand. Today handiwork is more of a hobby than a primary occupation, but a shift back in this direction would be a welcome one. If handiwork were prized and its products could be profitably sold, unemployment would cease to be a major problem. We would use fewer resources and own fewer goods, but what we would have would bring us greater satisfaction and its production would be a creative rather than a routine act.[18]

Management. From the perspective of the present, one can see more clearly that what Marx was calling for was limiting the dominance of capital—in part by redistributing power, and in part by building social structures around deeper sets of values. Naturally it's simpler to run a business if one chooses not to consider the quality of life of the workers; and the profits for the owners are higher as well. Similarly, management is simpler when one assumes that natural resources are unlimited, so that one does not have to consider environmental impact among the real costs of one's operations. The standard approach to the production of capital has been to limit the economics—the calculation of profits and losses—to short-term effects, filtering out the long-term, downstream costs of operations. By contrast, sustainable management is more challenging, since it calls for taking a systemic or holistic perspective and managing toward long-term societal and environmental benefits.[19]

"Market Socialism": reforms within the capital-based model. The literature is replete with social reforms that advocates believe can be made within the capitalist economic model.[20] Some argue either for full ownership of firms by workers, or for shared ownership between the workers and "their clients, suppliers, and representatives of local communities and of the planning committee."[21] Both options retain the framework of capitalist competition, merely modifying patterns of ownership.

Other scholars suggest that corporations be reconceived in a more democractic and participatory way. In the "participatory economics" model of Albert and Hahnel, for example, power is shared (and pricing is accomplished) through a kind of equilibrium between workers' councils and consumers' councils.[22] A model put forward by John Roemer in A *Future for Socialism* retains something like "shares" in corporations but does not allow the shares to be converted into cash; they can only be traded for other shares.[23] These and similar models offer compromises between market and socialist economies.

We worry about the extent of the compromises that are being called for. It's crucial to track the actual power relations. The ideology of a firm or culture can pretend that all employees are counted, when in fact a very small number of people (e.g., top management and board) actually make the decisions. One of the marks of real shared power is when value assessments are labor-based. For example, Cockshott and Cottrell argued two decades ago that it's possible to calculate the labor value of products and then to adjust prices to labor value over the long term.[24] With more recent advances in computing, software, and "big data," their thesis has become even more plausible today.

Banking: credit, not capital. Abolishing the current banking system is the first step toward achieving a genuinely socialist economy. Current capitalist nations have made themselves deeply dependent on the largest banks, private institutions whose sole goal is profit-making. Because they have the power to create capital through lending and to freely move their profits across national boundaries, these banks carry out functions once reserved for governments only.

In a series of articles, John Roemer has proposed a credit-based economic system. Because in this proposal the "shares" in corporations could not be converted to cash, they couldn't be used to raise capital. Instead, publicly owned banks would provide credit to businesses.[25] These would be "public banks that could not transform themselves into merchant banks—that is to say, acquire an interest in the capital of non-financial or financial institutions."[26] As Roemer writes in A *Future for Socialism,*

The bank's profits (including its share of firms' profits in its group) would return in large part to the government, to be spent on public goods, health services, education, and so on: this would constitute one part of a citizen's consumption of social profits.[27]

In effect, Roemer's proposal treats banks like utilities. Many capitalist nations have different rules for major utilities because they provide indispensable services to society, such as water, natural gas, and electricity. This proposal recognizes that providing credit to enterprises should also be done in the public interest.

Some theorists prefer the idea that banking reforms could be rolled out slowly, building upon their current capitalist foundations. For example, Thomas Weisskopf has suggested that privately owned banks could be part of an "enterprise-based" form of market socialism.[28] Marc Fleurbaey also supports a hybrid form of free enterprise, one based on credits rather than on capital. Banks, he proposes, could continue to be privately owned but would be far more constrained in the kind of business they could carry out. In some ways Fleurbaey's proposal sounds like the old "savings and loan" model in the Unites States: families deposit cash with banks, which in turn make loans to households and extend credit to enterprises.[29]

Similarly, Tony Andreani would allow banks to be privately managed and to compete with one another. He believes that it is sufficient if they are placed under

> a national financing fund, which allocates sums of credit to banks depending on the quality of their management (management whose yardstick is always the maximisation of labour incomes) … This form therefore rests on a public bedrock: all loan capital is ultimately centralised and allocated by the fund. Moreover, the model comprises supervision of the labour market.[30]

Like the preceding models, Andreani believes that a credit-driven economy can be centrally (though indirectly) planned, so as to avoid the excesses of the current system in the West, where massive for-profit banks control the fates of entire societies. Centrally *managed* economies, he argues, are less efficient and cannot be responsive enough. By contrast, planning is "the privileged site of democratic decisions—the site where the major social choices about working time, the balance between consumption and investment, income bands, priority programmes, and so on, are made and implemented."[31] Central planning without centralized management also allows for local economies and local businesses to emerge, which bring the same sorts of advantages that local agriculture, family farms, and village societies bring.

We are however less sanguine about achieving the level of reform that is needed in places like the United States without first challenging the dominant control of a small number of extremely wealthy individuals and the corporations that serve their interests. The evidence of the last twenty years—especially the global financial meltdown of 2008, in which bank-caused abuses played the central role—bring evidence against the optimistic view that the extremely wealthy will voluntarily limit their gains and act in the interest of the non-wealthy classes. Any real reforms will have to move away from control by capital and by those few who possess most of it. Such reforms are impossible without a radical redesign of the banking system. In particular, we are skeptical that self-managed banks will freely choose to maximize labor income.

More attractive is the suggestion by David Schwieckart that banks function as "second-degree cooperatives (directed by representatives of their workforces, of the funds, and of the client enterprises)."[32] On Schwieckart's model, like Roemer's, banks would be "public institutions, financed out of taxes, whose members are civil servants, interested only in the benefits."[33] Only if they are created in this way can one expect them to genuinely promote social goods, such as the creation of jobs and sustainable investment. Banks driven by the profit motive simply aren't motivated to serve the public good.

NOTES

1. Jean-François Lyotard, *The Postmodern Condition: A Report on Knowledge* (Minneapolis: University of Minnesota Press, 1984).

2. Peter Childs and R.J. Patrick Williams, *An Introduction to Post-Colonial Theory* (London and New York: Prentice Hall/Harvester Wheatsheaf, 1997), 21. Cf. p. 5: "the unrelenting, if uneven, expansion of capitalism from its West European base has been a constant—some might say *the* constant—of world history, to the point where there is now no part of the globe left untouched by it ... This larger, still incomplete project of the globalization of capitalism is what a number of post-colonial critics, especially those working with Marxist, or Marxist-derived concepts, understand as imperialism. For them, it is perhaps the key explanatory concept." See also Robert J.C. Young, *Postcolonialism: An Historical Introduction* (Oxford: Blackwell Publishers, 2001); Chinese translation 2006.

3. Elizabeth Gudrais, "What We Know about Wealth," *Harvard Magazine* Nov-Dec 2011, pp. 12-14, <http://harvardmag.com/pdf/2011/11-pdfs/1111-12.pdf>. The data is drawn from survey work done by Harvard Business School professor Michael Norton.

4. Niel Shah, "Only Richest 7% Saw Wealth Gains From 2009 to 2011," *The Wall Street Journal*, April 23, 2013. The data is drawn from a Pew Research Center report.

5. David Harvey, *Seventeen Contradictions and the End of Capitalism* (London: Profile Books, 2014).

6. See the Native American Foundation, The Seventh Generation Fund, at <SeventhGenerationFund.com>.

7. "U.S. to build climate hubs against changing climate," Xinhua News Agency, February 6, 2014, <http://news.xinhuanet.com/english/world/2014-02/06/c_133094910.htm>.

8. Data about the control of capital by an increasingly small number are summarized in Thomas Piketty, *Capital in the Twenty-First Century*, trans. Arthur Goldhammer (Cambridge, MA: Belknap Press/Harvard University Press, 2014). Piketty demonstrates the increased concentration of wealth in a smaller and smaller number of family dynasties, an outcome that he describes as "patrimonial capitalism."

9. Again, the data is powerfully laid out in Piketty's recent work (see previous note).

10. See Mark Anielski, *The Economics of Happiness: Building Genuine Wealth* (Gabriola, B.C.: New Society Publishers, 2007).

11. See details at <http://www.grossnationalhappiness.com/>.

12. Leong Wai Kit, "Singapore Needs Both Financial and 'Social' Reserves to Thrive: President Tony Tan," *Today*, November 5, 2013, <http://www.todayonline.com/singapore/spore-needs-both-financial-and-social-reserves-thrive-president-tony-tan>.

13. See the Agricultural Sustainability Institute, <http://asi.ucdavis.edu/front-page>; the Land Institute, <http://landinstitute.org/>; and the Sustainable Agriculture, Biodiversity and Livelihoods Programme of the International Institute for Environment and Development (IIED), <http://www.iied.org/food-agriculture>.

14. See Wes Jackson, *New Roots for Agriculture* (Lincoln: University of Nebraska Press, 1985); Wes Jackson and William Vitek, eds., *Rooted in the Land: Essays on Community and Place* (New Haven, CT: Yale University Press, 1996); and Jackson, *Nature as Measure: The Selected Essays of Wes Jackson* (Berkeley, CA: Counterpoint Press, distributed by Publishers Group West, 2011).

15. See the beautiful example in "Thoughts on the Natural History of Eden," chapter 16 of Wes Jackson, *Consulting the Genius of the Place: An Ecological Approach to a New Agriculture* (Berkeley, CA: Counterpoint Press, distributed by Publishers Group West, 2010). But the example

also shows how nature is never the same after our interventions.

16. Among Dean Freudenberger's publications, see *Global Dust Bowl: Can We Stop the Destruction of the Land before It's Too Late?* (Minneapolis: Augsburg Publishing House, 1990), *Food for Tomorrow?* (Minneapolis: Augsburg Publishing House, 1984), and (with Paul Minus) *Christian Responsibility in a Hungry World* (Nashville: Abingdon Press, 1976). See also John B. Cobb, Jr., "Ecological Agriculture," at <http://www.religion-online.org/showarticle.asp?title=3603>.

17. Traci Viinanen, "Breeding for Sustainability: Utilizing High-Throughput Genomics to Design Plants for a New Green Revolution," in *Sustainable Agriculture and New Biotechnologies*, ed. Noureddine Benkeblia (Hoboken: Taylor and Francis, 2011), 57.

18. Cobb, "Ten Ideas for Saving the Planet."

19. See Philip Clayton, "Process Philosophy and Systems Management," in *Science and Ecological Civilization: A Constructive Postmodern Approach* (Chinese translation forthcoming in 2015).

20. For a good overview, see Tony Andréani, "Market Socialism: Problems and Models," in Bidet and Kouvelakis, *Critical Companion to Contemporary Marxism* (Leiden: Brill, 2008), 233-54; available online at <http://www.marx.be/Prime/ENG/Books/Bidet_Contemporary_marxism.pdf>.

21. Pat Devine, *Democracy and Economic Planning: The Political Economy of a Self-Governing Society* (Cambridge, UK: Polity, 1988). Devine's concept of participatory planning combines existing market indicators with socially oriented measures.

22. Michael Albert and Robin Hahnel, *The Political Economy of Participatory Economics* (Princeton: Princeton University Press, 1991).

23. John Roemer, *A Future for Socialism* (Cambridge: Harvard Univ. Press, 1994).

24. Paul Cockshott and Allin Cottrill, *Towards a New Socialism* (Nottingham: Spokesman, 1993); see also Jacques Bidet and Stathis Kouvelakis, eds., *Critical Companion to Contemporary Marxism*, 236.

25. See Pranab Bardhan and John Roemer, eds., *Market Socialism: The Current Debate* (Oxford: Oxford University Press, 1993). See also John Roemer, "Can There Be Socialism after Communism?" *Politics and Society* 3 (1992): 269, as quoted in Bidet and Kouvelakis, *Critical Companion to Contemporary Marxism*, 243: "Firms belong to groups, each associated with a main bank, whose job is to monitor the firms in its group and arrange loan consortia for them. There would be a very limited stock market. Banks would own shares of firms, and each firm in a group would own some shares of the other firms in its group as well. The board of directors of a firm would consist of representatives of the main bank and of the other firms who hold its shares. The bank's profits (including its share of firms' profits in its group) would return in large part to the government, to be spent on public goods, health services, education, and so on: this would constitute one part of a citizen's consumption of social profits. In addition, each firm would receive dividends from its shares of other firms in its group, and these would be distributed to its workers, constituting the second part of the social dividend. Because a citizen's income would come in part from the profits of other firms in her keiretsu, she would have an interest in requiring those firms to maximize profits, an interest that would be looked after by her firm's representatives on the boards of directors of the other firms . . . If [firms] started performing badly, [the other firms] would be able to sell their stock . . . to the main bank, who would have an obligation to buy it. This would put pressure on the bank to discipline [the firm's] management."

26. Andréani, "Market Socialism," in Bidet and Kouvelakis, *Critical Companion to Contemporary Marxism*, 244.

27. Roemer, *A Future for Socialism*, 269.

28. Thomas Weisskopt, "A Democratic Enterprise-Based Market

Socialism," in Pranab Bardhan and John Roemer, eds., *Market Socialism: The Current Debate* (Oxford: Oxford Univ. Press, 1993).

29. Bidet and Kouvelakis, *Critical Companion to Contemporary Marxism*, 252.

30. Ibid., 252-53.

31. Ibid.

32. Ibid., 251.

33. Ibid.

Chapter 14

WHAT DOES ECOLOGICAL CIVILIZATION LOOK LIKE?

WHY BELIEVE IN THE POSSIBILITY OF POLITICAL CHANGE?

Organizing ourselves into social systems is a basic feature of human existence. Among the most significant of these systems are political systems—the formal structures by which humans govern themselves or are governed by others.

Decisions about political systems are never made in a vacuum. They reflect the beliefs and values of a group of people (city, state, or nation), they are influenced by what people see as realistic options at a given time, and they are largely determined by which people and which ideas have power. Power comes in many forms, including wealth, armies, ownership of land, and control of major public and private institutions.

In history it's very rare that people with power choose to share it with those who don't have it. Even though many different types of political systems exist in today's world, in most of them the people who hold power exercise it largely for their own benefit. Some of these are Communist states; some elect socialist parties to power from time to time; and many are purely and unabashedly based on capitalist assumptions, such as the United States. What they share in common is that their actual policies tend to favor the interests of those who hold the most power.

So if the powerful rarely give up power, why should one believe that reforms are possible? Karl Marx is famous for advocating higher and more noble goals than capital-based political systems ever have. In the state that he dreamed of, individuals would not exercise power for their own interests; each one would contribute to the best of his ability; and the resources would be shared across the society in ways that would best serve the common good.

It is time, here at the conclusion of our book, to be frank. In light of the historical facts that we have just summarized, we do not think it likely that capitalists will freely agree to support a socialist system. The masses of people on the planet already recognize that the super-rich are being selfish and that a more equitable distribution of wealth would be more just. But what can possibly compel them to release their power and wealth in the interest of promoting the greater good?

We believe that the coming environmental catastrophe will provide the needed catalyst. Experience shows that it's usually unwise to bet against well-established scientific models when they are supported by scientific consensus. (Over the last decades and centuries, it's often been religious believers who have bet against science, and generally they have lost this bet.) The scientific models agree that human-induced climate change will stretch, and eventually break, the social and economic structures on which humans currently depend. If the well-established scientific models are accurate—and they generally are—then change is coming . . . whether we are ready for it or not.

Humanity may react in three very different ways. One possibility is that this crisis—the first truly global crisis that our species has ever faced—will bring out the worst in our species. If so, the powerful will use their power to protect themselves, no matter how many people are hurt as a result. Rich nations will use their technology and their wealth to feed and protect their wealthy citizens, fighting off the starving millions on their borders with armies and bombs. Decisions will be short-sighted and selfish. Animals, nature, and the poor will suffer the most. Many people will die and many species will become extinct. Unfortunately, if human history is any indication, this scenario is the more likely one.

There are, however, two other possible scenarios. As civilizational collapse gets closer and closer, and as those in power begin to see that no miracle will erase it, it's also possible that the global crisis will bring out the more noble side of those in power, so that they use their wealth and influence for the sake of the planet and its inhabitants. Even if their motivations are not purely selfless, it may be that capitalists and corporations will feel pressure to respond constructively to the crisis, as benevolent rulers sometimes do.

Finally, it's possible that the masses will see that the rich are protecting themselves and abandoning the rest, and that they will rise up against this treatment. Recognizing that they are becoming the victims of the catastrophe, they may have new motivation to act together in their common interest. Because of our numbers, we could indeed change the system if we were united in action. As the eye of the storm bears down upon us, the 99 percent may indeed become the source of revolutionary change.

It Is Never Too Late

In 1972 John Cobb published a book with the title, *Is It Too Late?*[1] Given the evidence of environmental destruction that was already emerging in the 1960s, Cobb asked prophetically: is it too late for humans to turn things around and begin to build an ecological civilization? Although the book was published over forty years ago, it is clear that humanity has not yet made this turn.

Noam Chomsky, one of the most famous and most outspoken critics of U.S. foreign policy, spoke recently to sold-out audiences across Asia. One of his talks was entitled, "Capitalist Democracy and the Prospects for Survival." At one stop, Professor Chomsky was asked how he would answer the question posed in the title of his lecture: what are the prospects for the planet if capitalism continues to dominate human interactions? Chomsky's answer was unmistakable: "The quick answer is 'dim.'" If it was almost "too late" four decades ago, then mustn't it be too late now?

The answer is no, it's never too late. Of course, it *is* too late to stop the climate from changing, the glaciers from melting and the oceans from rising, many species from going extinct, and many people from dying as a result of what's coming. *But it is not too late to lay the foundations for a new kind of civilization.* With each passing year, more and more people become aware that humans in the modern period have built an unsustainable mode of living on this planet and that it is beginning to collapse all around us. To realize this fact is to recognize the need for us to start building a new kind of society. Now is the time to lay the foundations for a different kind of civilization.

WHAT DOES ECOLOGICAL CIVILIZATION LOOK LIKE?

The ancient Chinese religion known as Daoism is famous for its focus on harmony. Nature consists of competing interests, forces pulling in different directions. The wise person is the one who recognizes that contrasting ideas don't need to exclude one another. Recognizing in them complementary dimensions of the one Way, Daoists look for approaches that allow different perspectives to work together productively.

The wisdom of the Dao contrasts with the "common sense" of modernity, which consistently turns complementary ideas into philosophies (religions, nations) that are at war with one another. Private property represents an excellent example. For John Locke and Adam Smith, property was the foundation of human interaction, and protecting it was the cornerstone of the state. But for their French Enlightenment opponent, Rousseau, private property was the social equivalent of the Christian concept of original sin—the moment when all manner of evil entered into and disrupted humankind's natural harmony:

The first man who, having enclosed a piece of ground, bethought himself of saying "This is mine," and found people simple enough to believe him, was the real founder of civil society. From how many crimes, wars, and murders, from how many horrors and misfortunes might not anyone have saved mankind, by pulling up the stakes, or filling up the ditch, and crying to his fellows: "Beware of listening to this impostor; you are undone if you once forget that the fruits of the earth belong to us all, and the earth itself to nobody."[2]

Over the ensuing centuries, the followers of both camps became more critical of each other and, as a result, more extreme. Socialism came to be identified with the denial of all private property, and libertarianism came to be identified with the denial of social services, even to those most in need. As we look for the Dao in this debate, the middle way, we do not need to demand a complete communitarianism in which no one is allowed to own anything. The human drive toward ownership and competition is not inherently evil; it's the excesses that need to be restrained.

Consider another example. Many in the West recognize the damage that consumerism and radical individualism have caused: the injustice, the environmental destruction. They support radical reforms, including changes to the system itself. But they have been taught that the only alternative is a violent and abusive form of Communism, the kind that the world saw during the darkest years of Stalin's rule or in some of the excesses of China's Red Guard.

Why would the formal debates proceed as if these were the only two alternatives? By demanding a forced choice between extreme alternatives, leaders in the East and the West have backed us into a corner. We cannot lay the foundations for a new type of social (and global) organization unless we challenge the assumptions on which the faulty structures have been built. First among the assumptions that must go is the belief that modernity has forced the world to choose between mutually exclusive options: capitalism *or* old-style socialism, individualism *or* communalism, unlimited wealth for the powerful *or* the abolition of private property, humans *or* nature.

Throughout this book we have challenged that assumption. If there is hope in the postmodern turn, as constructive postmodernists believe, it lies in the renewed openings for hybrid solutions. For example, like most philosophy students in the West, in our classes we debated "individualism" versus "communalism" and wrote papers defending the one position against the other. Why did the professors treat these as exclusive options? Isn't *meaningful community* in fact an answer to the emptiness that individual isolation creates in cities around the world? Must it not be our goal to explore new possibilities for living creatively in community with each other?[3] Modern capitalist societies have brought about the collapse of the village community, the clan of relatives, and the extended family; today fewer and fewer children grow up in intact nuclear families. Our technologized lifestyle, and the pace of life that it produces, have further whittled down opportunities for meaningful face-to-face interaction. People also feel the loss of deep encounters with nature and with other species.

Organic Marxism is not only an economic and political philosophy, then; it is also a response to this yearning for community with each other and with nature. Of course, issues of wealth, power, and injustice don't just go away; they have to be dealt with.[4] Still, the idea that people and environment might come together again is not a romantic dream; it's a basic yearning that stems from the nature of our species. We seek participation in vibrant, organic communities because humans are social animals. We seek fulfilling work experiences because we actualize ourselves through what we do. We seek creative and artistic expression because it is our nature to dream of a better world than what we see around us.

ORGANIC MARXISM: A THIRD WAY

In this exploration we have sought to examine the resources of Karl Marx's philosophy with fresh, postmodern eyes. Like Tom Rockmore in his famous *Marx After Marxism*, we have not accepted that the history of Marxism offers the last word on Marx. Rockmore insists that most contemporary philosophies

> pale in comparison with Marxist theory of modern society. In this respect, Marx is very obviously a true giant, the author of the most impressive overall theory of the modern world we currently possess, a theory which, despite its many flaws, really has no obvious competition . . . Marx for the first time provides a credible theoretical framework to comprehend modern life as a whole. In this, he has no real competition, no theory of similar size and breadth with which his own could be compared.[5]

Also like Rockmore, we have treated Marxism not as a "closed system" but rather as an "open system." Read in this more open-ended way, many details of Marx's analysis speak more strongly today than in the past: what it means to distribute wealth and power justly, why the 1 percent becomes richer while the 99 percent become poorer, how the tragic gap between use value and exchange value can be narrowed, why capitalism is connected with ecological devastation, etc. In particular, we've seen, the ecological reformulation of Marxist principles opens doors to contemporary insights that one does not find in other systems. Marxist analyses of social ecology, such as the now-classic arguments in Murray Bookchin's *Remaking Society: Pathways to a Green Future*, demonstrate why class-domination patterns must be corrected simultaneously with the domination of nature.[6]

We speak of a "third way" because this fusion of socialist and ecological principles is not identical to classical Marxism. The policies of Organic Marxism do not center on huge state-run industries, nor do they seek to eliminate all private property, family and small-business production, and market exchange. Remember that one of the most organic socioeconomic systems in the history of humanity was the small farming community, which combined family-centered production and local markets with high levels of cooperation and collaboration for the sake of the community as a whole.

Three features in particular characterize this middle way. Organic Marxism advocates the (re)emergence of hybrid systems, with the acquisition of wealth constrained by societal needs. It supports the ownership of private property within limits set by the carrying capacity of the planet, which means that both values and constraints are based on the (communal and planetary) common good. It endorses educational systems—at the university level as well as in primary and secondary schools—that function to instill knowledge and values that reflect the needs of ecology and the demands of justice. Since these three principles sum up our central conclusions, each one deserves a word of elaboration in these closing pages:

(1) *The emergence of hybrid systems.* In earlier chapters we endorsed a hybrid system in which markets are structured so as to support thriving on all levels: local collaborations, regional associations, and the global community. Neither of the "pure" economic forms—pure capitalism and pure socialism—has consistently benefitted all three levels. One must acknowledge that, historically, the inefficiencies of fully socialized economies have not produced adequate gains for their citizens. Certainly the level of corruption in completely socialized economies such as the former East Germany or North Korea is not in the people's interest. Such economies, we suggest, will increasingly be replaced by hybrid systems that combine profit-making activities with regulations that are designed to prevent corruption, environmental abuse, and the inordinate acquisition of wealth by a small number of citizens.

Managing hybrid socioeconomic models requires an "open systems" approach. Hybridity is a distinguishing feature of multiple interlocking and interdependent systems: human and nonhuman, economic and cultural, and of course market-driven and regulatory. Whereas Marxism in the industrial age was synonymous with massive state-run economies that were centrally managed, Organic Marxism is adapted to the information age. Here the focus shifts to smaller-scale communities, micro-economic systems, and capacity-centered planning. In deterministic systems, managers seek to control outcomes through targeted interventions. In so-called chaotic systems, by contrast, managers (including the state) are co-participants in evolving systems that no one can completely control or predict.[7]

(2) *Beyond the private–public dichotomy.* Debates in political theory have tended to prioritize either the private or the public sector as their primary focus. Some seek to broaden the realm of what is considered private and to protect it from public scrutiny (liberals, libertarians); others tend to project family values outward onto the nation as a whole (the religious right). As Organic Marxists, we recognize that neither of these tendencies provides the solution. On a planet in peril, one needs to ask how *the values of the whole* can guide individual and family decision making, and one needs to explore how the support structures of family and local community can help build local and regional self-reliance. Both of these responses have been typical of traditional rural and small town economies through human history.

"Back to Marx" scholars have researched and presented the values and commitments that are expressed across Marx's work, for example in his portrayal of the capitalists, the bourgeoisie, and the proletariat. Because of the standards for "scientificness" (*Wissenschaftlichkeit*) that dominated in his day, Marx believed that he had to ground all values in objective historical and socioeconomic studies. This modernist conviction led him to downplay the important role of transformative values within specific cultures, emphasizing instead the universal laws of the class struggle. These modernist convictions have compromised the effectiveness of previous Marxist movements, for they prevent them from becoming fully culturally embedded. Never underestimate the power of ancient stories and classic texts to challenge the status quo and to motivate change.

Put differently, Organic Marxism means embedding Marx's dream of an egalitarian society within the organic context of a given people and culture. Contrast this approach with the libertarian tendencies in American society. Libertarians limit the "public interest" to protecting the life, liberty, and property of citizens, moving concerns about quality of life and deeper values to the private sphere. [8] The trouble is, such values are the glue that holds a society together, lifting attention above self-interest to the interests of the community as a whole. As Michael Walzer has recognized, nations cannot survive on such a "thin" platform of values.[9] Many of the sustaining values are birthed in home and hearth; they are captured by the religious or "folk" beliefs of the people; and they are nurtured by the arts and literature. Drawing absolute lines between private and public prevents the core values of a people from flowing into its public institutions and from nourishing and guiding its public square debates.

Overly sharp line-drawing also blocks public or national values from working their transformative power on individuals, families, and communities. The United States since the 1980s, and other developing nations more recently, have begun to see a generation of young professionals—some of the most gifted and well-educated citizens of the country—pursuing careers based only on the gains for themselves. (This was the class of people responsible for the global financial crisis of 2008.) Under a libertarian ideology, of course, this is expected; career decisions are "private" decisions, relevant only to the individual and his friends and family. But in an age of global climate disruption and of unsustainable economic practices, questions of career and lifestyle are no longer purely private. It's not only governments that need to take a systemic or organic view of the global situation; individual citizens, especially at higher educational and professional levels, must do likewise.

When one concedes this point, the heated battles over ownership and private property look rather different. A society gains from a healthy private sphere and from reasonable levels of private ownership.

Yet acquiring and caring for possessions works for the common good only in the context of shared civic values. Individuals can only thrive when the whole system thrives.

(3) *Beyond value-free education.* No area more clearly represents the fusion of private and public interests than the field of education. It is no coincidence that, in countries dominated by capitalist and libertarian strategies, universities sought to become "value free." Individuals wanted to get the best education for themselves; disciplines were responsible for their own standards of excellence but not for any "external" values; and businesses profited from the university-based production of knowledge and technology, which they could later market to their advantage.

Of course, universities were never really value free. The best British universities trained and socialized the servants of the British Empire, who looked back on their time at Oxford or Cambridge as their formative period for national leadership. Liberal arts programs at American universities taught the "canon" of classic texts, which imparted not only a sense of what constitutes excellence in writing, but also clear statements regarding the values by which one should live. (American universities were more Confucian then they admitted.) The growing crisis in American higher education has come as those canons of knowledge and values that every educated citizen "must have" have come under attack. Government officials are now looking for cheaper ways to train workers in the skills of the marketplace, for example through online professional degrees. For many, values training has now become too expensive and has been eliminated.

Organic Marxism calls for an educational system—universities as well as primary and secondary education—that functions to instill knowledge and values that are consistent both with the continued existence of life on earth and with just ways of distributing resources and opportunities. At every level, from child to adult, the process of education cannot help but instill values, whether explicit or implicit.

While pretending to be value free, many Western universities in fact fostered the values of competition, nationalism, and the free market.

Today, most acknowledge, the planet needs global citizens, not individuals driven solely by the interests of their particular community or nation, or by the desire for personal profit. Arguably, university reform in this direction is one of the most urgent changes necessary in the West, since the impact of the university experience sets the values for people's lives and work, not only in the early years of their careers but throughout most of their adult life. Studies continue to show that individuals with a strong liberal arts education—individuals trained in clear thinking, strong writing, and values-based reflection—are most likely to rise to the highest positions over the course of their careers. If the roots of ecological civilization do not grow during the university years, it is very unlikely that they will be able to do so later. Clearly, the need is not for superficial indoctrination, which often has the opposite effect from what it intends. Far more useful are educational reforms based on fostering deep reflection on values and on how they can influence subsequent actions. Far-reaching reforms are needed if education is to provide a rich foundation of *shared values* for the global citizens of the future.

In each of these three important areas, Organic Marxism clearly stands as a third way. It is not a romantic retreat into a primitive past, or an anti-technological stance that robs humanity of tools we will need. But neither does it endorse unrestrained consumerism and personal gain as the only motivation. Upon reflection, what's surprising is that we would have reduced the rich range of complementary options to just two competing opposites in the first place. The real alternative to consumerism, for example, is to discover a deeper set of social values—organic values—that link one again to the land, to nature, and to those cultural traditions that support them. Similarly, the real alternative to radical individualism is the rediscovery of vibrant, transformative community.

Final Conclusions

We live in an era when stronger and stronger forms of individualism are coming to dominate, even in highly communal cultures such as China and India. This unremitting focus on the individual is a byproduct of the new global dominance of Western capitalism and consumerism. As the *Worker's Vanguard* wrote recently:

> By reducing the human relation to nature purely to possessive-individual terms, capitalism thus represents (in spite of all of its technological progress) not so much a fuller development of human needs and powers in relation to the powers of nature, as the alienation of nature from society in order to develop a one-sided, egoistic relation to the world.[10]

Organic Marxism represents an important force of resistance against radical individualism and consumerism. It places a strong emphasis on the importance of communities, within which individual identity and resistance to the status quo is fostered, grown, and developed. Community exists at very many different levels: family, school, work, sports association, village, town, province, and nation. The nature of community at each of these specific levels is different. But the shared principles of organic community hold in every case. The goal of this movement is to wed the positive features of thriving organic communities with a consistent Marxist emphasis on the common good.

Ours is a strange time. To science, and to citizens around the world, it is painfully clear what must be done to avoid global climate catastrophe. Yet citizens are frustrated to find the obvious steps being blocked by big business, which is unwilling to let its profits go, and by the inaction of governments, which place their national interests above the needs of the planet.

Why, when faced with the urgent need for change, do humans continue to create in-groups and out-groups, claiming that good values are to be found only within one's own group and vilifying all others? In national and global debates, leaders set up false oppositions and then insist that the true answers are found only in their particular camp. In each chapter above, we've seen how the path to wise and just policies is blocked by ideological battles. Observers of Washington witness perhaps the most painful examples of inaction due to the inability to compromise. But it is not difficult to add examples from other parts of the world as well.

With the help of contemporary Marxist analyses, we recognize that the reasons for the stalemate are systemic. It's not that leaders are opposed to sustainable, earth-centered policies. It's that the system of modern capitalism is incapable of making the switch. The nations with the largest GDPs don't want to change the rules of the global economy because the current rules bring their citizens so much wealth and comfort. Developing nations have to play by the economic rules established in Europe and North America, since there's no other way to raise the standard of living for their citizens. Thanks to the IMF, the World Bank, and other international organizations established by the wealthiest nations, the poor nations find themselves falling more and more under the control of the dominant powers.

Once we understand the fixed rules of the global system, and whom they serve, we recognize that there is no "quick fix." The goals of the environmental movement can no longer be limited to symbolic steps, supplying band-aids to a dying planet. Nothing less than civilizational change will suffice. Movement leaders around the planet are beginning to lay the foundations for a new ecological civilization because they realize the need for fundamental changes in how people think and how we organize human society, both locally and globally.

In these pages we have traced the history and the concepts on which the new ecological civilization is being built. The social, political, and economic principles of modernity are (sadly) still often unrecognized. Marx provided some of the most effective tools for uncovering them, which is why we have argued that Marxist analyses are indispensable. But transformative socialist principles need to be embedded in cultures and embodied in post-capitalist communities. For that reason we have used "organic" as the umbrella term to express the central features of the civilization that is even now being born on this planet: sustainable, culturally and historically embedded, constructively postmodern, process-based, fundamentally local, communal in its orientation—in a word: ecological.

The momentum toward civilizational change is now building across the planet; people-based movements for revolutionary change are visible in virtually every country.[11] The movements are being driven by daily news of the growing environmental catastrophe, driven by the very air that we breathe (what should be life-giving has become toxic!), driven by our inborn sense of justice and common sense. The citizens of this planet will not watch it destroyed before our eyes, robbing our children and grandchildren of a healthy habitat, just because the wealthy and powerful are unwilling to change.

We believe that this growing momentum for change will not stop until many features of late modern European civilization have been replaced. The conditions for such radical transformation were not yet in place at the time that Marx wrote. Sadly, it has taken the first truly global crisis since human civilization arose—a humanly caused crisis—to create the necessary global momentum. Only as this organic movement becomes global will Marx's dream of transnational reforms finally be realized.

It is the dawn of a new form of human civilization. Individuals, societies, and nations are now deciding whether to keep fighting to preserve the dying order, or whether to take leadership in building the new. It's not a matter of waiting for more data; we already know what the old practices are doing to our planet, and we know what it takes to build a global society that is socially, economically, and environmentally sustainable. The ones who will make the greatest difference are those who work and live with wisdom, with diplomacy, and with restraint, placing the good of the whole planet first.

NOTES

1. John B. Cobb, Jr., *Is It Too Late? A Theology of Ecology* (Beverly Hills, CA: Bruce, 1972).

2. Jean-Jacques Rousseau, *A Discourse on Inequality: On the Origin and Basis of Inequality among Men* (Waiheke Island: Floating Press, 2009), 63.

3. We are grateful for conversations with Brianne Donaldson that have influenced this section.

4. To emphasize community is not, of course, an answer by itself. Capitalism creates "communities" of consumers so that advertising campaigns can be more effectively targeted at them. Freely choosing between the products and "lifestyle choices" that businesses offer to your community does nothing to bring fundamental changes to the system; it only increases corporate income. See Joerg Rieger, *No Rising Tide: Theology, Economics, and the Future* (Minneapolis: Fortress Press, 2009). As Rieger points out (personal correspondence), one can choose to belong to the Rotary Club or to a gated community. These communities actually reinforce the class differences of the status quo, rather than undercutting them.

5. Tom Rockmore, *Marx After Marxism: The Philosophy of Karl Marx* (Oxford: Blackwell Publishers, 2002), 197.

6. Murray Bookchin, *Remaking Society: Pathways to a Green Future* (Boston: South End Press, 1990).

7. Philip Clayton, *Science and Ecological Civilization: A Constructive Postmodern Approach*, (forthcoming in Chinese translation), especially Chapter 7, "Process Philosophy and Systems Management."

8. For the foundational concepts behind American libertarianism, see John Stuart Mill, *On Liberty*, ed. David Bromwich and George Kateb (New Haven, CT: Yale University Press, 2003).

9. Michael Walzer, *Thick and Thin: Moral Argument at Home and Abroad* (Notre Dame: University of Notre Dame Press, 1994).

10. *Workers Vanguard* 1032 (October 18, 2013), <http://www.icl-fi.org/english/wv/1032/ecosocialism.html>. In endorsing this statement, we do not endorse the hostile claims that the authors make against Ecological Marxism elsewhere in the article.

11. See the photographs at <www.350.org>, which show pictures of climate change activism around the planet.

Index

Lightning Source UK Ltd.
Milton Keynes UK
UKOW04f1854050116

265870UK00001B/71/P